# WELCOME TO PARIS

The Obelisk on Place de la Concorde.
A. Chicurel/hemis.fr

M

# Arriving in Paris

## By Train

**Gare de Lyon** (12e arr.), **Gare de Bercy** (12e arr.), **Gare d'Austerlitz** (13e arr.), **Gare Montparnasse** (15e arr.), **Gare du Nord** (10e arr.), **Gare de l'Est** (10e arr.) and **Gare Saint-Lazare** (9e arr.).
*Train Connections: see p. 156.*

## By Air

### From Paris-Charles de Gaulle Airport

**Roissybus** – Every 15-20 min. from 6am to 12:30am - 60-75 min. ride - €16.20 one way - www.parisaeroport.fr - Terminates at Opéra Garnier (Lines 3, 7, 8 and RER A).
**RER B** – Dir. Robinson–St-Rémy-lès-Chevreuse - every 10-20 min. from 4:45am to 1am - 30 min. ride - €11.45 one way - www.transilien.com - Stops at Gare du Nord, Châtelet-Les-Halles, Saint-Michel-Notre-Dame, Denfert-Rochereau, etc.
**350 Bus** – Dir. Porte de la Chapelle - every 15-30 min. from 6am to 10:30pm - 60-80 min. ride - €2.10 one way - www.ratp.fr.
**Bus 351** – Dir. Place de la Nation – every 15-30 min. from 7am to 9:30pm - 70-90 min. ride - €2.10 one way - www.ratp.fr.
**Bus Noctilien** – N143 and N140 - Terminates at Gare de l'Est - 12:30am-5:30am - €4.20.
**Cab** – €55 (fixed price) for the Rive Droite (Right Bank), €62 for the Rive Gauche (Left Bank).

### From Orly Airport

NB: The métro Line 14 extension to Orly is planned to go into service mid-2024, putting the center of Paris 30 minutes from the airport.
**Orlybus** – Dir. Denfert-Rochereau - every 10-15 min. from 6am to 12:30am - 30 min. ride - €11.20 one way.
**Orlyval and RER B** – Driverless shuttle to Antony (every 4-7 min. from 6am to 11pm - 6 min. ride) then RER B dir. CDG2-TGV or Mitry-Claye (15-30 min. ride) - €14.10 combined ticket, one way. Stops at Denfert-Rochereau, Saint-Michel-Notre-Dame, Châtelet-Les-Halles, Gare du Nord, then transfer on to the métro.
**Tramway** – Line T7 to Villejuif-Louis-Aragon (every 8-15 min. from 5:30am to 12:30am - 30 min. ride - €2.10 one way), then transfer to the métro (Line 7).
**Bus Noctilien** – N31, N131, N144 dir. Gare de Lyon - N22 dir. Chatelet - 12:30am-5:30am - 60 min. ride - €4.20.
**Cab** – €41 (fixed price) for the Rive Droite (Right Bank), €35 for the Rive Gauche (Left Bank).

### From Beauvais Airport

Shuttles between the airport and Paris (Porte Maillot) are timed with the flights - 75 min. ride - €16.90 one way - www.aeroportparisbeauvais.com.

**"Paris Visite" Travel Pass**
Valid for 1, 2, 3, or 5 days. p. 163.

Entrance to the Paris métro.
carterdayne/Getty Images Plus

# Unmissable

## our selection of must-see sites

★★★ **Eiffel Tower**
Map AB5 - p. 70

★★★ **Notre-Dame de Paris**
Map F6 - p. 18

★★★ **Musée d'Orsay**
Map D5 - p. 73

★★★ **Champs-Élysées District**
Map BC3-4 - p. 81

★★★ **Louvre**
Map DE4-5 - p. 26

★★★ **Saint-Germain-des-Prés**
Map D5-6 - p. 56

★★★ **The Seine, Quays, and Bridges**
p. 24

★★★ **Latin Quarter**
Map E6-7 - p. 47

★★★ **Montmartre**
Map E1 - p. 88

★★★ **The Marais**
Map FG4-5 - p. 35

# Our Top Picks

Stroll around the **Palais-Royal** Garden and window-shop in the arcades. Then continue a little further north to discover the covered passages (des Panoramas, Jouffroy, Verdeau, Galerie Vivienne), filled with old-fashioned charm. *See p. 32.*

Climb the **Butte Montmartre** via the narrow stairs on the hill's northern flank, take a stroll through the winding cobbled lanes, and stop a moment on the tiny Place du Calvaire, at the top of the stairs that descend into Paris, to take in the sweeping view of the capital. *See p. 88.*

Antoine Mercusot/Musée Carnavalet – Histoire de Paris

The Salle des Enseignes, Musée Carnavalet - Histoire de Paris.

Enjoy a leisurely walk around the garden of the **Musée Rodin**, then take a beat under the trees amidst the master's magnificent statues: *The Thinker, The Burghers of Calais, The Gates of Hell.* *See p. 69.*

Relive the entire history of Paris at the **Musée Carnavalet**, from prehistoric times to the present day. A royal showcase, a revolutionary heroine, an intellectual powerhouse, a capital of the arts... Explore the myths and legends of the "City of Light" from one fascinating room to the next, occupying two *hôtels particuliers* in the Marais district. *See p. 40.*

Discover the latest trends in modern art at the **Bourse de Commerce-Pinault Collection**, the **Fondation Louis-Vuitton** or the **Palais de Tokyo**, veritable temples of contemporary creativity. *See pp. 44, 79 and 86.*

Conjure the splendors of the Belle Époque inside the opulent **Petit Palais**, relax in its sublime interior garden, and admire its rich collections of Parisian sculptures and paintings from the late 19th century. Just a stone's throw from the Champs-Élysées, and admission is free! *See p. 84.*

Mosey under the wisteria through the **Mouzaïa** neighborhood, where villas and cottages with gardens line paved streets punctuated by 19th-century-style streetlamps. The countryside in Paris! *See p. 101.*

B. Gardel/hemis.fr

Tango in the Jardin Tino Rossi on a balmy summer's evening.



Catch the **no. 75 bus** from the Hôtel de Ville, ride through the Marais district, along the Canal Saint-Martin, around the **Parc des Buttes-Chaumont**, and alight at the **Philharmonie de Paris**, at La Villette. *See pp. 96-100.*

Dive into the world of Parisian Haute Couture at the **Galerie Dior**, a fashion fairytale showcasing the most iconic pieces created by Christian Dior from 1946 to the present day. *See p. 84.*

On a bright, sunny day, go marvel at the shimmering stained-glass windows in **Sainte-Chapelle**, a dazzling display of red and blue light dating from the 13th century. *See p. 23.*

On Sundays, when the streets are banned to cars, cycle along the **Canal Saint-Martin** between République and Parc de la Villette. Make like a local and picnic in the park then, on the way back, sip an apéritif at La Rotonde, or play a game of pétanque on the canalside. *See p. 96.*

Take a stroll around the **Parc Rives-de-Seine** on the Seine quayside looking out to Île Saint-Louis and the Louvre (Right Bank) or to the Musée d'Orsay (Left Bank). Or perhaps around the Jardin Tino Rossi to dance rock, salsa, or tango beneath the stars. *See p. 149.*

# Three Days in Paris

Paris is a tourist epicenter and the lines can be endless outside the city's most iconic monuments. Plan your visit accordingly, and remember to book skip-the-line tickets in advance.

## Day 1

**Morning**

Begin where Paris began: Île de la Cité ★★★ *(p. 18)*. Admire Notre-Dame★★★, a jewel of Gothic art, destroyed by fire. Pass through Place Louis-Lépine where you will find a charming flower market. Continue on to Sainte-Chapelle ★★★ and the Conciergerie★★. Cross the Pont-Neuf★ to wander around and have lunch in Saint-Germain-des-Prés★★★ *(p. 56)*.

**Afternoon**

Take a tour of the Latin Quarter★★★ *(p. 47)*: the Église St-Séverin★★, Hôtel de Cluny★★, and Sorbonne★, a quick pause in the Jardin du Luxembourg★★, then on to the Panthéon★★, Église St-Étienne-du-Mont★★, and Rue Mouffetard★.

**Evening**

Saunter along the quays on the Rive Gauche and over to Île Saint-Louis★★ *(p. 25)* with its superb 17th-century abodes. It's then moments to the Marais★★★ district across the river for dinner *(p. 35)*. Or head into Montparnasse ★ *(p. 62)*, a buzzing neighborhood of cafés, cinemas, and theaters.

### One More Day

Head out towards Eastern Paris to wander around the city's bustling, down-to-earth neighborhoods, where the cool Parisians gather: the Canal St-Martin (p. 96), the villages of Belleville and Ménilmontant (p. 105), the Parc des Buttes-Chaumont (p. 100), and La Villette (p. 98).

## Day 2

**Morning**

Depending on your mood, take in the Musée d'Orsay★★★ *(p. 73)* or one section of the Louvre★★★ *(p. 26)* – cross the Passerelle Léopold-Sédar-Senghor to get from one museum to the other. On a sunny day, a picnic in the peaceful gardens of the Palais-Royal★★ *(p. 32)* makes for a pleasant lunch. Or why not do a Japanese restaurant on Rue Sainte-Anne, a 10-minute walk from the Louvre?

**Afternoon**

Continue by foot to Étoile by way of the Tuileries★, Place de la Concorde★★★ *(p. 81)*, the Champs-Élysées★★ *(p. 83)* and, at the top of the avenue, climb up to the roof of the Arc de Triomphe★★★ *(p. 86)* for incredible views of the French capital.

**Late afternoon and evening**

*From Charles-de-Gaulle-Étoile, take the métro to Pigalle (Line 2).* Scale the Butte Montmartre★★★ *(p. 88)*. Meander through the winding streets lined with gorgeous period houses, then stop to feel awestruck by the immense mosaic adorning the apse of the Sacré-Cœur★★ *(p. 93)* and by the panoramic views of Paris. Go back down to the Abbesses district (Rue des Abbesses, Rue des Martyrs, and Rue des Trois-Frères), where you will find plenty of restaurants.

## Day 3

### Morning

Not too hazy on the horizon? Head to the Eiffel Tower★★★ *(p. 70)* and its neighboring museum, the Musée du Quai-Branly - Jacques-Chirac★★ *(p. 72)*. To conserve your energy and still get to see the Seine, take a Batobus boat *(the 1-day pass lets you hop on and off all day)* at the Tour-Eiffel métro station. Once aboard, take in the sights along the way: the Grand★ and Petit Palais★★, the view of the Invalides★★★, Place de la Concorde★★★, the Musée d'Orsay★★★, the Louvre★★★, and Île de la Cité★★★. Get off at the Hôtel de Ville métro stop for lunch around Beaubourg, or a little further in the Marais★★★.

### Afternoon and evening

Enjoy a stroll around the Marais district★★★ *(p. 35)* to admire its beautiful buildings. Don't miss the Place des Vosges★★★ and its sumptuous *hôtels particuliers* (private mansions), and visit one of the museums in the neighborhood: the Musée Picasso★★, the Musée Carnavalet★★ (all about the history of Paris), or the Musée d'Art et d'Histoire du Judaïsme★★. No trip to the Marais would be complete without a spot of shopping or a bite to eat in one of the area's plethora of bars and restaurants.

EoNaYa/Getty Images Plus

The Jardin des Tuileries.

# One More Day in Greater Paris

Here are some suggestions for day trips beyond the *périphérique* (Paris ring road), in spitting distance from the Olympic sites and well connected by public transport.

## Versailles

*RER C or SNCF train.*

### ▶ The Palace★★★

*www.chateauversailles.fr*

A symbol of classical perfection, the world's largest palace was, from the late 17th century to the French Revolution, a never-ending construction site. Versailles reflected the flourishing creativity of the period and denoted the excessive extravagance of royal power, from Louis XIV through Louis XVI. Highlights: the Grand Apartments, the Hall of Mirrors, and the King's Private Apartments.

### ▶ The Palace Gardens★★★

With sweeping perspectives, elegant topiary, and majestic statues adorning the fountains, renowned landscaper Le Nôtre designed the most sumptuous of gardens for the Sun King, surpassing even the resplendent handiwork of Fouquet at Vaux-le-Vicomte. Over several years, the Gardener to the King achieved quite a feat—all the more remarkable given he was working on marshland: a meticulous arrangement of gardens, fountains, and ponds in perfect symmetry, myriad statues and artificial caves, and piles of rocks where water, one of the true passions of the Grand Siècle, spouts everywhere you look. Attending a Musical Fountains Show is the best way to appreciate this landscaping masterwork.

### ▶ The City of Versailles★★

This is a city planned to allow the sun to shine down the three wide avenues that all converge towards the palace. Featuring stunning period facades, fine examples of classical and baroque architecture, and somewhat bumpy cobbled streets that still resonate with its past as a "royal city", Versailles forms an extraordinary ensemble, originally designed to accommodate courtiers who hated to be too far from their king.

### Versailles Palace in Figures

The palace occupies an area of 721,206 sq.ft, of which only about 172,000 sq.ft is open to visitors! It contains 700 rooms, 67 staircases, 352 fireplaces, 2,153 windows, and 27 acres of roof, not to mention countless works of art and paintings. Outdoors, the grounds (2,100 acres) comprise almost 27 miles of paths, 250,000 trees, 172,000 sq.ft of boxwood shrubs, more than 10.5 miles of bowers, 55 fountains, and 600 water features. To enjoy the treasures of Versailles in 3D: www.gvn.chateauversailles.fr.

H. Milas/Alamy/hemis.fr

Ceiling of the Salon de Vénus, Château de Versailles.

## Saint-Denis

*Getting there: Métro Line 13, RER B or D, Tramway T1 or T5.*
The centuries collide in this multicultural and spirited working-class Paris suburb.

▶ **Basilique St-Denis★★★**
*1 r. de la Légion-d'Honneur*
*www.saint-denis-basilique.fr*
Since the 12th century, this basilica has occupied a special place in the history of France as well as the history of art: each period of its construction or reconstruction represents a veritable artistic revolution. The cemetery where the kings of France since the Capetian dynasty were laid to rest harbors a collection of recumbent statues and tombs unique in Europe. Also worth a look is the ambitious project to resurrect the spire and northern tower, planned for completion in 2030. This original construction site-school is open to apprentice stone masons *(www.suivezlafleche.com).*

▶ *The* **Stade de France★**
*www.stadefrance.com*
Designed by the architects Zublena, Macary, Regembal, and Costantini, this Olympic stadium opened in 1998 is a multi-record breaker: a total footprint of 17 hectares, 886 ft long, 755 ft wide, 115 ft high, 28 miles of staircase, holding over 80,000 spectators for football and rugby, 96,000 for concerts! To learn all its secrets, a visit to its museum is a must-do.

## La Défense

*Métro Line 1, RER A (NB: t+ ticket not valid), Tramway T2.*
Developed 60 years ago, Europe's largest (in terms of office stock) purpose-built **business district★★** is a showcase of contemporary architecture and an open-air museum. It is an extension of the perspective of the historic axis stretching from the Louvre to the Grande Arche, an immense 300,000-ton, 360-foot-high concrete arch, designed by the Danish architect Otto von Spreckelsen. Its panoramic elevator leads to a viewpoint with breathtaking vistas of Paris and Nanterre.

# Paris along the River by Bike

In recent years, Paris has come to rival bike-crazy cities like Amsterdam, and now boasts hundreds of miles of cycle paths—over 600 miles, in fact! The capital seems much smaller when you explore it on two wheels. The 10-mile journey west to east—along the riverbanks and quaysides—takes in some of the city's most grandiose monuments.

### ▶ Champ-de-Mars - Invalides

Depart from the École Militaire *(p. 69)* for an epic stroll through the Champ-de-Mars all the way to the Eiffel Tower *(p. 70)*. From the iconic tower, follow the cycle path that runs along the quayside on the Rive Gauche to reach the Esplanade des Invalides *(p. 66)*.

### ▶ Invalides - Tuileries

Cross the sumptuous Pont Alexandre-III *(p. 66)* towards the Petit and Grand Palais *(p. 83-84)*. The cycle lane on the Rive Droite leads straight to Place de la Concorde *(p. 81)*, where you can stand to admire the Champs-Élysée *(p. 83)* and the Jardin des Tuileries *(p. 82)*.



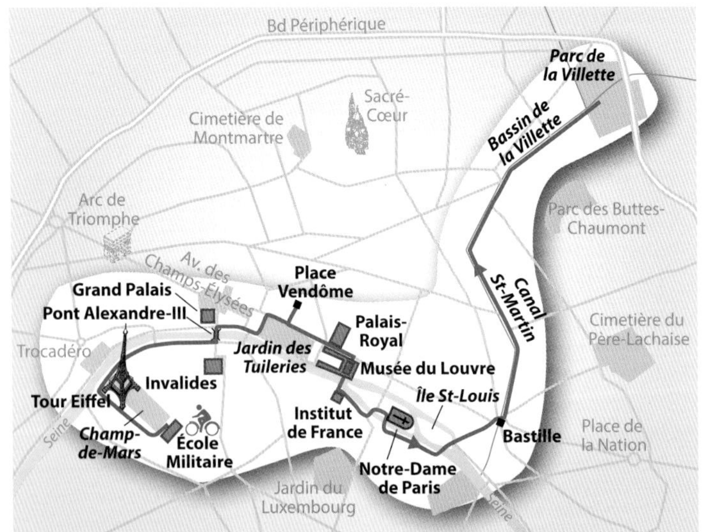

olrat/Getty Images Plus

Paris Plages on the Seine's Rive Droite (Right Bank).



## ▶ Tuileries - Louvre

After a quick tour of Place Vendôme *(p. 30)*, peddle up Rue de Rivoli, now reserved for cyclists, to Place du Palais-Royal *(p. 32)*. On the right, the Passage Richelieu leads to the monumental Pyramide du Louvre and its impressive Cour Carrée courtyard *(p. 26)*.

## ▶ Louvre - Bastille

From the Cour Carrée, it's a short ride to the Pont des Arts pedestrian bridge, which takes you over to the Institut de France *(p. 59)*, where you can switch to the Rive Gauche cycle lane. Carry on heading east, keeping your eyes peeled for the Pont-Neuf *(p. 24)*, Notre-Dame *(p. 18)* and Île Saint-Louis *(p. 25)*, whose eastern tip you'll cross by taking the Boulevard Henri-IV, direction Bastille *(p. 102)*.

## ▶ Bastille - La Villette

Boulevard Richard-Lenoir stretches to the Canal Saint-Martin *(p. 96)*, which you can follow all the way to the artificial lake and park of La Villette *(p. 97)*. One of the best places to see the more real and less glitzy side of Paris.

### Top Tip

The Vélib Pass *(Terms & Conditions and prices, p. 164)* lets you pick up and drop off a bicycle at any of the 1,400 stations scattered across the city. Opt for the mechanical bikes (green) or electric bikes (blue).

# VISIT PARIS

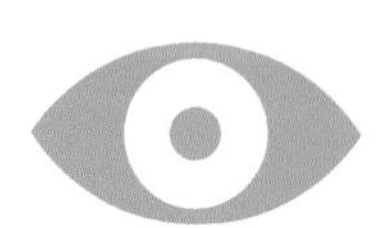



Montmartre and Sacré-Cœur Basilica.
espiegle/Getty Images Plus

# Paris Today

Not too long ago, there was a growing fear about the future of Paris. Ever more touristy, ever more popular, would the French capital turn into a mere living museum, a glossy but vapid version of its former self? Au contraire is the resounding verdict! Even after the recent pandemic that knocked Paris for six, the French capital has never looked so electrified, eclectic, and exuberant. More and more café and restaurant terraces are spilling onto the streets, neighborhood stores—and consuming local—are coming back in favor in every arrondissement, pedestrians and cyclists are reclaiming public spaces, and Parisians are even getting their fingers green by planting around the urban trees outside their buildings. More than ever, Paris has become a livable city for its residents who are fully embracing everything the capital has to offer.



## A Community Space

The change is most palpable on the highways: long the exclusive domain of cars, now the streets are chock full of bicycles (70% more bike traffic since the lockdown of spring 2020). The "slow travel" revolution is gaining momentum, helped along by new technologies (self-service bicycles) and municipal policy that has, it's fair to say, massively disrupted the city infrastructure (more than 600 miles of cycle paths built to date, compared with 2.6 miles in 1995). In addition, the city council has announced plans to fully pedestrianize the city center (from Boulevard St-Germain in the south to the Grands Boulevards in the north) by the time of the 2024 Olympic Games—a project that has, however, raised more than a few eyebrows at Paris' police headquarters...
Another appealing takeover of the public space comes courtesy of the rise of the outdoor apéritif! No sooner does the clement weather arrive than parks and gardens all over Paris—not to mention the quaysides along the Seine and Canal Saint-Martin—turn into one giant picnic blanket! Just go for an evening stroll to see for yourself: far from growing old gracefully, Paris is still a city that loves to have fun!

## A Living Mosaic

With rumbles in the press that rural living is coming back into vogue, might the capital have found the magic formula? To remain a cluster of villages where provincial charm has the upper hand over urban living.
Some will want to stroll around the **Latin Quarter**, between Maubert and the Seine, past the wonky period houses, through quaint squares where café terraces invite you for a rest stop, and along the winding alleyways that give the impression of being in a small town–until you catch a glimpse of the colossal Notre-Dame as you round a bend!
Others might prefer to explore **Saint-Germain-des-Prés**, with its maze of narrow streets between the Seine and Boulevard Saint-Germain: the food market on Rue de Buci, Cour du Commerce-St-André, Place Saint-Sulpice. The former bastion of the city's intellectuals remains an enclave

of resistance to the craziness of modern life!

Esthetes will appreciate, too, **Île Saint-Louis**, irresistibly drawn by its classical architecture and peaceful charm. Take a tour of its art galleries and boutiques before going for a walk along the Seine where the shadows of the past still cast their spell.

The same sense of enchantment can be found around Place des Vosges and along Rue des Francs-Bourgeois, in the **Marais**, a Jewish quarter and gay village, whose majestic *hôtels particuliers* have been restored to life, among antique shops, fashion boutiques, bars, and bookstores.

And what's left to say about the mythical village of **Montmartre**, in the north of the city? The flights of steps up the Butte lead to sweeping vistas and charming tiny parks hidden beyond the tourist streets. It's the countryside in the city!

In the northeast of Paris, the former blue-collar districts have been given a new lease of life, too: **Ménilmontant** and **Belleville**, as well as the **Canal Saint-Martin** and around the **artificial lake** at **La Villette** have been taken over by artist studios, new-generation bakeries, coworking spaces, community-run bars, and health-conscious restaurants.

## A Cultural Melting Pot

Paris is renowned for being a city of art and culture, and major events in recent years have further cemented its reputation, such as the long-awaited opening of the Bourse de Commerce-Pinault Collection, or that of the Hôtel de la Marine, not forgetting the reopening, after extensive facelifts, of the Musée

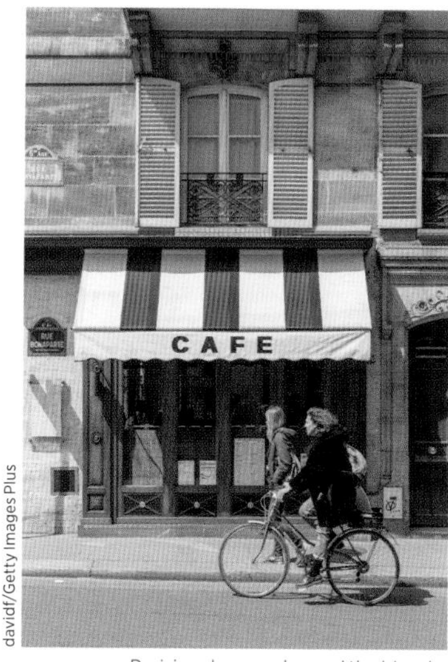


davidf/Getty Images Plus

Parisians have embraced the bicycle.

Carnavalet, the Musée de Cluny, and the La Samaritaine department store.

But to discover Paris is also about soaking up the festive atmosphere that permeates the city during big annual events: Paris Plages and other summer festivals (open-air cinema at La Villette, Paris l'Été, the Tuileries funfair), the Nuit Blanche in fall when museums stay open late into the night, and the magical Christmas lights and decorations that twinkle all over the city.

Paris is an incredibly creative, fiercely free city that is constantly reinventing itself and pushing boundaries! Figuratively but also physically as it spills over the city's ring road and expands into Grand Paris (Greater Paris).

# Île de la Cité★★★ and Île St-Louis★★

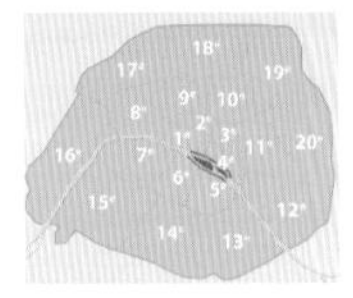


**Île de la Cité, the historic birthplace of Paris, is the French capital's beating heart: who can resist the romantic setting of its flower market, the iconic apse of Notre-Dame Cathedral, or the awe-inspiring stained-glass windows of Sainte-Chapelle? More secluded, the neighboring Île Saint-Louis is lined with magnificent 17th-century mansions along its ancient quays in the leafy shade of centuries-old plane trees. Surrounded by the Seine, you'll be captivated!**

▶**Getting there:** Ⓜ Cité (Line 4), Châtelet (Lines 1, 4, 7, 11, and 14; Lines A, B, and D) - RER Saint-Michel-Notre-Dame (Lines B and C).

**Local Map p. 20-21. Detachable Map EF5-6.**

▶**Tip:** Visit Sainte-Chapelle on a sunny day to appreciate the full splendor of its stained-glass windows. Save money with the Sainte-Chapelle/ Conciergerie twin ticket.



## ÎLE DE LA CITÉ

**EF5-6** Strategically located between two branches of the Seine, the island is the site of the original settlement of Lutetia, the heart of its civil, military, and religious authority.

### Cathédrale Notre-Dame de Paris ★★★

**F6** Ⓜ *Cité or RER B Saint-Michel-Notre-Dame - 6 parvis Notre-Dame - ✆ 01 42 34 56 10 - www.notredamedeparis.fr - Closed for restoration until late 2024.*
The fire on April 15, 2019 that set Notre-Dame ablaze (thankfully no one was hurt) will forever remain etched in people's memories. Starting in the eaves, the fire spread throughout the roof and the spire, designed by Eugène Viollet-Le-Duc in the 19th century, which eventually collapsed. Some 1,300 works, many priceless, were rescued and are now being stored at the Louvre or in secure warehouses. Almost one billion euro in donations were raised for the cathedral's reconstruction, slated for completion by late 2024.
The Bishop of Paris **Maurice de Sully** began building Notre-Dame in 1163 to give the capital a cathedral worthy of its standing. The cathedral was completed in around 1300. Notre-Dame was one of the first large churches built to be supported by flying buttresses, which take all the weight of the structure on the outside to maximize the space and light on the inside. The flying buttresses were fitted with a drainage system designed to protect the stone foundations from rainwater runoff: the famous **gargoyles**. But what makes the cathedral so exceptional is more to do with its beauty and symmetry. Everything has its place; nothing is superfluous.

It's such a marvel of harmony that you can easily forget that its construction spanned more than a century. The intricate portals on the **facade** are true works of art. On the left, the Portal of the Virgin is adorned with a moving depiction of the Dormition of the Mother of God and the Coronation of Mary. In the center is the Last Judgment. The archivolts represent the heavenly court.

## LA CITÉ

0 — 100 m

### WHERE TO EAT

Les Fous de l'Île........................ 1

Maison Maison........................ 3

### WHERE TO DRINK

Berthillon........................ 2

Hoct&Loca........................ 15

Le Liquorium........................ 26

Le Tout-Paris........................ 29

### SHOPPING

Le Piéton de Paris........................ 15

### WHERE TO STAY

Hôtel Andréa........................ 2

At the bottom, heaven and hell are symbolized by Abraham saving souls and by terrifying demons. On the right is the Portal of Saint Anne, where the Virgin is seated on a throne holding the infant Jesus, in true Romanesque style. Above the portals, the **Gallery of Kings** is a row of the kings of Judah and Israel, Christ's ancestors. Removed and partially destroyed during the French

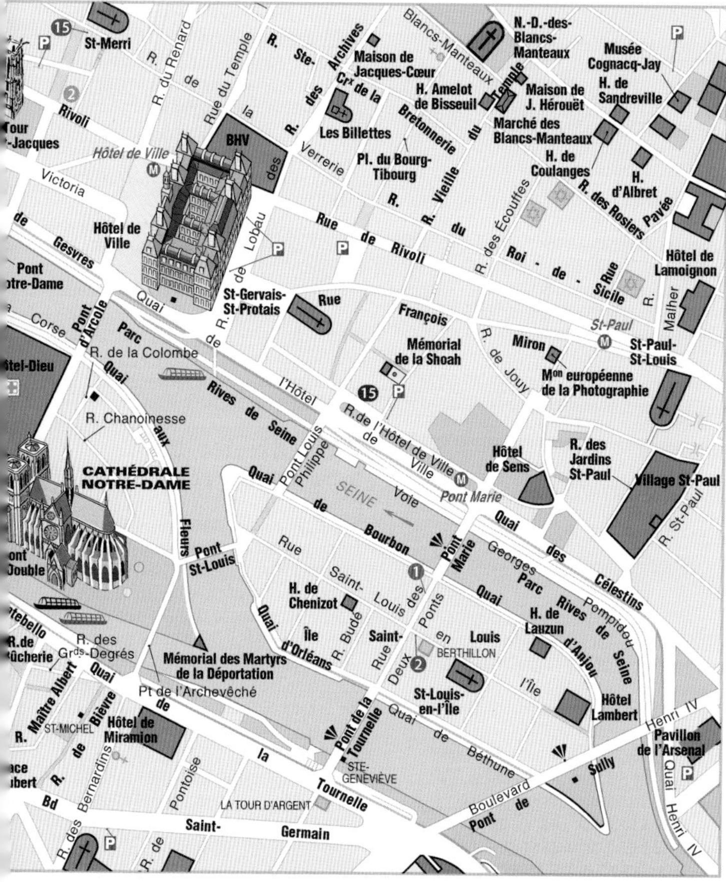

### A Colossal Construction Site

After many long months spent making the site safe, the restoration of Notre-Dame picked up pace at the end of 2022. On this scaffolding-clad Gothic behemoth, up to a thousand journeymen, artisans, and laborers are beavering away! The vaults above the nave, which collapsed during the fire, were rebuilt in spring 2023, just as the reconstruction of the spire began. Meanwhile, the entire monument has undergone a painstaking restoration including its stained-glass windows, Grand Organ, statues, frescoes, and other features. Under the square in front, the exhibition **Notre-Dame de Paris: au cœur du chantier** *(rebatirnotredamedeparis.fr - Tue-Sun 10am-8pm - free)* takes visitors into "the heart of the worksite" to discover the trades and crafts of the men and women working on this ambitious project. **Éternelle Notre-Dame** *(www.eternellenotredame.com - booking req. - 45 min. - €30)* is a terrific virtual reality experience that transports you through the history of the monument from the 12th century to the present day. Amazing!



Revolution (they were mistaken for the kings of France!), the original sculptures are now preserved in the Musée du Moyen Âge *(p. 50)*. The ones you can admire at the cathedral today date back to the restoration work of French architect Viollet-le-Duc. Almost 33 feet in diameter, the large rose window resembles a halo above the statue of the Virgin and Child. The interior, whose graceful and bold elevation is a testament to the talents of the French Gothic school of architecture in the early 13th century, should regain its former glory once the current renovation work is completed.

**Tours** – *1 r. du Cloître-Notre-Dame - 01 53 40 60 80 - Closed until late 2024.* The summit reveals one of the most glorious panoramas of the capital. The tower on the right holds the famous bourdon, the oldest bell weighing in at 13 tons, with its half-ton clapper.

**Crypte Archéologique★** - *7 pl. Jean-Paul-II - 01 55 42 50 10 – www.crypte.paris.fr – daily ex. Mon 10am- 6pm - €9 (-18s free).* Beneath the square in front of Notre-Dame, expanded during Haussmann's major renovation of Paris, the foundations of monuments from the 3rd to the 19th centuries were unearthed. Notable highlights include remains of two Gallo-Roman rooms heated by hypocaust, the foundations of the Late Roman city wall, as well as the cellars and basements of medieval houses and monuments.

## Around Notre-Dame

To the north of the cathedral, the old Chapitre district (Rue Chanoinesse and Rue de la Colombe), although modernized through the ages, remains the only true medieval vestige on Île de la Cité. To admire Notre-Dame's magnificent apse, the **Pont de l'Archevêché** is the best vantage point. Close by, at the eastern tip of the island, the **Mémorial des Martyrs de la Déportation** *(10am-7pm, 5pm Oct-Mar – free)* is a moving tribute to all those who perished in the Nazi concentration camps. The crypt, composed of stone, metal and concrete, was designed in 1962 by the French modernist Georges-Henri Pingusson as a place for somber

Inna Zabotnova/Getty Images Plus

Sainte-Chapelle



reflection. A tomb contains the remains of an unknown deportee.
Finish your tour at the **Marché aux Fleurs**, an institution in the heart of Île de la Cité, a flower market set within stunning iron and glass pavilions. The bird market there had its swan song several years ago.

## Sainte-Chapelle ★★★

**E5** Ⓜ *Cité. 8 bd du Palais - ✆ 01 53 40 60 80 - www.sainte-chapelle.fr - 9am-7pm (5pm Oct-Mar) - €11.50 (-25s free) - €18.50 combined ticket with the Conciergerie - expect crowds at peak times.*
Built in the 13th century by **Saint Louis** (King Louis IX) in the heart of Île de la Cité to house the Relics of the Passion (including the Crown of Thorns of Christ), just acquired by the French monarchy, Sainte-Chapelle is close to perfection. Designed as a shrine of stone and glass, this Radiant Gothic masterpiece took six years to complete. The lower chapel is all the more impressive given it is scarcely 23 feet tall. The **stained-glass windows**★★★ in the upper chapel are the oldest in Paris. They depict 1,113 scenes inspired by the Passion and Exaltation of Christ, the announcement of His birth by the great prophets and John the Baptist, and various biblical scenes. The western rose window from the 15th century illustrates the Apocalypse of Saint John.
The sun's rays passing through these 49-foot-high windows make for an unforgettable spectacle.

## Conciergerie ★★

**E5** Ⓜ *Cité – 2 bd du Palais - ✆ 01 53 40 60 80 - www.paris-conciergerie.fr - 9:30am-6pm - €11.50 (-25s free); €18.50 combined ticket with Sainte-Chapelle.* Head over to Quai de la Mégisserie, on the other side of the Seine, to enjoy the best view of the Conciergerie, its four towers reflected in the river that once covered their foundations. First a palace for the kings of France, before the Louvre, it was used as a courthouse from the 14th century and then a prison. In the center of the Seine-facing facade, the two twin towers once guarded the entrance to the royal palace. The right-hand tower housed the royal treasury, hence its name of **Tour d'Argent** (Silver Tower). At the corner of Boulevard du Palais, the square tower is named the **Tour de l'Horloge** after the first public clock (which still works) was installed there in 1370. Containing beautifully preserved Gothic rooms, in particular the **Salle des Gens d'Armes**★★ (Soldier's Hall), the interior of the Conciergerie evokes the history of the French Revolution: many of those convicted by the Revolutionary Court (including Danton and Robespierre) were imprisoned there. The cell where **Marie-Antoinette** spent her final days was converted to an expiatory chapel in 1815. Between January 1793 and July 1794, more than 2,600 prisoners were put on carts and taken from the Conciergerie to the square where the guillotine awaited.

Cross the Cour du Mai to get to the **Palais de Justice**★ *(8 bd du Palais - ✆ 01 44 32 52 52 - www.cours-appel.justice.fr - daily ex. weekend 8:30am-6:30pm - inquire about tours).* The building you visit today has come a long way since it was the palace of the Kings of France. The **Salle des Pas Perdus** (Hall of Lost Causes) was commissioned by Philip the Fair and was the first civil chamber in the apartments of Saint Louis. The **high court**, which shared this site, was moved in 2018 to a new building designed by Renzo Piano, in the Clichy-Batignolles district (➲ *p. 87*).



## Place Dauphine ★

**E5** Ⓜ *Pont-Neuf.* For a long time, Île de la Cité ended in the west with an archipelago cut off from the main island by the marshy branches of the Seine. In 1607, at this spot **Henry IV** ordered the construction of this triangular square flanked by uniform houses. The land was divided into lots and sold off to merchants, such as goldsmiths who lent their name to the quay that was built in the 19th century. From 1913 to 2017, the Paris Judicial Police had their HQ at 36, Quai des Orfèvres, a now legendary address.

## Pont-Neuf ★

**E5** Ⓜ *Pont-Neuf.* The "new" bridge is actually the oldest bridge in Paris, completed in 1604, and the first without houses built along its quays, yielding unobstructed views over the river. The half-moon alcoves were taken up by open-air stalls, attracting tooth pullers, clowns, and throngs of idle onlookers and pickpockets. Below, enjoy the idyllic setting of Square du Vert-Galant, surrounded by the Seine at the western tip of Île de la Cité, looking out to the Louvre (Right Bank), the Hôtel de la Monnaie, and the Institut de France (Left Bank).

## Quai Saint-Michel

**E6** Here, between Place St-Michel and Notre-Dame, a community of **booksellers**, working from their famous green boxes, tout vintage and rare books, engravings, drawings, magazines, etc., offering one of the most picturesque images in the city. The center of Paris counts nearly 220 booksellers and 900 boxes filled with books and various other publications dotted along the Left and Right Banks.

## ÎLE SAINT-LOUIS ★★

**F6** Ⓜ *Pont Marie or Sully-Morland.* A popular spot with Parisians on a Sunday, who come to stroll past its gleaming stone buildings or picnic along Quai de Béthune and Quai de Orléans. A haven of calm away from the bustle of the city.
In the Middle Ages, Île Saint-Louis was split in two: Île aux Vaches (Island of Cows) and Île Notre-Dame. In the 17th century, entrepreneur Christophe Marie was granted permission from **Louis XIII** and the Chapter of Notre-Dame to join the two islands, build bridges across the river, and sell off plots of land. The real-estate operation would turn this squalid land into an island with a medieval grid pattern of streets, adorned with classical mansions each one more sumptuous than the next. The residences with their beautiful facades and elegant wrought-iron balconies once belonged to wealthy bankers and magistrates. Rue St-Louis-en-l'Île is home to some of the most sublime mansions in the district, such as Hôtel Chenizot with its ornately sculpted balcony (at no. 51).
**Église Saint-Louis-en-l'Île★** – Feel free to push open the door to this beautiful church, a fine example of French Baroque architecture, completed in 1725. The interior is a veritable museum, filled with paintings and sculptures from the 15th to the 18th centuries.
**Pont de Sully** – This bridge, at the eastern tip of the island, dates from 1876. From the northern branch, the view takes in the Quai d'Anjou and the Hôtel Lambert (built by Le Vau in 1640), the Port des Célestins, the **Pont Marie★** *(see below)* and the bell tower of Saint-Gervais; from the southern branch, admire the glorious **view★** of Notre-Dame and Île de la Cité. At 17, Quai d'Anjou, the **Hôtel de Lauzun** (17th c.), its gutters adorned with dolphins, was the one-time meeting place of the "Club des Haschischins", whose members included author Balzac and poet Théophile Gautier. Gautier wrote a magazine article about the drug-induced experiences that went on there. Baudelaire lived in the building from 1843 to 1845, writing part of his poetry anthology, *Les Fleurs du Mal*, there.
**Quai de Bourbon** – At the western tip of the island, the chained bollards and the view of Église Saint-Gervais-St-Protais and the Hôtel de Ville make this a spellbinding **site★**.

## Pont Marie ★

**F6** Ⓜ *Pont-Marie.* The oldest bridge in Paris, after the Pont-Neuf, and arguably one of the most stunning for its simplicity. It was commissioned by Christophe Marie and completed in 1635, but it had to be partially rebuilt in 1670 after major floods swept away two of its arches.

## Pont de la Tournelle

**F6** Ⓜ *Pont-Marie.* Across from the period houses on Quai de la Tournelle (Left Bank), this bridge grants magnificent **views★★★** of Notre-Dame. The statue (1928) of Saint Geneviève, the patron saint of Paris, stands on one of its stone columns.

# Musée du Louvre★★★

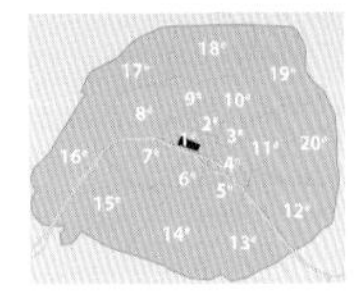

**With over 400 rooms, nine miles of corridors, two miles of external facade, and 480,000 works in total, the Louvre is the world's largest museum in more ways than one! Today symbolized by its famous glass pyramid, the former palace of the Kings of France encapsulates 800 years of architecture and 10,000 years of art history. A masterpiece at the service of masterpieces!**

▶ **Getting there:** Ⓜ Louvre-Rivoli (Line 1) or Palais-Royal-Musée-du-Louvre (Lines 1, 7).

**Detachable Map DE4-5.**

▶ **Practical information:** Reception/Ticket Office - main entrance via the pyramid - ✆ 01 40 20 53 17 - www.louvre.fr - 9am-6pm, Fri 9am-9:45pm - closed Tue - €17 (-26s free).

▶ **Tip:** The museum is so vast that not every room is open at the same time. Go to the reception under the pyramid or check the website to see which rooms are going to be closed during your visit. In any case, you won't get to see everything in one day!



## THE PALACE

Its story began in 1190, when King Philip II of France chose to build, in the west of Paris, a fortress that Charles V would later transform into an elegant royal residence, in the 14th century. It all changed in the 16th century when Francis I razed the medieval palace to the ground and commissioned the architect Pierre Lescot to create a Renaissance-inspired castle, the beginnings of the sublime **Cour Carrée★★★** that Louis XIV would complete in the 17th century, with its main feature, facing the city, a lavish **colonnade★★**, the handiwork of Perrault. In the same period, Henry IV built a gallery stretching over 1,600 feet along the Seine to link the Louvre to the Palais des Tuileries, as per the wishes of Catherine de' Medici in the 1560s. Uniting these two palaces was the "Grand Design" of every French monarch up to Napoleon III, who finally succeeded in enclosing the **Cour Napoléon★★**. Alas, in 1871, the Communards set fire to the Palais des Tuileries, leading to the rather original shape of the current Palais du Louvre, its two wings embracing the **Jardin des Tuileries★** (*p. 82*).
In 1981, France's president François Mitterrand launched the "Grand Louvre" project, which saw the museum reorganized around the iconic pyramid designed by the Chinese-American architect Ieoh Ming Pei, a laudable union of French classicism and contemporary design.

## THE MUSEUM

**Maps** – In the Hall Napoléon, the reception lobby beneath the pyramid, you'll find free maps to guide you around the museum's three wings: Sully, Denon, and Richelieu.
**Visitor Trails** - Themed self-guided tours give you insights into a dozen artworks. Collect maps at the museum reception.
**Audio guides** – *✆ 01 40 20 53 17 - www.louvre.fr - for adults, children and people with disabilities, commentary on selected artworks in 9 langs. - €5.*
**Guided Tours** – *✆ 01 40 20 53 17 - www.louvre.fr - guided tours, check times - €9/12 - introductory museum tours ("Welcome to the Louvre", 1hr30) or themed tours, in English or French. Buy tickets in the group reception area under the pyramid.*
**Events** - See the "What's On" section of the museum's website for the latest news and programming.

### The Must-See Rooms

A visit to the Louvre is as much about the building—a marvel of classical architecture—as the artworks it houses. Don't miss the remains of the medieval Louvre (walking past the ancient ditches of the original keep is mind-blowing!), the magnificent Marly and Puget courtyards (for French sculpture), the glittering Galerie d'Apollon ordered by Louis XIV (featuring the crown jewels), and the sumptuous apartments of Napoleon III, a riot of gold and tassels!

## The Major Masterpieces

**Sully Wing** – **The Venus de Milo**, Level 0, Salle 16 - *The Great Sphinx*, Level -1, crypt - *The Seated Scribe*, Level 1, Salle 22 - *Amenhotep IV*, Level 1, Salle 25 - *The Turkish Bath*, by Ingres, Level 2, Salle 60 - *The Card Sharp*, by Georges de La Tour, Level 2, Salle 28 - *The Bolt*, by Fragonard, Level 2, Salle 48.
**Denon Wing** – **The Mona Lisa**, by Leonardo da Vinci, Level 1, Salle 6 - **The Wedding at Cana**, by Veronese, Level 1, Salle de la Joconde - **Winged Victory of Samothrace**, Level 1, top of the Daru staircase - *Cycladic Idol*, Level -1, Salle 1 - *Borghese Gladiator*, Level 0, Salle B - *Psyche Revived by Cupid's Kiss*, by Canova, Level 0, Salle 4 - *The Dying Slave* and *The Rebellious Slave*, by Michelangelo, Level 0, Salle 4 - *The Coronation of Napoleon I*, by David, Level 1, Salle 75 - **The Raft of the Medusa**, by Géricault, Level 1, Salle 77 - *Crown of King Louis XV*, Level 1, Galerie d'Apollon - *Pyxis of al-Mughira*, Level -1, Espace A - *Mamluk Porch*, Level -1, Espace B - *Baptistry of Saint Louis*, Level -1, Espace B.
**Richelieu Wing** – **Human-Headed Winged Bull**, Level 0, Cour Khorsabad, Salle 4 - *Marly Horses*, by Guillaume Coustou, Cour Marly - *Tomb of Philippe Pot*, Cour Marly - *Erasmus*, by Hans Holbein, Level 2, Salle 11 - *Gabrielle d'Estrées and One of Her Sisters*, École de Fontainebleau, Level 2, Salle 10 - *Bathsheba at Her Bath*, by Rembrandt, Level 2, Salle 32 - *The Lacemaker*, by Vermeer, Level 2, Salle 38 - *The Rape of the Sabine Women*, by Nicolas Poussin, Level 2, Salle 11.

# Opéra★★ - Palais-Royal★★

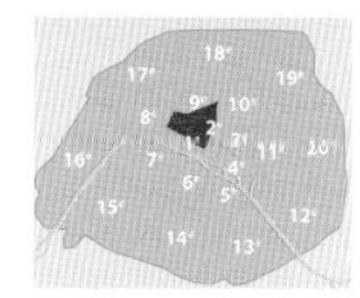


**By day, the Opéra and Grands Boulevards district is manic, thronged with tourists and traffic. At night, theater, dance, and music take center stage. The area around the Jardin du Palais-Royal, known for its designer boutiques and covered passages, is much calmer.**

▶**Getting there:** Ⓜ Opéra (Lines 3, 7, and 8), Pyramides (Lines 7 and 14), Palais-Royal-Musée-du-Louvre (Lines 1 and 7), Quatre-Septembre (Line 3).

**Local Map p. 31. Detachable Map DF3-4.**

▶**Tip:** The department stores are crowded at the weekend, so go on a weekday morning if you can.

## Palais Garnier - Opéra National de Paris ★★

**D3** Ⓜ *Opéra. Pl. de l'Opéra (entrance at the corner of Rue Scribe and Rue Auber) - ✆ 0892 89 90 90 - www.operadeparis.fr - 10am-5pm (ex. performance days) - €14 (-12s free).*
An undeniable success of the Second Empire, this building erected in 1860 by **Charles Garnier**, then aged just 35, presents its monumental and lavish facade to Place de l'Opéra. Noteworthy sculptural features include *The Dance (arcade)*, by Jean-Baptiste Carpeaux and, at the top of the opera house, Apollo holding aloft his lyre, a nod to the building's vocation. **Inside★★★**, Garnier demonstrated his originality by using marble, sourced from quarries all over France, in a wide spectrum of colors: white, blue, pink, red, and green. The **Grand Staircase** and the **Grand Foyer** are opulent works of art, as dramatic as the operas performed on stage.

## Around the Opéra

**DE3-4** From **Place de l'Opéra★★**, Boulevard des Capucines leads to the Église de la Madeleine, Rue de la Paix takes you to Place Vendôme, and **Avenue de l'Opéra★** to the Palais-Royal. Constructed between 1854 and 1878, the Avenue soon

### The Opéra Garnier in Figures

Covering 118,404 sq.ft, the Opéra Garnier actually only has room for 2,200 spectators, so big are the backstage and performance areas; the stage alone can hold 450 performers at a time. The opera house employs around 1,100 staff. The guided tour is fascinating and includes a glimpse of the main auditorium, its ceiling painted by Chagall.

became one of the city's most prestigious thoroughfares. This business and duty-free-shopping district is a magnet for tourists from overseas who flock to the upmarket department stores. **Printemps** (opened in 1865) and **Galeries Lafayette** (originally a small haberdasher's shop set up by Alphonse Kahn in 1895) have spawned imitations as far as Japan. Galeries Lafayette oozes old-world charm with its centuries-old dome and gilded railings. Head to the roof terrace for a terrific **view** of the back of the Garnier opera house. Dazzling lights and decorative window displays bring the streets and stores to life during the festive period.



## La Madeleine ★

**D3** Ⓜ *Madeleine.* A majestic colonnade and colossal sculpted pediment mark the front of this Roman temple-inspired church, consecrated in 1842. From the monumental steps, take in beautiful **views**★ of Rue Royale, the Obélisque, Palais-Bourbon, and the Invalides dome.

## Place Vendôme ★★

**D3 Rue de la Paix**, feted for its luxury storefronts—Cartier, Van Cleef & Arpels, Boucheron to name a few—, leads to Place Vendôme. Quite possibly one of the most beautiful squares from the final days of Louis XIV's reign in Paris, this square, with its octagonal layout, designed by Jules Hardouin-Mansart, was to serve as the backdrop for a colossal statue of the king. While this equestrian statue, by François Girardon, was unveiled in 1699, the square itself wasn't finished until 1702. By 1720, the square had achieved its harmonious appearance graced with uniform avant-corps and colossal Corinthian pillars. The royal statue was destroyed during the French Revolution, but in 1810 Napoleon I commissioned a **column** modeled on Trajan's column in Rome. Standing 145 feet tall, it is wrapped by a bronze spiral made out of 1,250 smelted cannons taken from Austerlitz, and crowned with a statue of the Emperor. The **Hôtel Ritz** occupies no. 15.

## Musée des Arts Décoratifs ★★

**DE4** Ⓜ *Palais-Royal-Musée-du-Louvre. 107 r. de Rivoli - ✆ 01 44 55 57 50 - www.madparis.fr - daily ex. Mon 11am-6pm, Thu 11am-9am - €14 (-26s free) - €20 combined ticket with the Musée Nissim-de-Camondo (p. 87).*
Set in a wing of the Louvre Palace, this museum presents a comprehensive panorama of the decorative arts—graphic arts, jewelry, toys, wallpaper, glass, fashion and textiles, advertising and graphic design—from the Middle Ages to the present day.
All the names that have contributed to the history of style feature: Boulle, Sèvres, Aubusson, Christofle, Lalique, Guimard, Mallet-Stevens, and so on. The interiors are faithfully recreated, including Jeanne Lanvin's private apartment and Eugène Grasset's dining room. The museum also puts on temporary exhibitions.
**Rue de Rivoli**★, its arcades lined with shops touting reasonably priced souvenirs, leads to the Jardin des Tuileries (*p. 82*).

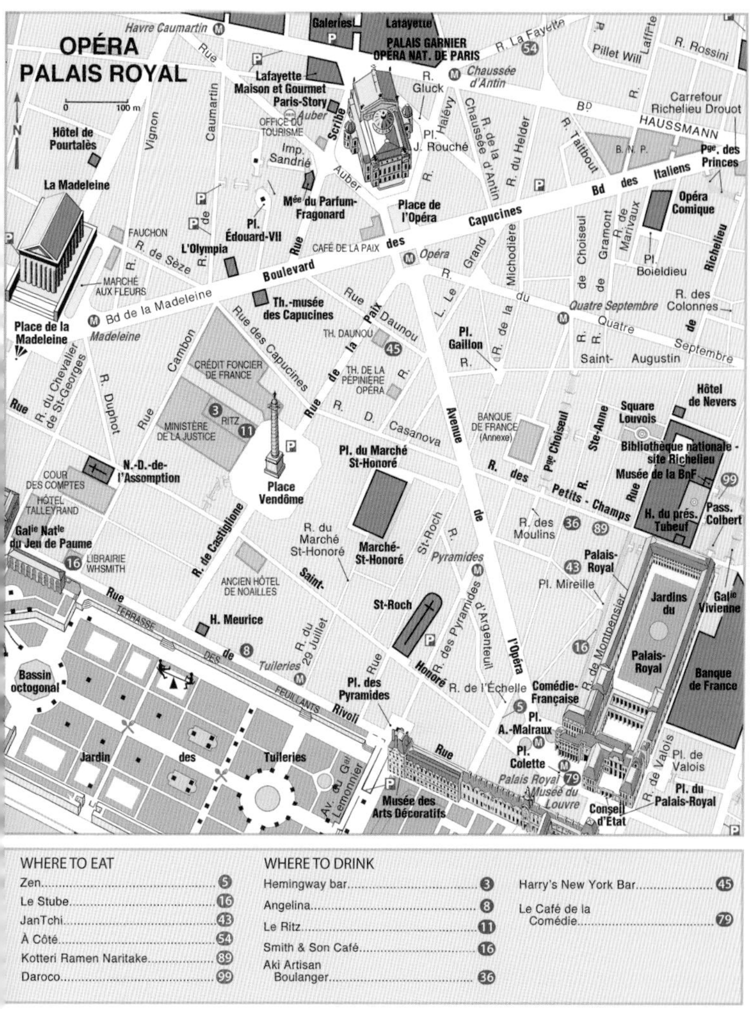


## WHERE TO EAT

| | |
|---|---|
| Zen | 5 |
| Le Stube | 16 |
| JanTchi | 43 |
| À Côté | 54 |
| Kotteri Ramen Naritake | 89 |
| Daroco | 99 |

## WHERE TO DRINK

| | |
|---|---|
| Hemingway bar | 3 |
| Angelina | 8 |
| Le Ritz | 11 |
| Smith & Son Café | 16 |
| Aki Artisan Boulanger | 36 |
| Harry's New York Bar | 45 |
| Le Café de la Comédie | 79 |

## Palais-Royal ★★

**E4** Ⓜ *Palais-Royal-Musée-du-Louvre.* North of the Louvre, the Palais-Royal (the seat of France's Constitutional Council and Ministry of Culture) overlooks a fantastic **garden★★**, an unexpected refuge in the center of Paris. A vast and sublime complex built for Richelieu in 1624, the Palais-Cardinal was renamed Palais-Royal when Anne of Austria came to live there with the young Louis XIV. In 1780, the palace was gifted to Louis-Philippe II, Duke of Orléans, who began a major development phase. Along three sides of the garden, he erected rows of town houses with uniform facades and arcades lined with shops—later turned into gambling halls and brothels, the height of fashion until they were banned in 1836. The architect behind this remarkable complex was Victor Louis. From 1786 to 1790, Louis Philippe II commissioned the same architect to build the Salle du Théâtre-Français, today's **Comédie-Française★**, and the **Théâtre du Palais-Royal★**.

In the Cour d'Honneur (interior courtyard), 260 sections of black-and-white-striped marble column, a controversial installation by **Daniel Buren** (1986), are a contemporary echo of the 19th-century colonnades. Adjacent is the garden with rows of perfectly manicured silver linden trees and arcades bordered with dozens of classic French brands, designer boutiques, and art galleries. The covered passages connecting with the neighboring streets *(to the north)* add to the distinctive charm of the place. On Place du Palais-Royal, which lies opposite the Louvre, a huge building undergoing renovation is set to house, by 2025, an ambitious offshoot of the **Fondation Cartier pour l'Art Contemporain** (*p. 64*).

To the west of the Palais-Royal, a little Tokyo has developed around **Rue Sainte-Anne**, with Japanese sushi and barbecue restaurants, bookshops, and grocery stores. Wander around the area to the east to discover 17th-century architecture, boutiques selling rare or luxury items, and covered passages built during the 1800s, like **Galerie Véro-Dodat★★** and its neoclassical interior *(access via Rue Montesquieu and Rue Croix-des-Petits-Champs).*



## Galerie Vivienne and Passage Colbert ★★

**E4** Ⓜ *Pyramides.* These passages were built in the 1820s. **Galerie Vivienne**, north of the Jardin du Palais-Royal *(main entrance on 4,*

### The "Home of Molière"

Founded in 1680 by Louis XIV, the Comédie-Française boasts one of the most ornate auditoriums in Paris. Although the repertoire performed there is mostly classical, the world's oldest theater company has gradually opened up to contemporary playwrights. Inside, you can see the famous statue of Voltaire by Houdon, and the chair where, on February 17, 1673, **Molière** was taken ill and carried off stage for the last time while playing the title role in his final comedy, *Le Malade Imaginaire*.

*Rue des Petits-Champs)*, flooded with natural light thanks to its glass roof, is opulently decorated with moldings of nymphs and goddesses as well as mosaics. Vidocq, a former wild child turned famed detective, lived at no. 13. **Passage Colbert** *(main entrance at 6, Rue des Petits-Champs)*, restored to how it was with its Pompeian decor, is today a hub of academic excellence in the cultural field, and home to France's National Institute of Art History and National Institute of Heritage.
Not far away, the relatively long **Passage Choiseul** *(main entrance at 40, Rue des Petits-Champs)* deserves a look-see for its old-fashioned charm.

## Bibliothèque Nationale de France-Musée de la BnF ★★

**E3-4** Ⓜ *Bourse. 58 r. de Richelieu - ✆ 01 53 79 49 49 - www.bnf.fr.*
Across from the pretty Square Louvois stands the main building of the **Bibliothèque Nationale de France**★★ which, in 1998, transferred part of its collection to the Bibliothèque François-Mitterrand, in the 13e arrondissement. At this historic site, notably in the sumptuous **Galerie Mazarine**★★★, dating from the 17th century, the **Musée de la BnF**★★ *(entrance at 5 r. Vivienne - daily ex. Mon 10am-6pm, Tue 8pm - €10, -26s €8)* presents in rotation the most precious pieces in its collection, including the Prisse Papyrus (the oldest of its kind discovered), ancient pottery and statues, old coins, the legendary Throne of Dagobert, the Charlemagne chessmen, treasures from Sainte-Chapelle, the Coronelli globes (17th c.), and manuscripts by Flaubert, Rimbaud, and Proust.

legna69/Getty Images Plus

The dome ceiling at Passage Colbert.

## Place des Victoires ★

**E4** Ⓜ *Bourse.* It was commissioned by Maréchal La Feuillade, a courtier to Louis XIV, as a sign of admiration for the king. Decorated with the royal effigy, the square designed by Jules Hardouin-Mansart has retained its harmonious original layout. On the other side, admire the square in front of the Notre-Dame-des-Victoires Basilica (17th c.), emanating Italian charm *(Rue des Petits-Pères)*.

## The Grands Boulevards

**DEF3** The Grands Boulevards replaced the ancient walls that once encircled Paris *(➲ p. 176)*. Cheap fast-food joints and souvenir stores have taken over the elegant 19th-century coffee houses. Here, you'll also find theaters, the Musée Grévin, a popular waxworks, the Grand Rex, an iconic movie theater, and multiple covered passages, a chance to see Paris of old.

### Hôtel des Ventes Drouot-Richelieu

**E3** *9 r. Drouot - ✆ 01 48 00 20 00 - drouot.com - times vary, inquire - free - see website for auction program.*
Drouot transforms the showrooms and later auction rooms into veritable cabinets of curiosities. Even if you're not there to buy, it's worth stepping inside to soak up the atmosphere.

### The Passages★

The original shopping malls, **Passage Jouffroy** *(no. 10 bd Montmartre)* and **Passage des Panoramas** *(at no. 11)* offer a fascinating glimpse of Paris of yesteryear, like something out of a black-and-white photograph. Yet the passageways are a-changing, with outmoded boutiques closing down and chic, organic, fine-dining eateries taking their place. These glorious arcades are entering a new era. After Passage Jouffroy, take **Passage Verdeau**, less crowded, its quaint charm intact. On Boulevard des Italiens, **Passage des Princes** (no. 5) has been fully restored. Then continue on to the peaceful **Cité Bergère** *(enter at 6 r. du Faubourg-Montmartre)*, where Chopin and Henrich Heine once lived, after admiring the Art Nouveau decor at **Bouillon Chartier** *(at no. 7)*, in business since 1896.
Further along *(entrance at 14-18 r. Richer)*, the elegant **Cité de Trévise**, a fine example of Renaissance Revival architecture, feels wonderfully frozen in time.



### Musée Grévin★

**E3** Ⓜ *Grands-Boulevards. 10 bd Montmartre - ✆ 01 47 70 85 05 - www.grevin-paris.com - Jul-Aug: 9:30am-7pm; rest of year: 10am-6pm, wknd 9:30am-7pm - €19 (-18s €16.50), discounts online.*
In 1881, Arthur Meyer, founder of daily newspaper *Le Gaulois*, came up with the idea of presenting to the public the celebrities that graced the front pages of his paper as full-size wax statues. He hired Alfred Grévin, sculptor, cartoonist, and costume designer, to create the museum. It was an instant success. Today, the collections are regularly updated and more interactive than ever.

### Grand Rex★

**F3** Ⓜ *Bonne Nouvelle. 1 bd Poissonnière – www.legrandrex.com.*
With 2,650 seats on three levels and a star-studded vaulted ceiling, this Art Deco cinema (1932) is one of the icons on the Grands Boulevards.
**Rex Studios** - *School vac.: 10am-7pm; rest of year: inquire - €11 (-26s €9).*
This 50-minute experience takes you behind the scenes of the Rex on a journey through the world of cinema—from the shoots to the big screen.

**Bouillon Chartier, Where Dinner Won't Break the Bank**

Here, the "old style" waitstaff, dressed in black and white, spin around the room serving classics like grated carrots, beef bourguignon, and chocolate mousse. *p. 109.*

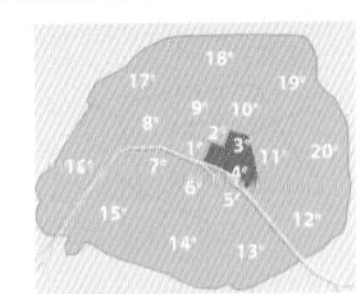


# The Marais★★★ and Les Halles★

The Marais, one of the few areas of Paris not eyed by Baron Haussmann for his urban renewal program, has kept its medieval streets, squares, and private mansions from the 17th and 18th centuries. In this hip and avant-garde neighborhood, art galleries and designer shops vie for attention among luxury ready-to-wear labels and the kosher restaurants and grocery stores along Rue des Rosiers. On Sundays, the boutiques are open (rare in Paris), the streets full of leisurely walkers there to shop or do brunch. What was once also Paris' "gay village" is slowly beginning to disappear under the strain of soaring rents. Is the Marais losing its soul? Just up the road, Les Halles is the largest pedestrian area in Paris, a major draw for its hundreds of stores and fast-food outlets.

▶**Getting there:** The Marais spans both sides of the Rue de Rivoli/Rue Saint-Antoine, between Bastille and Hôtel de Ville, up to République in the north. The "Northern Marais" refers to the triangle bound by Rue Pastourelle, Rue du Temple, and Boulevard du Temple. M Saint-Paul (Line 1), Rambuteau (Line 11).

**Local Map p. 38-39. Detachable Map EG4-6.**

▶**Tip:** Expect crowds during the day. Come in the morning for a moment of calm, or the evening for a fun night on the tiles.



## THE SOUTHERN MARAIS

**FG5-6** One of Paris' most popular districts was built on old money, as you can tell from the abundance of *hôtels particuliers* (private mansions) .

### Hôtel de Ville ★

**F5** M *Hôtel de Ville. Pl. de l'Hôtel-de-Ville (reception 5 r. Lobau) - ☏ 01 42 76 40 40 - www.paris.fr - tours suspended, inquire.*

The "Palace of All Revolutions", Paris' former City Hall did not escape the dramatic events of the Paris Commune, going down in flames on May 24, 1871. Rebuilt in a Renaissance Revival style not short on bombast, the building has retained the original spirit impressed upon it by the Italian architect Boccador in the 1530s. Inside, its huge, richly ornate reception halls remain emblematic of the decorative codes of France's Third Republic.

The famous **Bazar de l'Hôtel de Ville**, now known simply as the "BHV", has been thriving across the way since 1856.

### Église Saint-Paul-Saint-Louis ★★

**G5-6** M *Saint-Paul. 99 r. St-Antoine - ☏ 01 42 72 30 32 - www.spsl.fr - 8am-8pm.*

The plan of this **Jesuit** church, built from 1627 to 1641, was inspired by the Church of the Gesù in Rome, a model of Baroque architecture. The facade's three levels of Corinthian columns conceal the dome within. Inside, don't miss *Christ in the Garden of Olives*★★ by Delacroix.

## Village Saint-Paul

**G6** Ⓜ *Saint-Paul.* The village is bounded by Rue des Jardins-Saint-Paul, Rue Charlemagne, Rue Saint-Paul, and Rue de l'Ave-Maria. It's actually a building complex interconnected by interior courtyards flanked by period houses and antique stores. On **Rue des Jardins-Saint-Paul**, which once looked out over the city walls, a long stretch of stone, flanked by two towers, is the biggest surviving fragment of the **Wall of Philip Augustus**★. It used to connect the Tour Barbeau, which was located at no. 32, Quai des Célestins, to the Poterne Saint-Paul.



## Hôtel de Sens ★

**F6** Ⓜ *Saint-Paul. 1 r. du Figuier.* This sublime *hôtel particulier* was constructed from 1475 to 1507 as a residence for the archbishops of Sens, before Paris became an archdiocese in 1622. Passing through the porch, in the Flamboyant style, you enter the courtyard. The square tower containing a spiral staircase features a bretèche (a balcony with machicolations). The exterior facades are adorned with turrets and beautiful dormer windows. The Hôtel de Sens is home to the **Bibliothèque Forney**, a library specializing in the fine arts, decorative arts, and professional crafts. It regularly hosts exhibitions *(inquire on www.paris.fr).*

## Maison Européenne de la Photographie ★

**F5** Ⓜ *Saint-Paul - 5-7 r. de Fourcy - ✆ 01 44 78 75 00 - www.mep-fr.org - Wed-Fri 11am-8pm (Thu 10pm), wknd 10am-8pm - €10 (-26s €6).* This center of contemporary photographic art occupies the Hôtel Hénault de Cantobre (1704), restored and enlarged by the architect Yves Lion. The collection, which is renewed with each temporary themed exhibition, comprises around 20,000 works. In the basement, check out the library, video library, and auditorium after seeing an exhibition, always of excellent quality.

## Place du Marché-Sainte-Catherine ★

**G5** Ⓜ *Saint-Paul.* This pedestrian square is bordered by impressive uniform buildings. Thanks to its terraces, it's one of the most stunning small squares in Paris.

## Rue Saint-Antoine

**G5-6** Ⓜ *Saint-Paul.* A major thoroughfare to the east, Rue Saint-Antoine was frequently taken by royalty. From the 14th century, its uncommon width attracted the hoi polloi as a popular spot for promenading and general revelry. In the 1600s, it was considered the fanciest street in all Paris.

## Hôtel de Sully ★★

**G6** Ⓜ *Saint-Paul. 62 r. St-Antoine - ✆ 01 44 61 20 00 - www.hotel-de-sully.fr -*

R. Mattes/hemis.fr

Place des Vosges.



*courtyard and garden: 9am-7pm - bookstore: daily ex. Mon 1pm-7pm.* Constructed from 1625, the building—the base of France's institute for historic monuments—was bought in 1634 by **Sully**, the trusted minister of Henri IV. With its pediments, sculpted dormer windows, and figures representing the four elements and two seasons, the **courtyard**★★ is a notable ensemble in the Louis XIII style. At the bottom of the garden, the orangery gives access on to Place des Vosges.

## Place des Vosges ★★★

**G5** Ⓜ *Saint-Paul.* The oft-described "most beautiful square in Paris" is a vision of harmony, thanks to the alternating real stone and fake brick on the facades, all identical. Each of the 36 town houses *(pavillons)* has two floors set above arcades and slate roofs dotted with dormer windows. The Pavillon du Roi (King's Pavilion) *(south side)* is mirrored by the Pavillon de la Reine (Queen's Pavilion), with a delightful garden between the two. Henry IV, who wished to bestow a beautiful neighborhood on his capital, had a royal square built between 1605 and 1612. The area became the epicenter of elegant Parisian society, a place for carousels, secret trysts, and duels. Past residents include Madame de Sévigné (at no. 1B), Bossuet (no. 17), Richelieu (no. 21), Théophile Gautier and Alphonse Daudet (no. 8). The place's current name has honored the French department of Vosges

## WHERE TO EAT

L'As du Fallafel ........ 9
Soma ........ 10
Breizh Café ........ 11
Eataly Paris ........ 15
Paris New York ........ 23
Notre Café Marais ........ 27

## WHERE TO DRINK

L'Ébouillanté ........ 1
Mariage Frères ........ 4
Carette ........ 12
Comme à Lisbonne ........ 14
La Belle Hortense ........ 73

## SHOPPING

Fleux ........ 2
Épicerie Izraël ........ 4
Paris Rendez-Vous ........ 13
Calligrane ........ 14
Le Piéton de Paris ........ 15

## WHERE TO STAY

Hôtel du Petit Moulin ........ 4



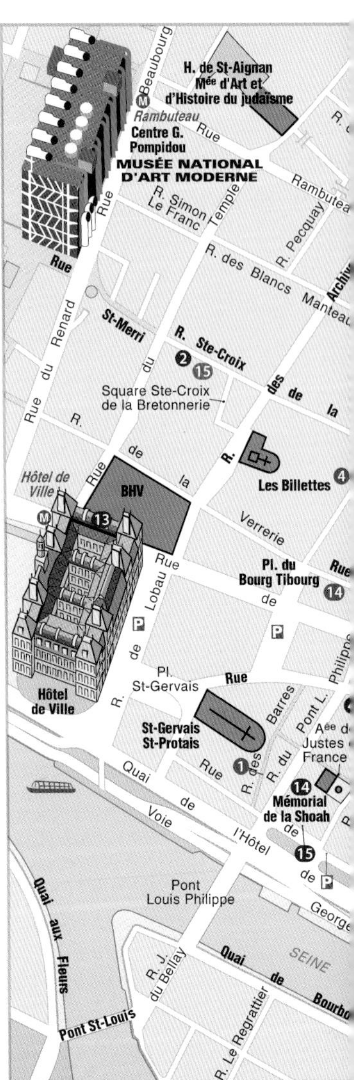

LE MARAIS
0
100 m
N
Pge de Retz
St-Jean-St-François
Porte Clisson
H. de Soubise-Clisson-Mée des Archives nat.
Hôtel de Rohan
Hôtel Salé
Musée Picasso - Paris
St-Denys du St-Sacrement
TOUR H. AUGUSTE
Pl. de Thorigny
N-D. des Blancs Manteaux
Hôtel Amelot de Bisseuil
Musée Cognacq-Jay
H. Le Peletier de St-Fargeau
Musée Carnavalet - Histoire de Paris
Hôtel Carnavalet
H. de Coulanges
H. d'Albret
Hôtel de Lamoignon
PAVILLON DE LA REINE
PLACE DES VOSGES
Mon européenne de la Photographie
Saint-Paul
Pl. du Marché Ste-Catherine
Lycée Charlemagne
St-Paul-St-Louis
Hôtel de Sully
PAVILLON DU ROI
Maison de Victor Hugo
Enceinte de Ph. Auguste
Lycée Charlemagne
Hôtel de Sens
Village St-Paul
Musée de la Magie et des Automates
Pont Marie
R. des Haudriettes
R. des 4 Fils
R. de Saintonge
R. de Poitou
Vieille du Temple
R. du Perche
R. des Coutures St-Gervais
R. Saint-Claude
R. de Thorigny
R. de la Perle
R. Barbette
R. Elzévir
R. du Parc Royal
Rue Saint-Gilles
Rue des Francs Bourgeois
R. Payenne
R. de Sévigné
Rue des Minimes
R. du Foin
R. de Béarn
R. de Turenne
Rue des Rosiers
R. Pavée
R. des Écouffes
R. Vieille du Temple
R. du Roi de Sicile
Rivoli
R. Malher
R. de Jarente
Miron
François
G. l'Asnier
R. de Jouy
R. du Prévôt
R. Caron
Rue Saint-Antoine
R. Charlemagne
R. Saint-Paul
R. Neuve St-Pierre
R. de Birague
R. du Figuier
R. des Jardins St-Paul
R. Beautreillis
R. du Petit Musc
R. Castex
Quai de l'Hôtel de Ville
Quai des Célestins
Pompidou
R. des Lions St-Paul
R. Charles V
Pont Marie
R. de Bretonnerie
4
10
11
23
73
9
27
12

since 1800, the first to pay taxes to the Empire. Today, people come to stroll under the arcades, gaze in the windows of art galleries and boutiques, and enjoy a glass of something. Street orchestras provide the soundtrack on Sundays.

### Maison de Victor-Hugo★

*6 pl. des Vosges - ✆ 01 42 72 10 16 - www.maisonsvictorhugo.paris.fr - daily ex. Mon. 10am-6pm - free.* Victor Hugo is another former famous occupant of Place des Vosges. The interior of the apartment he lived in from 1832 to 1848 is beautifully intact, its decor as richly profuse as the celebrated Romantic writer's imagination. It's an intimate museum, made all the more poignant by his death bed.



### Rue des Francs-Bourgeois ★

**FG5** Ⓜ *Saint-Paul and Rambuteau.* Once a major artery through Paris, it is today one of the main and busiest streets in the Marais, linking the Place des Vosges and the Centre Pompidou, drawing in tourists and locals alike to shop in its multitude of designer boutiques. Look out for several *hôtels particuliers* from the 16th and 17th centuries, including, at no. 31, the **Hôtel d'Albret,** at no. 26, the **Hôtel de Sandreville** and, at no. 30, the **Hôtel d'Alméras**. At no. 16, the **Hôtel Le Peletier de Saint-Fargeau** and Hôtel Carnavalet together house the Musée Carnavalet *(see below)*.

### Musée Carnavalet - Histoire de Paris ★★

**G5** Ⓜ *Saint-Paul. 23 r. de Sévigné - ✆ 01 44 59 58 58 - www.carnavalet.paris.fr - daily ex. Mon 10am-6pm - free.* All of Paris' history under two roofs! After four years of renovations, the institution reopened its doors in 2021, providing an even more impressive showcase for its rich collection of more than 600,000 pieces! From prehistoric times to the present day, you see the city emerging, expanding, rebelling, spreading... The journey through history is captivating, documented by all kinds of models, historic photographs, works of art, as well as superb reconstructions of period interiors, from aristocratic salons to Art Nouveau boutiques—and even Marcel Proust's bedroom! Forming the entrance to the museum, the main courtyard of the **Hôtel Carnavalet★★** remains one of the most beautiful architectural ensembles in the Marais, with its bas-reliefs by Jean Goujon depicting the four seasons.

## THE NORTHERN MARAIS

**FG4-5** The architectural style and trendy vibes of the Marais district in the 4e arrondissement continue into the Northern Marais. Here too you'll find a plethora of carefully curated concept stores, hip bars, and healthy restaurants.

### Musée d'Art et d'Histoire du Judaïsme ★★

**F4-5** Ⓜ *Rambuteau. 71 r. du Temple - ✆ 01 53 01 86 53 - www.mahj.org - mid-Jul-mid-Oct: Tue-Fri 11am-6pm, wknd 10am-6pm; rest of year, inquire - closed on Rosh Hashanah and Yom Kippur - €10 (-18s free).* The **Hôtel de Saint-Aignan★** is now a modern and enlightening museum displaying an exceptional array of ancient and contemporary

D. Giancatarina/Musée de la Chasse et de la Nature, Paris

The Musée de la Chasse et de la Nature, the Stag and Wolf Room.



works—archaeological objects, paintings, and even ritual objects– that give a window into the Jewish cultures of Central Europe and the Mediterranean. Among the exhibits are a beautiful collection of Hanukkah menorah, two paintings by Chagall, and an exquisite assortment of finely crafted clothing and jewelry. One section is dedicated to the Dreyfus affair, told through press clippings and black-and-white photographs.

## Archives Nationales-Hôtels de Soubise and de Rohan ★★

**F5** Ⓜ *Rambuteau.* These two private mansions now form a single ensemble connected by magnificent **gardens★★**, fully renovated and open to the public. They house the state's public archives, from the Middle Ages to the Ancien Régime, as well as the **Musée des Archives Nationales★** *(entrance at 60 r. des Francs-Bourgeois - ✆ 01 40 27 60 96 - www.archives-nationales.culture.gouv.fr - daily ex. Tue 10am-5:30pm, wknd 2pm-7pm, if temporary exhibition on - free).* The horseshoe-shaped **courtyard★★** and peristyle of the Hôtel de Soubise *(60 r. des Francs-Bourgeois)* are pure majesty. The building occupies the site of the oldest (14th c.) *hôtel particulier* in the Marais. You can still admire the **Porte Clisson★** *(58 rue des Archives)*, the entrance with its two corbelled turrets, the only surviving remnant of private architecture from

14th-century Paris. The **apartments★★** were decorated from 1732 by the finest painters and sculptors of the period *(✆ 01 40 27 60 71 - guided tours on Sat and Mon, inquire for times - €8).* Entrusted in 1927 to the National Archives, the handsome **Hôtel de Rohan** *(87 r. Vieille-du-Temple)* was built in 1705 as a residence for the Prince and Princess of Soubise, Bishop of Strasbourg and the future Cardinal de Rohan. In late 2021, decorative elements from the Chancellerie d'Orléans, a private mansion set at the edge of the Palais-Royal and demolished in 1923, found a new home there. Crafted by some of the most renowned artists of their day, they feature exceptional examples of decorative arts from the second half of the 18th century *(closed for renovation, inquire on ✆ 01 40 27 60 71).*



## Musée de la Chasse et de la Nature ★★

**F4-5** Ⓜ *Rambuteau. 62 r. des Archives - ✆ 01 53 01 92 40 - www.chassenature.org - Tue-Sun 11am-6pm (9:30pm certain Wed) - €10.* Among the most beautiful residences in the Marais, the **Hôtel de Guenegaud** was built by François Mansart around 1650 and redesigned in the 18th century. With the **Hôtel de Mongelas** (18th c.) next door, it houses the highly original hunting and nature museum. Displayed from room to room, the collection of ancient, modern, and contemporary art (paintings, sculptures, objets d'art, furniture, installations, videos, etc.) is designed to explore the relationship between humans and animals throughout the ages. A surprising and quirky museum, one of a kind in Paris.

## Fondation Henri Cartier-Bresson ★

**F4** Ⓜ *Rambuteau. 79 r. des Archives - ✆ 01 40 61 50 50 - www.henricartierbresson.org - daily ex. Mon 11am-7pm - €10 (-18s free).* The Fondation, its mission to preserve the legacy of photographers Henri Cartier-Bresson (1908-2004) and Martine Franck (1938-2012), hosts superb temporary exhibitions dedicated to the work of the two artists in connection with the city or landscapes, along with other renowned photographers.

## Carreau du Temple ★

**G4** Ⓜ *Temple. 2 r. Perrée - ✆ 01 83 81 93 30 - www.carreaudutemple.eu - ticket office: Mon-Sat 10am-9pm - prices vary by what's on.* Umpteen times earmarked for demolition and saved by the local community, this former market, its wrought-iron structure dating from 1860, is now a multipurpose sports and cultural center.

## Marché des Enfants-Rouges

**G4** Ⓜ *Temple. 39 r. de Bretagne - closed Mon.* Foodies should make a beeline for this market, the oldest in Paris (1615), especially at the weekend. Its colorful aisles are packed with all kinds of food stalls and a handful of restaurants *(◉ p. 111)*. Its name "Red Children" comes from the color of the clothes worn by the children in the neighboring orphanage in the 17th century.

## Musée Picasso ★★

**G5** Ⓜ *Saint-Sébastien-Froissart. Hôtel Salé - 5 r. de Thorigny - ✆ 01 85 56*

*00 36 - www.museepicassoparis.fr - daily ex. Mon 10:30am-6pm, wknd 9:30am-6pm - €14.*
A magnificent setting to honor the creative genius that was Pablo Picasso, the **Hôtel Salé** was constructed between 1656 and 1659 for Pierre Aubert, Lord of Fontenay, a wealthy financier who made his fortune from the salt tax, hence the mansion's "salty" name. Surviving features include the stunning grand **staircase** with its wrought-iron railings and sculpted ceiling. Completely refurbished in the early 2010s, today it houses the world's biggest collection of works by Picasso: nearly 300 paintings, over 250 sculptures, including the famous *Baboon and Young* (1951), papiers collés, relief constructions, and nearly 4,000 drawings and prints. It hosts temporary exhibitions, too.

## Musée Cognacq-Jay ★★

**F5** Ⓜ *Chemin-Vert. 8 r. Elzévir - ✆ 01 40 27 07 21 - www.museecognacqjay.paris.fr - daily ex. Mon 10am-6pm - free.*
This impressive collection of 18th-century European art occupies the **Hôtel Donon**. In perfect harmony and taste, the building and artworks evoke the elegant lifestyle of the Age of Enlightenment. This is one of the capital's most charming museums, its beautifully wood-paneled rooms a pleasure to wander around.

## BEAUBOURG DISTRICT

**F4-5** The Beaubourg plateau—lined with old, dilapidated houses until the late 1960s–has, since 1977 with the arrival of the Centre Pompidou, become one of the city's liveliest squares. Artists of all genres set up on the forecourt outside the modern art center. In summer, it's a suntrap all through the afternoon. The major exhibitions at Beaubourg tend to draw an international crowd, the atmosphere always vibrant and upbeat. To the right, the **Fontaine Stravinsky★** is adorned with black sculptures by Tinguely and colorful ones by Niki de Saint Phalle. On this same square you'll find the **Église Saint-Merri★**, from the 15th century, in the Flamboyant Gothic style.

## Centre Georges-Pompidou ★★

**F5** Ⓜ *Rambuteau - Pl. Georges-Pompidou - ✆ 01 44 78 12 33 - www.centrepompidou.fr - daily ex. Tue 11am-9pm (Thu 11pm) - €15 - closed 2025-2030 for planned renovations.*
Architects Richard Rogers and Renzo Piano completed the construction of this avant-garde building, with its steel framework, glass walls, and bold colors, in 1977. In its glass tube, the main escalator, or "caterpillar" as it's known, travels diagonally up the side of the building. The sixth and final floor grants magnificent **views★★** over the rooftops of Paris. The Center's programming promotes every creative discipline through retrospectives, exhibitions, and festivals.

### The Museum★★★

*Levels 4 and 5, entered via Level 4.* The museum's collection, made up of more than 9,000 artworks, covers every artistic movement **from 1905 to the present day**. The selection of works

on display is renewed every two years.
**Modern Art** - The rooms present the major trends in modern art in chronological order: Fauvism (Derain, Matisse, Dufy), Cubism (Braque, Picasso), Dadaism represented by Marcel Duchamp and his ready-mades, Abstraction (Kandinsky, Klee, Mondrian), Surrealism (Dalí, Magritte, Ernst, Miró, Breton), then abstract art from the 1950s (Hartung, de Staël, Soulages), American avant-garde (Pollock, Newman), CoBrA, sculptures by Brancusi and, on the terraces, monumental works by Miró, Ernst, Calder, and Takis.
**Contemporary Art** - The most significant works of contemporary art from the 1960s onwards are on display, pieces by the likes of Beuys, Boltanski, Bourgeois, Hantaï, Mitchell, Soulages, Twombly, Warhol, Viola, and Rauschenberg.



## LES HALLES ★

**EF4-5** This pedestrian district is one of the most animated areas in Paris. Les Halles, once described as the "belly of Paris", is the market where grocers, butchers, fishmongers, and alike have been feeding Parisians since 1135. In 1969, the market was moved to the suburb of Rungis, and the Baltard-designed market pavilions, with their steel structure and glass roof, made way for the Forum des Halles.

### Forum des Halles

**EF4** Ⓜ *Les Halles*
Beneath its 270,000 sq.ft glass **canopy** (designed by Patrick Berger and Jacques Anziutti), the Forum is an enormous mall with 150 stores plus sports and leisure facilities. At its center, the patio, a feat of architecture, grants views of the Centre Pompidou, while outside, the 10 acres of greenery of the **Jardin Nelson-Mandela** is bordered by the colossal Église Saint-Eustache and the Bourse de Commerce (former stock exchange).

### Bourse de Commerce-Pinault Collection ★★

**E4** Ⓜ *Les Halles. 2 r. de Viarmes - ✆ 01 55 04 60 60 - www.pinaultcollection.com - daily ex. Tue 11am-7pm (Fri 9pm) - €14 (18-26s €10) - free late night opening every first Sat of the month 5pm-9pm.*
*To gain insight into the practices of the artists on show, take a guided tour or ask one of the knowledgeable educators on duty in the rooms.*

**Place de Grève: the Meeting Point to Find Work in Les Halles**

Flanked by a *grève* (sand and gravel beach) conducive to mooring, the Seine's Rive Droite (Right Bank) became a thriving hub for river trade. Commercial activity boomed given that, in the 12th century, the Paris Basin was the epicenter of the West's economic development thanks to its excellent wheat lands, its position as a crossroads between southern and northern Europe, and its wine production.
It was only natural to build the market Les Halles, in the early 13th century, just a stone's throw from this natural harbor, named Place de Grève (on the current Place de l'Hôtel-de-Ville), where one would go to find work. Ironically, today *se mettre en grève* means "to go on strike".

B. Gardel/hemis.fr

Église Saint-Eustache and Jardin Nelson-Mandela.



A building long overlooked despite its extraordinary circular design (18th-19th c.) and enigmatic Medici column (16th c.), the former Stock Exchange of Les Halles de Paris is now a destination in its own right. Since 2021, after years of renovation, the businessman François Pinault has taken the helm to present, in constantly updated exhibits, his fabulous collection of **contemporary art**, with a staggering 10,000 pieces (including 5,000 photos). Inside the building's main feature, namely the **central rotunda,** crowned with a magnificent glass dome and an immense painted fresco (to the glory of world trade) from the late 19th century, the Japanese architect Tadao Ando has inserted a concrete wall, 95 feet in diameter and 30 feet high. The space easily rivals the works on show that explore every trend and practice in today's art world. A dizzying display!

## Église Saint-Eustache ★★

**E4** Ⓜ *Les Halles - 146 r. Rambuteau - ✆ 01 42 36 31 05 - www.saint-eustache.org - 9:30am-7pm, wknd 9am-7pm.* Built between 1532 and 1640, the church, its Gothic architecture calling to mind Notre-Dame, only received its final facade in 1754. Its slender vaults and stained-glass windows have witnessed the christenings of Richelieu and Molière, and the funeral of La Fontaine. Among its treasure trove of artworks, keep an eye out for the bronze triptych by Keith Haring,

*The Life of Christ*, in the Chapelle Saint-Vincent-de-Paul, and the tomb of Colbert, sculpted by Coysevox and Tuby *(late 17th c.)*. The **facades of the transept★** have retained their Renaissance composition with their two stair turrets crowned by lanterns.

## Pedestrian area around the Forum des Halles

**EF4-5** Running from the Église Saint-Eustache, **Rue Montorgueil** is lined with period buildings sporting picturesque signs (no. 15, 17, 23, 25). From there, you can get, via Rue Tiquetonne and Rue Dussoubs, to the covered **Passage du Grand-Cerf**, its 19th-century decor beautifully intact. The other end takes you out onto **Rue Saint-Denis**, one of the capital's oldest streets. A commercial street since it opened in the 8th century, today it's an eclectic mix of stores, restaurants, and bars. Sex shops have replaced the sex workers who had lived in the area for decades. Heading south, you'll cross **Rue de la Grande-Truanderie**, once the site of a slum that was a refuge for Paris' criminal underbelly until the reign of Louis XIV. A little further along, the medieval **Rue des Lombards** is named for the Lombard moneylenders from Italy who sold silver at the price of gold. It's a vibrant area with thronging bar and jazz club terraces. You'll pass the **Fontaine des Innocents★** on your tour. This Renaissance masterpiece, built to commemorate the solemn royal entry of Henry II into Paris in 1549, is attributed to Pierre Lescot (design) and Jean Goujon (sculpture). It sat at the heart of the Saints Innocents Cemetery, the largest in Paris until 1786, when two million skeletons were transferred to the Catacombes *(p. 65)*. Henry IV was killed by Ravaillac on May 14, 1610, just a short walk away, at 11 **Rue de la Ferronnerie**. Between Rue de Rivoli and Pont-Neuf, after more than 15 years of closure, the iconic department store **La Samaritaine★**, established in 1870, at last reopened in 2021. Its sumptuous Art Nouveau and Art Deco buildings have been extended with a contemporary wing set behind an undulating glass facade (on the Rue de Rivoli side). Masterfully renovated and furnished, the complex houses an over 215,000-sq.ft shopping mall, luxury hotel, and multiple restaurants and cafés. Enjoy spectacular views atop the main building overlooking the Seine.

# Latin Quarter★★★

**Dominated by the Panthéon and gradually descending towards the Seine, the Latin Quarter is bisected north to south by Rue Saint-Jacques, which follows the ancient path of the main thoroughfare through Lutetia (ancient Paris). A center of academia and book-related trades in the Middle Ages, the district has retained its vibrant student buzz. The Sorbonne University is still surrounded by a cluster of prestigious schools, and Place Saint-Michel and Luxembourg remain popular student hangouts.**

▶**Getting there:** M Saint-Michel (Line 4), Cluny-la-Sorbonne (Line 10), RER Saint-Michel-Notre-Dame (Lines B and C).

**Local Map p. 48-49. Detachable Map EG6-8.**

▶**Tip:** Peckish? Avoid the super-touristy Rue de la Huchette; there's plenty of options along quieter streets close by.

## Place Saint-Michel

**E6** M *Saint-Michel.* A meeting point for students from all over the world. The fountain and square date to the 19th century. From there, wander along Rue de la Harpe, Rue de la Parcheminerie, Rue de la Huchette, and Rue Saint-Séverin to get a feel of medieval Paris. Think about visiting in the morning, before the streets are inundated with tourists. Fast-food outlets and souvenir shops have moved in en masse to these streets which are especially lively at night.

## Around Église Saint-Séverin ★★

**F6** M *Cluny-la-Sorbonne. 1 r. des Prêtres-St-Séverin.* The church, extended at the sides in the 14th and 15th centuries, is almost as wide as it is long. The bays pass from the Rayonnant to the Flamboyant Gothic style, the latter style found in the double **ambulatory**★★, multiple ribs spiraling down the columns with marble and wood facing. The **stained-glass windows**★ date from the late 15th century. Modern multicolored windows designed by Bazaine illuminate the chapels in the apse. Take **Rue Galande** to admire its medieval houses, and follow it round to the right and the **Église Saint-Julien-le-Pauvre**. Slightly older than Notre-Dame (1165-1220), this church was given over to the Melkite Greek Catholic Church in 1889. Right next door, **Square Viviani** is home to Paris' oldest tree, a locust tree planted in 1602 and now held up by concrete props. Next, head to Rue de la Bûcherie and Rue des Grands-Degrés, flanked by period buildings that conjure up images of bygone Paris. If your French isn't up to scratch, stock up on English-language reading matter for your trip at the bookstore **Shakespeare & Company** *(37 r. de la Bûcherie)*. An institution since 1951,

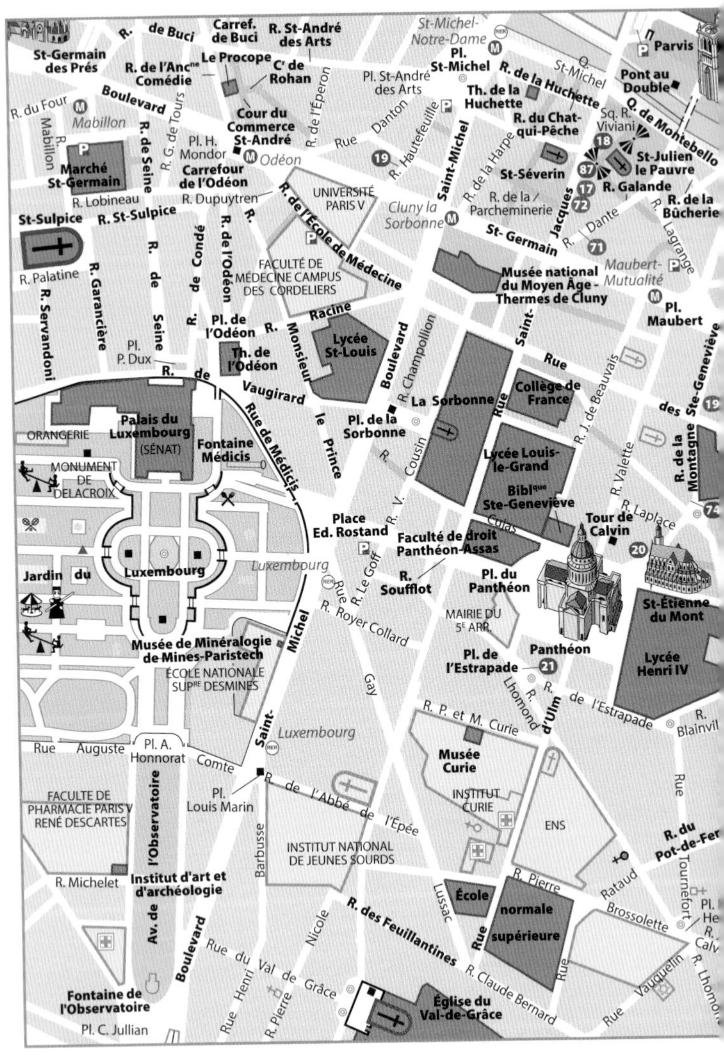
St-Germain des Prés
Boulevard
Carref. de Buci
R. St-André des Arts
Le Procope
Cour du Commerce St-André
Carrefour de l'Odéon
Marché St-Germain
St-Sulpice
R. St-Sulpice
UNIVERSITÉ PARIS V
FACULTÉ DE MÉDECINE CAMPUS DES CORDELIERS
R. de l'École de Médecine
Cluny la Sorbonne
St-Séverin
Musée national du Moyen Âge - Thermes de Cluny
Pl. St-Michel
Th. de la Huchette
Pont au Double
Parvis
St-Julien le Pauvre
Maubert-Mutualité
Pl. Maubert
Lycée St-Louis
Th. de l'Odéon
Pl. de l'Odéon
Palais du Luxembourg (SÉNAT)
Fontaine Médicis
Rue de Médicis
La Sorbonne
Pl. de la Sorbonne
Collège de France
Lycée Louis-le-Grand
Bibl. Ste-Geneviève
Tour de Calvin
Place Ed. Rostand
Faculté de droit Panthéon-Assas
Jardin du Luxembourg
Pl. du Panthéon
Panthéon
St-Étienne du Mont
Lycée Henri IV
MAIRIE DU 5E ARR.
Pl. de l'Estrapade
Musée de Minéralogie de Mines-Paristech
ÉCOLE NATIONALE SUPRE DESMINES
Musée Curie
INSTITUT CURIE
ENS
INSTITUT NATIONAL DE JEUNES SOURDS
FACULTE DE PHARMACIE PARIS V RENÉ DESCARTES
Institut d'art et d'archéologie
Av. de l'Observatoire
École normale supérieure
R. des Feuillantines
Fontaine de l'Observatoire
Pl. C. Jullian
Église du Val-de-Grâce
Boulevard Saint-Michel
Rue du Val de Grâce
R. Claude Bernard
Pl. Louis Marin
R. de l'Abbé de l'Épée
Rue Auguste Comte
Pl. A. Honnorat

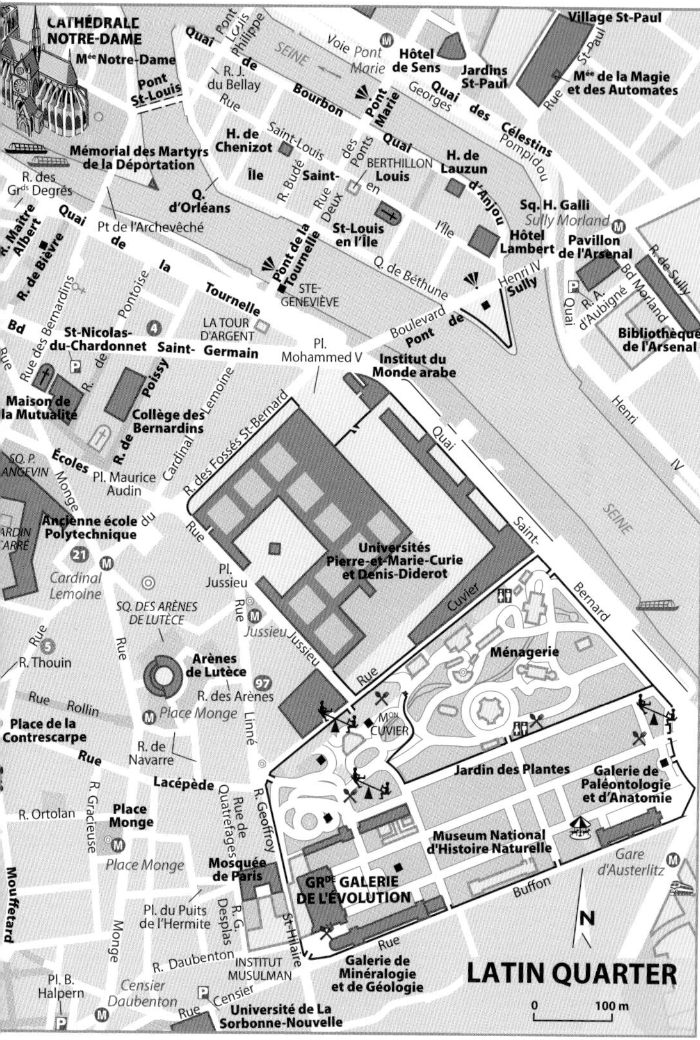

Cathédrale Notre-Dame
Mée Notre-Dame
Pont St-Louis
Quai de Bourbon
Pont Louis Philippe
Voie Pont Marie
Seine
R. J. du Bellay
Rue Saint-Louis en l'Île
Hôtel de Sens
Jardins St-Paul
Village St-Paul
Rue St-Paul
Mée de la Magie et des Automates
Pont Marie
Quai des Célestins
Georges Pompidou
H. de Chenizot
Mémorial des Martyrs de la Déportation
R. des Grds Degrés
Île Saint-Louis
R. Budé
Rue des Deux Ponts
Berthillon
Quai d'Anjou
H. de Lauzun
Q. d'Orléans
Pt de l'Archevêché
St-Louis en l'Île
Sq. H. Galli
Sully Morland
Hôtel Lambert
Pavillon de l'Arsenal
R. de Sully
R. Maître Albert
Quai de la Tournelle
R. de Bièvre
Pont de la Tournelle
Ste-Geneviève
Q. de Béthune
Henri IV
Pont de Sully
Boulevard Henri IV
R. A. d'Aubigné
Bd Morland
Quai Henri IV
Bibliothèque de l'Arsenal
Rue des Bernardins
Pontoise
4
La Tour d'Argent
Bd Saint-Germain
St-Nicolas-du-Chardonnet
Pl. Mohammed V
Institut du Monde arabe
R. de Poissy
Maison de la Mutualité
Collège des Bernardins
Cardinal Lemoine
R. des Fossés St-Bernard
Quai Saint-Bernard
Sq. P. Angevin
Écoles
Pl. Maurice Audin
Monge
Rue du Cardinal Lemoine
Ancienne école Polytechnique
Jardin Carré
21
Cardinal Lemoine
Pl. Jussieu
Universités Pierre-et-Marie-Curie et Denis-Diderot
Rue Cuvier
Rue Jussieu
Jussieu
Sq. des Arènes de Lutèce
5
R. Thouin
Arènes de Lutèce
R. des Arènes
97
Ménagerie
Rue Rollin
Place Monge
Linné
Mon Cuvier
Place de la Contrescarpe
R. de Navarre
Rue Lacépède
Jardin des Plantes
Galerie de Paléontologie et d'Anatomie
R. Gracieuse
R. Ortolan
Place Monge
Rue de Quatrefages
R. Geoffroy St-Hilaire
Museum National d'Histoire Naturelle
Place Monge
Mosquée de Paris
Gare d'Austerlitz
Grde Galerie de l'Évolution
Rue Buffon
Mouffetard
Pl. du Puits de l'Hermite
R. G. Desplas
N
Rue Monge
R. Daubenton
Institut Musulman
Galerie de Minéralogie et de Géologie
Latin Quarter
Pl. B. Halpern
Censier Daubenton
Rue Censier
Université de La Sorbonne-Nouvelle
0 100 m

49

aspiring writers passing through, affectionately called "Tumbleweeds", can find a bed for the night in exchange for a few tasks: reading a book a day, spending a few hours stocking shelves, and writing a one-page autobiography for the shop's archives.

## Musée National du Moyen Âge - Thermes de Cluny ★★

**E6** Ⓜ *Cluny-la-Sorbonne. 28 r. du Sommerard - ✆ 01 53 73 78 16 - www.musee-moyenage.fr - daily ex. Mon 9:30am-6:15pm - €12 (-18s free).*



Reopened in 2022 after an ambitious renovation program that resulted in a completely new visitor route—more modern and brighter—, the Musée de Cluny was extended with a new wing clad in cast aluminum, the handiwork of architect Bernard Desmoulin. The complex now encapsulates 2,000 years of Parisian architecture, courtesy of its original core that unites two symbolic buildings of the city's history: the ancient Gallo-Roman thermal baths from Lutetian times and the Hôtel des Abbés de Cluny.

**Thermal Baths★** - Only one third of the original footprint of this vast 2nd-century building has survived. This public bathhouse was plundered and burned down by the Barbarians in the late Roman Empire. Intact, the *frigidarium* room is particularly impressive, its ancient vaults rising over 45 feet high! Here you can see the famous Pillar of the Boatmen, unearthed beneath the nave of Notre-Dame in 1711 and which honors both Roman and Celtic gods.

**Hôtel de Cluny** – Built from 1485 to 1500 on top of the eastern section of the ancient baths, this is the last private dwelling from the Middle Ages in Paris to be standing today—along with the Hôtel de Sens in the Marais (*p. 36*). Although the medieval tradition is still reflected in classic details (crenels, turrets, etc.), their role is purely decorative: the building is above all the first example of a private mansion set between a courtyard and garden.

**Museum★★** - Connecting the Musée d'Archéologie National de Saint-Germain-en-Laye (in Yvelines) and the Musée National de la Renaissance d'Écouen (in Val-d'Oise), the collections bring the Middle Ages to life through textiles, goldsmithery, glassware, ironwork, ivory, sculpture, ceramics, paintings, and other finely crafted objects from the period. The permanent exhibition gives precious insight into various aspects of medieval civilization (daily life, economy, war, etc.), dominated by the pervasive Christian religion, with magnificent remains of Parisian churches, from Notre-Dame to Saint-Germain-des-Prés. The jewel in the museum's crown, the six **tapestries of the Lady of the Unicorn★★★**, exquisite examples of tapestry in the Millefleur style from the Netherlands (circa 1500), are enchanting.

## La Sorbonne ★

**E6-7** Ⓜ *Cluny-La Sorbonne. 17 r. de la Sorbonne - www.sorbonne.fr - guided tours (1hr30) to book ahead by email at visites.sorbonne@ac-paris.fr - €15.*
The prestigious Paris college, founded in the 13th century, was then reserved for students in theology. Today, it remains synonymous with excellence and... protest, since it was here that the student riots of May 68, sparked at the Nanterre campus, grew to epic proportions.
Crowned by a dome, its details painted by Philippe de Champaigne, the **chapel★** *(not open to visitors)* in the Jesuit style houses the **tomb of Cardinal de Richelieu★** (Girardon, 1694), principal of the institution in 1622.
Other prestigious institutions can be found in the environs: the Collège de France, the Saint-Louis, Henri-IV, and Louis-Le-Grand high schools, the École Normale Supérieure on Rue d'Ulm, the École des Mines, and so on.

The Jardin du Luxembourg.

## Jardin du Luxembourg ★★

**E6-7** *RER Luxembourg. R. de Fleurus, pl. Edmond-Rostand and r. de Vaugirard - ✆ 01 42 34 20 00 - www.senat.fr - ♿ - seasonal opening hours (7:30am/8:15am-4:30pm/9:30pm).*
A green lung steeped in history, close to the Sorbonne, the Odéon, and Montparnasse, the garden has a classical beauty that is instantly appealing. In 1612, Marie de' Medici bought the mansion from the Duke of Luxembourg along with the surrounding land, later turned into a vast park. The **garden** was landscaped in the French style: harmonious lines and perspectives, not to mention its shade, designed to delight walkers. Children pushing toy sailboats on the octagonal lake make for a familiar sight. The English style is present, too, in the serpentine paths running the length of Rue Guynemer and Rue Auguste-Comte. Keeping up the rustic tradition, arboriculture and beekeeping classes are taught in the old nursery garden *(near Rue d'Assas)*.

The **Fontaine Médicis★**, at the top end of the small pond, reflects the Italian influence. This is the most beautiful relic from the former garden of Marie de' Medici. Kids will be entertained by the swings, rides, and puppet shows on the Rue Guynemer side.

**Palais du Luxembourg★★** - Completed in 1615, this palace, commissioned by Marie de' Medici to escape the Louvre she detested, is now home to the upper chamber of the French parliament, the Senate. Debates, usually on Tuesdays, Wednesdays, and Thursdays, are open to the public.

## Église du Val-de-Grâce ★★

**E8** *RER Port-Royal. 1 pl. Alphonse-Laveran - Access to the church only as part of the visit to the Musée du Service de Santé des Armées.*



This magnificent church was commissioned by Queen Anne of Austria in thanks to God should he give her a son. The promise was fulfilled 21 years later when she gave birth to the future Louis XIV, in 1638. François Mansart and then Lemercier oversaw the construction. The rich decoration on the dome includes statues, angels, medallions, and fire pots. The interior has a Baroque style, with polychrome paving stones. The **dome★★** painted by Mignard depicts the *Fields of Heaven*. The former royal abbey to which the church was attached housed a military hospital from 1793 to 2016. In the cloister, the **Musée du Service de Santé des Armées** (*✆ 01 40 51 51 92 - evdg.sante.defense.gouv.fr - daily ex. Mon and Fri 12pm-6pm - closed Aug - €5 (6-18s €2.50)*) traces the healthcare history of the armed forces.

## Panthéon ★★

**E7** *RER Luxembourg. Pl. du Panthéon - ✆ 01 44 32 18 00 - paris-pantheon.fr - Apr-Sep: 10am-6:30pm; rest of year: 10am-6pm - €11.50 (-25s free).*

After recovering from a serious illness in 1744, **Louis XV** commissioned Soufflot to build a sanctuary on the highest point of the Left Bank to replace the dilapidated church of Saint Geneviève. The architect designed a grand building 361 feet long, 275 feet wide and 272 feet high. The **peristyle** is composed of fluted Corinthian columns, supporting a triangular pediment, the first of its kind in Paris. Inside, the walls are decorated with **paintings★** created from 1877. The most famous, by Puvis de Chavannes, depict the story of Saint Geneviève. In April 1791, the Constituent Assembly closed the church to worship and made it a mausoleum for the "ashes of the great men of the French era of liberty": the **Panthéon**. In the 19th century, it changed function several times: a church during the Empire, a necropolis under Louis Philip, again a church under Napoleon III, the city's general headquarters, then finally a secular temple in 1885 to hold the ashes of Victor Hugo. More than 80 personalities, from Voltaire, Jean Moulin, Louis Braille, and Jean Jaurès to Marie Curie, Germaine Tillion, and Simone Veil (and her husband), are buried in the crypt.

From the **dome ★★★**, you can access the highest parts of the monument (up 206 steps), from where you can enjoy a spectacular 360-degree panorama of Paris *(open Apr-Oct: 10am-4:30pm - €3.50 on top of Panthéon entrance ticket)*.

Christian Mueller/Getty Images Plus

The Panthéon.



## Église Saint-Étienne-du-Mont ★★

**F7** Ⓜ *Cardinal-Lemoine. 1 pl. Ste-Geneviève - ✆ 01 43 54 11 79 - www.saintetiennedumont.fr - 9:30am-12pm, 3pm-7:30pm, Sat 10am-12pm, 3pm-8pm, Sun 10am-1pm, 4pm-8pm.* This church from the 13th century, rebuilt between the 15th and 17th centuries, is known for its 16th-century **rood screen★★** (partition separating the choir from the nave, here intricately sculpted), its organ (the oldest in Paris), and the remains of Saint Geneviève, the patron saint of Paris. The mathematician Blaise Pascal and dramatist Jean Racine are buried here. The incredibly original **facade★★** has three superimposed pediments in its center, while the bell tower adds a light touch to the otherwise imposing ensemble. Thanks to its Gothic structure, large windows along the side aisles, in the choir (Flamboyant style), and the ambulatory, plus the window (Renaissance) in the nave, flood the place with light. In the Cloître des Charniers, contiguous to the church (two cemeteries bordered it in the past), stunning **stained-glass windows★** depict subjects related to the Eucharist (17th c.).

## Mouffetard District★

**F7-8** Ⓜ *Plage Monge.* This neighborhood was once a popular haunt with students and poets (the likes of Sade, Rabelais, Villon), travelers, and bandits. Don't miss

**Rue Mouffetard**★ with its daily market *(except Mondays)*, retailers (the sculpted sign "À la Bonne Source" at no. 122 dates from the 17th century), its village and touristy feel, and **Place de la Contrescarpe**★, with its bustling café terraces.

## Jardin des Plantes ★★

**FG7** Ⓜ *Gare-d'Austerlitz or Monge - ✆ 01 40 79 56 01 - www.jardindesplantesdeparis.fr - summer: 7:30am-8pm; Mar & Oct: 8am-6:30pm; rest of year: 8am-5:30pm (times vary according to sunrise and sunset) - free.* The Jardin des Plantes is an extraordinary conservatory that champions nature—a breath of fresh air and spot of culture in the city. Highlights include the **huge greenhouses**, the first in the world built on this scale, in 1834-1836, made of glass and metal *(daily ex. Tue 10am-5pm - €7, -25s €5 - ticket including entry to the Galerie de Botanique)*. You can also wander around the **Jardin Alpin** or see the animals in the **Ménagerie**, the zoo established in 1794 *(57 r. Cuvier - ✆ 01 40 79 56 01 - www.mnhn.fr - 10am-5pm - €13, -25s €10)*. The zoo is home to all kinds of small and medium-sized species, some endangered, including red pandas and orangutans.



## Muséum National d'Histoire Naturelle ★★

### Grande Galerie de l'Évolution★★★

**F7** Ⓜ *Gare-d'Austerlitz. 36 r. Geoffroy-St-Hilaire - ✆ 01 40 79 54 79 - www.jardindesplantesdeparis.fr - daily ex. Tue 10am-6pm - €13 (-25s €7).*
This magnificent museum located within the Jardin des Plantes explains the key stages of evolution through three main exhibits.
**La Diversité du Vivant** - Past the underwater environments, a beautiful caravan of taxidermied animals presents the world's terrestrial environments, from the warmest (with zebras, giraffes, buffaloes, antilopes) to the coldest (polar bears). The monkeys and birds (near the elevators) are from the rainforest.
**L'homme, facteur d'évolution** – The influence of human action on the natural environment is shown here, the **salle des espèces menacées ou**

### Key Milestones of the Jardin des Plantes

In 1626, Jean Héroard and Guy de La Brosse, doctors and pharmacists during the reign of Louis XIII, were granted permission to establish the Royal Garden of Medicinal Plants in the suburb of Saint-Victor. They turned it into a school for botany, natural history, and pharmacy. The garden was opened to the public in 1640. The botanist Tournefort and the three Jussieu brothers traveled the world to enrich its collections. It was under Buffon, the institution's director from 1739 to 1788, assisted by Daubenton and Antoine Laurent de Jussieu, nephew of the predecessors, that the botanical garden truly blossomed. So tremendous a success that a statue was erected in Buffon's honor—in his lifetime!

**disparues★★** (room of endangered or extinct species) the most alarming illustration.

**L'évolution de la vie** - From the early theories of naturalists (Lamarck, Darwin) to recent discoveries about DNA.

### Galerie de Paléontologie et d'Anatomie Comparée★

**G7** Ⓜ *Gare-d'Austerlitz. 2 r. Buffon - ✆ 01 40 79 56 01 - www.jardindesplantesdeparis.fr - daily ex. Tue 10am-6pm - €10 (-25 s €7).*
Located in an independent building in a typical 19th-century style, this gallery shows over 5,000 skeletons of vertebrates, from triceratops to humans and whales.
An impressive display!

### Galerie de Minéralogie et de Géologie★

**F7** Ⓜ *Gare-d'Austerlitz. 36 r. Geoffroy-Saint-Hilaire - ✆ 01 40 79 56 01 - www.jardindesplantesdeparis.fr - daily, ex. Tue 10am-5pm - €7 (-25s €5).*
One of the richest collections of crystals in the world, earth's treasures fit for jewelry!

## Mosquée de Paris ★

**F7** Ⓜ *Place-Monge. Pl. du Puits-de-l'Ermite - ✆ 01 45 35 97 33 - www.mosqueedeparis.net - daily ex. Fri 9am-6pm - closed on Muslim holidays - €3 (children €2).*
This handsome Moorish building was erected by the City between 1922 and 1926 to honor the Muslim soldiers who died during the Great War. An oasis of calm, with a pleasant tea room, restaurant, and Turkish baths *(www.la-mosquee.com).*

## Arènes de Lutèce ★

**F7** Ⓜ *Place-Monge.* This Gallo-Roman monument from the 2nd century—destroyed in 280 by the Barbarians—lay undisturbed for about 1,500 years: the only trace of this ancient 17,000-seater amphitheater was the name of a local vineyard (Clos des Arènes). The building of Rue Monge in 1869 unearthed the arena, which assumed its current appearance in 1910. Today, players of pétanque and football share the space.

## Institut du Monde Arabe ★

**F6** Ⓜ *Jussieu or Cardinal-Lemoine - 1 r. des Fossés-St-Bernard - ✆ 01 40 51 38 38 - www.imarabe.org - Tue-Fri 10am-6pm, wknd 10am-7pm -€8 (-26s free).*
The glass-and-aluminum building, designed by Jean Nouvel, blends the architectural styles of East and West. The southern facade displays the traditional geometry found in Arab countries: the 240 apertures, which open and close every hour, resemble mashrabiya. To the west, the Tour des Livres evokes the minaret of the Great Mosque of Samarra (Iraq).
The ninth floor (with panoramic bar and restaurant) and ground floor bookstore offer unspoilt **views★★** over Paris.

**The museum** - The chance to discover the countless facets of the Arab world and Islam, through religion, languages, culture, and history.
Hosts exhibitions of contemporary art from Arab countries.

# Saint-Germain-des-Prés★★★ - Montparnasse★

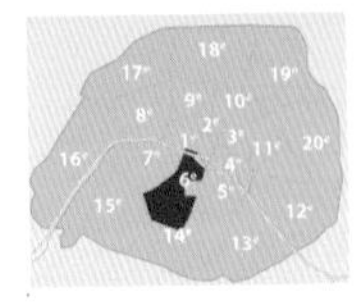


**Saint-Germain, Odéon, Montparnasse... you're in the heart of the Rive Gauche (Left Bank), walking in the footsteps of radical intellectuals and post-war writers, who would meet at the bars and cafés here. Boasting private mansions from the 17th and 18th centuries, magnificent Haussmannian facades, winding streets flanked by arcades, and luxurious storefronts, Saint-Germain too owes its charm to the special ambiance fostered by students of fine arts, medicine, and architecture.**

▶**Getting there:** Ⓜ Saint-Germain-des-Prés (Line 4), Mabillon (Line 10), Odéon (Lines 4 and 10), Saint-Sulpice (Line 4).

**Local Map p. 57. Detachable Map CE5-8.**

▶**Tip:** The art galleries are most likely to be open on Saturday.



## SAINT-GERMAIN-DES-PRÉS ★★★

**DE5-6** Following the Liberation of Paris, the district of Saint-Germain-des-Prés became popular for its nightlife, jazz cellars, and cafés frequented by artists and intellectuals, the likes of Sidney Bechet, Simone de Beauvoir, Boris Vian, Juliette Gréco, Sartre, Picasso, Apollinaire, Breton, Camus, and Prévert. While its golden days may be over, a stroll around its art galleries, antique shops, bookstores, iconic cafés, and timeless streets is a real treat.

### Église Saint-Germain-des-Prés ★★

**DE6** Ⓜ *Saint-Germain-des-Prés - 1 pl. St-Germain-des-Prés - ✆ 01 55 42 81 18 - www.eglise-saintgermaindespres.fr - 9:30am-8pm, Tue-Sat 8:30am-8pm.*

**WHERE TO EAT**
Au Pied de Fouet .......... 25
Blueberry Maki Bar .......... 29
Marcello.......... 30
Kodawari Ramen .......... 40
Tsukizi .......... 74
L'Avant-comptoir du marché .......... 94
Le Bon Saint-Pourçain .... 103

**WHERE TO DRINK**
La Palette .......... 25
Chez Georges .......... 28
Bread & Roses .......... 30
Freddy's.......... 76
Le Bar du Marché.......... 77

**SHOPPING**
Buly 1803 .......... 3

**WHERE TO STAY**
Hôtel de Nesle.......... 1

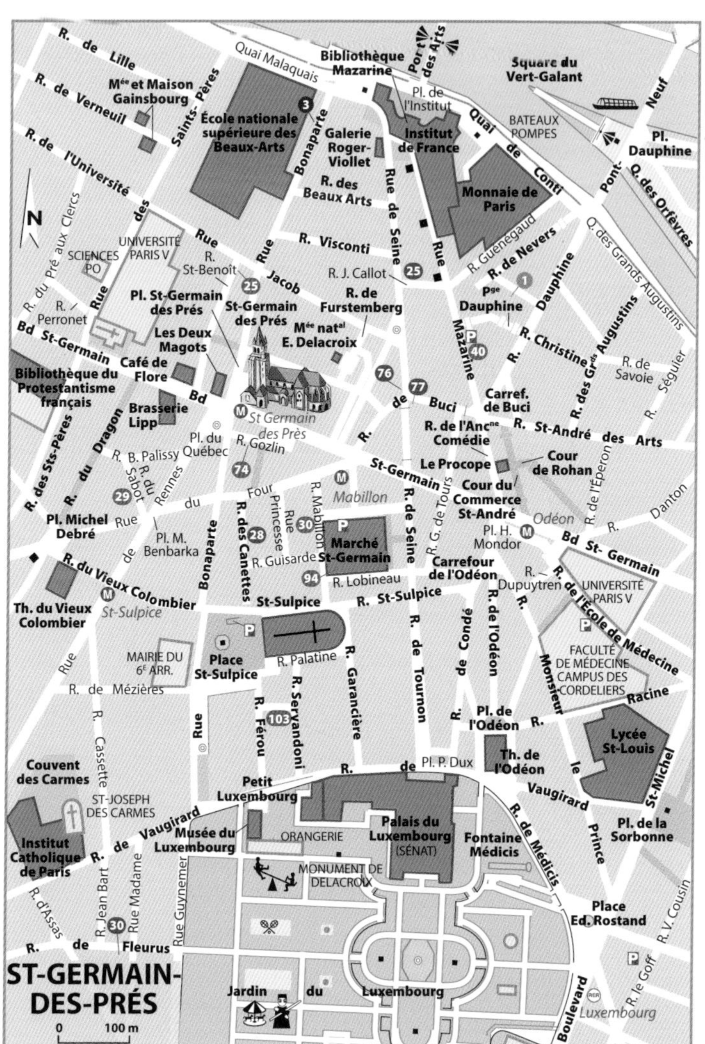
ST-GERMAIN-DES-PRÉS
0 100 m
N
R. de Lille
R. de Verneuil
R. de l'Université
Quai Malaquais
Bibliothèque Mazarine
Port des Arts
Square du Vert-Galant
Mée et Maison Gainsbourg
Saints-Pères
École nationale supérieure des Beaux-Arts
Bonaparte
Galerie Roger-Viollet
Pl. de l'Institut
Institut de France
Quai de Conti
BATEAUX POMPES
Neuf
Pl. Dauphine
Pont-
Q. des Orfèvres
Monnaie de Paris
R. des Beaux Arts
Rue de Seine
R. Visconti
Rue Mazarine
R. Guénégaud
R. de Nevers
Q. des Grands Augustins
Dauphine
UNIVERSITÉ PARIS V
SCIENCES PO
R. du Pré aux Clercs
Rue des
Rue Jacob
R. St-Benoît
R. J. Callot
Pge Dauphine
R. Perronet
Pl. St-Germain des Prés
St-Germain des Prés
R. de Furstemberg
Mée natal E. Delacroix
R. Christine
R. des Grds Augustins
Bd St-Germain
Les Deux Magots
Café de Flore
Bibliothèque du Protestantisme français
Brasserie Lipp
St Germain des Près
R. de Buci
Carref. de Buci
R. de Savoie
Séguier
R. du Dragon
R. des Sts-Pères
Pl. du Québec
R. Gozlin
R. B. Palissy
R. du Sabot
Rennes
R. de l'Ancne Comédie
R. St-André des Arts
Le Procope
Cour de Rohan
R. de l'Éperon
St-Germain
Cour du Commerce St-André
Danton
Four
Princesse
R. Mabillon
Mabillon
Odéon
Pl. Michel Debré
Rue de Rennes
Pl. M. Benbarka
R. des Canettes
Marché St-Germain
R. Guisarde
R. G. de Tours
Pl. H. Mondor
Bd St-Germain
R. du Vieux Colombier
Th. du Vieux Colombier
St-Sulpice
R. Lobineau
Carrefour de l'Odéon
R. Dupuytren
UNIVERSITÉ PARIS V
R. de l'École de Médecine
St-Sulpice
R. St-Sulpice
R. de Condé
R. de l'Odéon
R. de Tournon
R. Monsieur le Prince
MAIRIE DU 6E ARR.
Place St-Sulpice
R. Palatine
R. Garancière
FACULTÉ DE MÉDECINE CAMPUS DES CORDELIERS
Racine
R. de Mézières
R. Servandoni
R. Férou
Pl. de l'Odéon
Lycée St-Louis
R. Cassette
Rue Bonaparte
Couvent des Carmes
R. de Vaugirard
Pl. P. Dux
Th. de l'Odéon
St-Michel
ST-JOSEPH DES CARMES
Petit Luxembourg
Musée du Luxembourg
ORANGERIE
Palais du Luxembourg (SÉNAT)
Fontaine Médicis
R. de Médicis
Pl. de la Sorbonne
Institut Catholique de Paris
MONUMENT DE DELACROIX
R. d'Assas
R. Jean Bart
Rue Madame
Rue Guynemer
Place Ed. Rostand
R. V. Cousin
R. de Fleurus
Jardin du Luxembourg
Boulevard
Luxembourg
R. le Goff
Q.
3
25
25
1
40
76
77
74
29
28
30
94
103
30

Founded in the 6th century by King Childebert I, son of Clovis, the Benedictine Abbey of Saint-Germain-des-Prés became an important site for the prodigious Benedictine foundation from the 8th century, which numbered 17,000 abbeys and priories and supplied 24 popes. Despite the damage caused by the Norman invasions, the abbey was rebuilt every time, over the centuries becoming a veritable city at the gates of Paris (in the prés, or "fields"), complete with its own defense system, and even one of the major intellectual centers of medieval Europe. From 1674, it served as a state prison, before being wrecked during the French Revolution. Only the ancient abbey church remains intact. Most of the structure has survived from the 12th century. While the massive tower on the facade dates from the 11th century, the spire is from the 19th century. The original gate was concealed by an exterior gate in 1607. Inside, the walls and columns were painted in the 19th century with superb polychrome **decoration★★**, partly by Hippolyte Flandrin, to which a recent renovation has restored its splendor. At the entrance, note the Virgin and Child, a work dating from the 15th century, transferred from Notre-Dame.



## Literary Cafés

**Brasserie Lipp** *(151 bd St-Germain - ✆ 01 45 48 53 91 - www.brasserielipp.fr - 9am-12:45am)* was a hangout for academics and politicians. Regulars included Proust, Gide, and Malraux. Hemingway wrote *A Farewell to Arms* at the bar. In 1935, the owner Marcelin Cazes established an award for authors yet to win an award. The Prix Cazes is still held there every year. Made famous by clientele such as Sartre and de Beauvoir, **Café de Flore** *(172 bd St-Germain - ✆ 01 45 48 55 26 - www.cafedeflore.fr - 7:30am-1:30am)* and **Les Deux Magots** *(6 pl. Saint-Germain-des-Prés - ✆ 01 45 48 55 25 - lesdeuxmagots.fr - 7:30am-1am)* keep alive the literary tradition of Saint-Germain-des-Prés by hosting each year the jury and award-giving of the Prix de Flore and the Prix des Deux Magots.

### Alternative Art Trails

The **Carré Rive gauche** (www.carrerivegauche.com) is a nonprofit with around 120 members, bringing together gallery owners and antique dealers based between Quai Voltaire, Rue du Bac, Rue Saint-Pères, and Rue de l'Université since 1977. Their well-deserved reputation draws big-time collectors and museums to acquire pieces from them.

**Art à Saint-Germain-des-Prés**, a nonprofit founded in the late 1990s, operates on the same principle, with members located along Rue de Seine, Rue Mazarine, and Rue Dauphine.

Every November since 2010, the **Photo Saint-Germain Festival** (www.photosaintgermain.com) has brought together around fifty venues and institutions around a unifying theme such as literature or travel.

Place Saint-Sulpice also hosts various artsy events, like the **Marché de la Poésie** (www.marche-poesie.com), over five days in June.

The Mazarine Library at the Institut de France.



## Rue de Furstenberg ★

**E6** Ⓜ *Saint-Germain-des-Prés.* Peaceful narrow street with a pretty square shaded by paulownia trees. The **Musée Delacroix★** has taken up the apartment and studio the painter occupied from 1858 to 1863 *(6 r. de Furstenberg - ☏ 01 44 41 86 50 - www.musee-delacroix.fr - daily ex. Tue 9:30am-5:30pm, late nights first Thu of month 9pm €7 (-26s free) - €17 combined ticket with Musée du Louvre)*. The museum's major paintings include *Mary Magdalene in the Desert*, exhibited at the Salon of 1845, and *The Education of the Virgin*. There's a lovely garden in the courtyard.

As you head down Rue de Seine to the Institut de France, lovers of photography and historic Paris should make a beeline for the **Galerie Roger-Viollet** *(6 rue de Seine - ☏ 01 55 42 89 00 - www.roger-viollet.fr - Tue-Sat 11am-7pm)*, the HQ of the famous Parisian agency founded in 1938 by Hélène Roger-Viollet. It's an opportunity to discover part of its immense photographic collection during temporary exhibitions—and why not treat yourself to a print?

## Institut de France ★★

**E5** Ⓜ *Saint-Germain-des-Prés. 23 quai de Conti - ☏ 01 44 41 44 41 - www.institutdefrance.fr - Sat 10am-6pm - free.*

This majestic classical building is in harmonious keeping with its right-bank neighbor, the Louvre, to which it is connected by the delightful

**Pont des Arts**. The property is courtesy of **Cardinal Mazarin**, who bequeathed a sum for the construction of a college to school 60 students from the provinces united in France during the Treaty of the Pyrenees (Piémont, Alsace, Artois, and Roussillon). It was Napoleon who transferred the Institut de France to the site, which includes the **Académie Française** (established by Cardinal Richelieu in 1635), Académie des Inscriptions et Belles-Lettres (Colbert, 1663), Académie des Sciences (1666), Académie des Beaux-Arts (1816), and Académie des Sciences Morales et Politiques (1832). Adorned with beautiful woodwork, the **Bibliothèque Mazarine**★ is the oldest public library in France *(23 quai de Conti - ✆ 01 44 41 44 06 - www.bibliotheque-mazarine.fr - Mon-Sat 10am-6pm - guided tours: sign up on the website - free).*



## Monnaie de Paris ★

**E5** Ⓜ *Saint-Germain-des-Prés. 11 quai de Conti - ✆ 01 40 46 56 66 - www.monnaiedeparis.fr - daily ex. Mon 11am-6pm (Wed 9pm) - €12 (-26s free).* *Café Frappé par Bloom - daily ex. Mon 11am-7pm, brunch at the weekend.* Founded in 864, this is the oldest active factory in the world!

Since 1775, it has occupied this majestic neoclassical palace, extended by workshops at the rear, specially built by architect Jacques-Denis Antoine. Extending 384 feet along Quai Conti, the main building is noted for the simple lines of its design. Dedicated to the mint, the **Musée du 11 Conti** invites visitors to discover the history of coins, striking techniques, and the trades associated with the production of coins and objets d'art fabricated locally and in Pessac, in Gironde. A section of the palace's sumptuous rooms house the much-feted fine-dining restaurant Guy Savoy (upper level, west wing).

## Place Saint-Sulpice ★★

**DE6** Ⓜ *Saint-Sulpice.* All the facades around this square built in the mid-18th century were supposed to resemble that of **no. 6**, the work of Servandoni, but that was wishful thinking. The fountain erected by Visconti in 1844 stands in the center, featuring the great Christian preachers of the 17th century: Bossuet, Massillon, Fléchier, and Fénelon. Generations of religious folk have purchased objects of devotion from the neighboring stores. "Saint-Sulpice Art", the style of these kitsch holy objets d'art, flourished until the 1960s. Today, religious objects have been replaced by fashion.

## Église Saint-Sulpice ★★

**E6** Ⓜ *Saint-Sulpice - Pl. St-Sulpice - ✆ 01 46 33 21 78 - www.paroissesaintsulpice.paris - 8am-7:45pm.*
Founded by the Abbaye de Saint-Germain-des-Prés, the church was rebuilt multiple times and enlarged in the 16th and 17th centuries (six architects worked on it in 134 years). Inside, the proportions are impressive. **Frescoes★ by Delacroix**, the height of Romanticism (1849-1861), festoon the Chapelle des Saints-Anges *(first on right)*: on the vaulted ceiling, *St. Michael Defeating the Devil;* on the walls, *Heliodorus Driven from the Temple* and *Jacob Wrestling with the Angel.* The **Chapelle de la Vierge**★

*(in the axis of the apse)* was decorated under the direction of Servandoni. In the niche of the altar, *The Virgin and Child* is the handiwork of Pigalle. The **organ case★** was designed by Chalgrin (1776). Rebuilt by Aristide Cavaillé-Coll in 1862, it is the largest in France (102 stops over five keyboards) and one of the finest. During the reconstruction of Notre-Dame, Saint-Sulpice is serving as a cathedral, temporarily hosting major ceremonies, including Jacques Chirac's state funeral in 2019.
The narrow streets to the right of the church leading to the Jardin du Luxembourg (*p. 51*) are particularly charming: **Rue Férou★**, **Rue Servandoni★** and **Rue Garancière**.

## FAUBOURG SAINT-GERMAIN ★★

**D5-6** A très chic and tranquil neighborhood linking Saint-Germain-des-Prés with the Invalides, this "noble suburb" was one of the great strongholds of the Parisian aristocracy from the 16th century. Its sumptuous private mansions are now home to myriad embassies and ministries—including the French prime minister's residence, the Hôtel Matignon, at 57, Rue de Varenne.

### Maison Gainsbourg

**D5** Ⓜ *Rue du Bac. 5 bis r. de Verneuil - www.maisongainsbourg.fr - daily ex. Tue 9:30am-8pm (10:30pm Wed and Fri) - booking advised - €25 (-16s €16), museum only €12 (-16s €6).*
In September 2023, the home of the famous singer from 1969 to 1991 opened its doors to visitors for the first time. The original furnishings are intact! In addition, there's a museum recounting his life and a piano bar *(at no. 14)*. A few weeks before the opening, fans had already flocked to Rue de Verneuil when Jane Birkin's death was announced on July 16.

### Musée Maillol (Fondation Dina-Vierny)

**D5-6** Ⓜ *Rue-du-Bac. 59-61 r. de Grenelle - ☏ 01 42 22 57 25 - www.museemaillol.com - 10:30am-6:30pm (10pm Wed) - €16 (-6s free).* The museum, named for Maillol's muse, presents his works, paintings, and larger-than-life sculptures. Major exhibitions of modern and contemporary art also held there.

### Le Bon Marché

**D6** Ⓜ *Sèvres-Babylone. 24 r. de Sèvres - ☏ 01 44 39 80 00 - 10am-7:45pm.* At the corner of Rue du Bac and Rue de Sèvres, the first department store in Paris, designed by Aristide and Marguerite Boucicaut, opened in 1852. The instant and colossal success went on to inspire many entrepreneurs... and even authors like Émile Zola, in his novel *The Ladies' Paradise*. Its Art Deco decor makes an elegant backdrop for the upscale goods. Don't leave without swinging by **La Grande Épicerie de Paris**, a haven for foodies.

## THE ODÉON DISTRICT ★★

**E6** Ⓜ *Odéon.* The **Carrefour de l'Odéon** is dominated by a statue of French Revolutionary figure Danton (19th c.) erected on the site of the court building, where he was arrested in 1794. It's the center of the neighborhood, between Saint-Germain and the Sorbonne, where most of the local action is concentrated. Cinemas, coffeehouses, old bookstores, art galleries, and shops make it a very lively place.

### Cour du Commerce-St-André ★

**E6** *Enter at no.130 bd St-Germain.* It was along this charming passage that in 1790 Dr. Guillotin tried his "philanthropic decapitation machine" on… sheep. There, Jean-Paul Marat printed his radical newspaper, *L'Ami du peuple*.

### Rue de l'Ancienne-Comédie

**E6** This was the stage for the first plays by Racine and Molière. In 1770, with the theater on the verge of bankruptcy, the company moved to the Théâtre du Palais des Tuileries before taking over the Odéon. At no. 13, **Le Procope** (1686) is the oldest café in Paris, a hub of the capital's literary life, from La Fontaine to Verlaine.



### Rue de l'École-de-Médecine

**E6** Dominated by the neoclassical buildings of the Paris-Descartes School of Medicine, no. 15 is the site of the **Réfectoire des Cordeliers** (16th c.), the last remaining vestige of the convent taken over in 1791 by the Danton-headed revolutionary club.

### Rue Monsieur-le-Prince

**E6** This street runs along the School of Medicine and Lycée Saint-Louis, towards Luxembourg. The Polidor restaurant (no. 41) is an institution, as is the Bouillon Racine (3, Rue Racine), in the Art Nouveau style, founded by the Chartier brothers in 1906. Their interiors are worth a peek inside. At no. 4, spot the beautiful porte-cochère of the former Hôtel de Bacq (mid-18th century.). The apartment on the third story of no. 10 is where the philosopher **Auguste Comte** died in 1857, and is open to visitors *(✆ 01 43 26 08 56 - augustecomte.org - Tue-Wed and second Sat of month 2pm-5pm - €4).*

### Place de l'Odéon ★

**E6** Its buildings with concave facades contribute to the harmony of this semi-circular square, unchanged since it opened in 1779. Café Voltaire at no. 1 was beloved by encyclopedists. The **Odéon-Théâtre de l'Europe**, designed by Peyre and Wailly (1782), was inaugurated by Marie-Antoinette. It was renovated in the 20th century, a stunning ceiling by André Masson (1965) among the new features. The first performances held there include: *The Marriage of Figaro* by Beaumarchais, *Golden Head* by Paul Claudel, *Rhinoceros* by Ionesco, and *Waiting for Godot* by Samuel Beckett. TheOdéon-Théâtre de l'Europe was, together with the Sorbonne lecture halls, one of the venues of the student general assemblies of May 68.

## MONTPARNASSE ★

**CD7-8** Walk up **Rue de Rennes** or through the Jardin du Luxembourg *(p. 51)* to reach Montparnasse. Although the neighborhood wasn't unscathed from major urban development projects in the 1970s, it still draws crowds for its cinemas and crêperies (Bretons who settled in Paris arrived at Montparnasse train station), or to have a drink in brasseries made famous by 1920s Bohemian Paris. These restaurants were frequented by

Church and fountain, Place Saint-Sulpice.



a host of artists and intellectuals who abandoned Montmartre: Modigliani, Chagall, Light, Kisling, Picasso, Apollinaire, Stravinsky, Miró, Satie, Ezra Pound, Hemingway...

## The Historic Brasseries

**Le Dôme** – *108 bd du Montparnasse - ✆ 01 43 35 25 81 - www.restaurant-ledome.com - 12pm-2:45pm, 7pm-10:30pm.* Created around 1906, it was the favored meeting place for American Bohemians.

**La Coupole** – *102 bd du Montparnasse - ✆ 01 43 20 14 20 - www.lacoupole-paris.com - 8am-midnight.* A famous dance hall in the early 20th century, this bar has retained its magnificent frescoes, bar, and long picture windows.

**Le Select** – *99 bd du Montparnasse - ✆ 01 45 48 38 24 - www.leselectmontparnasse.fr - 7am-2am (Fri-Sat 3am).* The Art Deco setting of this bar, opened in 1925, lured the likes of Max Jacob, Apollinaire, Picasso, Modigliani, Cocteau, Zadkine, Henry Miller, Miró, Soutine, and Breton.

**La Rotonde** – *105 bd du Montparnasse - ✆ 01 43 26 48 26 - www.larotonde-montparnasse.fr - 7:30am-midnight.* Opened in 1903, this venue continues the tradition of Parisian brasseries. Lenine, Trotsky, Picasso, Chagall, Léger, Modigliani, Matisse and others mingled in this retro-style venue.

The theaters, bars, and restaurants on **Rue de la Gaîté** are the focal point of the neighborhood's nightlife.

The Théâtre Montparnasse (no. 31), Théâtre de la Gaîté-Montparnasse (no. 26), Bobino (no. 20) and Théâtre Rive-Gauche (no. 6) keep its reputation going today.

### Tour Montparnasse ★

**D7** Ⓜ *Montparnasse-Bienvenüe. 33 av. du Maine - ✆ 01 45 38 52 56 - www.tourmontparnasse56.com - 9:30am-10:30pm (Fri-Sat 11pm) - €15-18 (12-17s €13.50) - rooftop terrace closed indefinitely (access to the 56th floor only).* From the top of this 698-foot (59-floor) tower, the **view★★★** of Paris is incredible. The 1973-built skyscraper is in the throes of a major facelift by the architectural firm Nouvelle AOM.



### Musée Bourdelle ★

**C7** Ⓜ *Montparnasse-Bienvenüe. 18 r. Antoine-Bourdelle - ✆ 01 49 54 73 73 - www.bourdelle.paris.fr - daily ex. Mon 10am-6pm - free.* This museum is set in the former dwelling of the sculptor Antoine Bourdelle (1861-1929). His beautiful, practically untouched studio is definitely worth a look! With an extension designed by Christian de Portzamparc, the museum shines a light on the compelling work of this former student of Rodin.

### Musée Zadkine ★

**DE7** Ⓜ *Vavin. 100 bis r. d'Assas - ✆ 01 55 42 77 20 - www.zadkine.paris.fr - daily ex. Mon 10am-6pm - €9.*
The studio and lush garden once used by Russian sculptor Ossip Zadkine (1890-1967) is now a museum, tucked away and pleasantly calming compared with other museums.

### Cimetière du Montparnasse ★

**D8** Ⓜ *Edgar-Quinet. 3 bd Edgar-Quinet - 8am-6pm, Sat 8:30am-6pm, Sun 9am-6pm (closes at 5:30pm in winter).* This cemetery (1824) is the final resting place of scores of artists, writers, and intellectuals: Baudelaire, Saint-Saëns, Maupassant, Sartre, de Beauvoir, Duras, Gainsbourg, Pialat, Ionesco, César, Wolinski, Langlois... Spread over almost 50 acres, it's the second largest cemetery in the city of Paris, after Père-Lachaise.

### Fondation Cartier pour l'Art Contemporain ★

**D8** Ⓜ *Raspail. 261 bd Raspail - ✆ 01 42 18 56 50 - www.fondationcartier.com - daily ex. Mon 11am-8pm (Tue 10pm) - €11 (-25s €7.50) - new annex in the 1e arr. planned in 2025.*
The design of this building by Jean Nouvel blurs the boundaries between the real and virtual, with sheet-glass facades that extend the view along Boulevard Raspail. The exhibitions intersect with the rich diversity of creative disciplines, with a particular focus on environmental issues.
**Rue Campagne-Première** saw many artists pass through in the 1920s-30s. Note, at no. 31-31B, the building with large windows and clad in multicolored flamed sandstone tiles. Here, from 1922 to 1940, Man Ray rented a studio where the who's who of Paris' artistic society came to be photographed. At no. 17 is a passage lined with small buildings occupied by studios.

The Catacombes.



## Place Denfert-Rochereau

**Off Map by D8** Ⓜ *Denfert-Rochereau.* In the center, the **Lion de Belfort** (bronze sculpture by August Bartholdi) pays tribute to Colonel Pierre Philippe Denfert-Rochereau, who defended the city of Belfort in 1870 during the Franco-Prussian War. To the south of the square, you can go shopping along **Rue Daguerre**, a charming pedestrian street and beloved home of filmmaker Agnès Varda, who lived at no. 88. Not far away, on Rue Victor-Schœlcher, is the **Institut Giacometti**, an exhibition venue and reconstruction of the workshop at Rue Hippolyte Maindron where Alberto Giacometti (1901-1966) lived and worked for 40 years *(www.fondation-giacometti.fr - Tue-Sun 10am-6pm - €8.50, -18s free)*.

## Catacombes ★

**Off Plan by D8** Ⓜ *Denfert-Rochereau. 1 av. du Col.-Henri-Rol-Tanguy - ✆ 01 43 22 47 63 - www.catacombes.paris.fr - daily ex. Mon 9:45am-8:30pm - advance tickets online €29 (-18s €5), last-minute tickets €15 (-18s free). No toilets or cloakrooms - not recommended for young children, sensitive individuals, or people with heart or respiratory conditions. 130 steps down, 83 steps up, temperature: 14°C/57°F.*
These Gallo-Roman limestone quarries converted into an ossuary from 1785 to 1810 hold millions of skeletons from Paris' parish cemeteries. Goose bumps guaranteed!

# Invalides★★★ - Eiffel Tower★★★

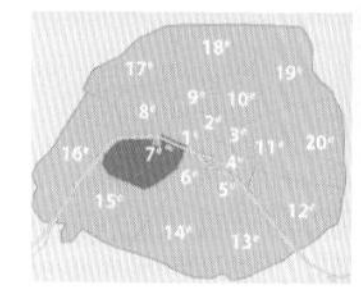


**Here, leafy avenues are bordered by ministries, embassies, and mansions ringed by sprawling grounds and gardens. Your gaze is never far away from stunning views of one of the world's most prominent silhouettes, the Eiffel Tower, and the glow from the Invalides dome. The Musée du Quai-Branly - Jacques-Chirac, with its fascinating collections from far-flung places, brings a contemporary touch to the opulent environs.**

▶**Getting there: Invalides:** Ⓜ Invalides (Lines 8 and 13), Varenne (Line 13), La Tour-Maubourg (Line 8). RER Invalides (Line C). **Eiffel Tower:** Ⓜ Bir-Hakeim (Line 6), École-Militaire (Line 8), Trocadéro (Lines 6 and 9). RER Champ-de-Mars-Tour-Eiffel (Line C). By Batobus, Tour-Eiffel and Musée-d'Orsay station.

**Detachable Map AD4-6.**

▶**Tip:** Have a picnic on the Seine's Left Bank, now pedestrianized and integrated into the Parc Rives-de-Seine. Or in the garden of the Musée Rodin *(admission fee)*. If you're looking for some retail therapy, quite rare in the neighborhood, head to Place de l'École-Militaire and Rue Cler. The latter, car-free and animated, is thronged with terrific bars, restaurants, and independent stores.



## Pont Alexandre-III ★★

**C4** Ⓜ *Invalides.* Tsar Nicholas II laid the first stone of this bridge on October 7, 1896, planned to symbolize the Franco-Russian Alliance, signed in 1892. Inaugurated at the 1900 Paris Exposition, it was designed to meet strict technical specifications: the single arch, with a span of 358 feet, would allow river traffic to pass under while supporting a flat apron that did not obstruct the perspective. The work is ornately decorated with lighting columns and volutes. The two golden Pegasuses—symbolizing War (Rive Gauche) and Peace (Rive Droite)—frame the view towards the Invalides.

## The Invalides ★★★

**C5** From the Pont Alexandre-III, wander around the **esplanade** at the Invalides, built from 1704 to 1720 by Robert de Cotte, architect François Mansart's brother-in-law. Then, take a look at the magnificent vista of the Hôtel des Invalides, its majestic dome commanding the view. Rows of silver linden trees border the lawns.

### Hôtel des Invalides

Ⓜ *Varenne. Access via 129 r. de Grenelle or pl. Vauban.* Founded by **Louis XIV**, this masterful ensemble was successively a hospice for destitute war veterans, hospital, fire station,

and convent before reclaiming its primary vocation at the turn of the 20th century: to care for wounded soldiers. It houses several military agencies and museums, including the Musée de l'Armée.

The 643-foot northern **facade★★**, designed by Libéral Bruant, makes for an arresting sight. At its center, a monumental door, under its triumphant arch pediment (one of a kind in France), gives access to the **cour d'honneur★★** (courtyard). The austere beauty of the place is striking. It was here that Napoleon would inspect his veterans. In the middle stands the statue of the "little corporal", as Napoleon was known, by Seurre.



## Église Saint-Louis des Invalides★

*Free admission.* The "church of the soldiers" was built by **Jules Hardouin-Mansart**, who took inspiration from Libéral Bruant's plans. Inside, flags captured from the enemy provide the only decoration. Through the window behind the master altar and its baldachin, you can make out the Église du Dôme.

## Église du Dôme★★★

*For visitor conditions, see "Museum de l'Armée".* A former private royal chapel in the French Baroque style, it was built between 1677 and 1706 by Jules Hardouin-Mansart. The grandeur of the double-drum dome is matched by the rigorous design of the church, built to the plan of a Greek cross. The dome, a thing of spectacular height and majesty, was allowed to gleam once again for the occasion of the bicentennial of the French Revolution: 555,000 pieces of gold leaf (27.9 lb) were required for its restoration. Transferred there in 1861, the remains of **Emperor Napoleon I** lie, in the center of the crypt, in a tomb made of red quartzite surrounded by a dozen winged allegories of Napoleonic victories, crafted by Pradier.

An augmented reality tour reveals the secrets of the building by immersing you in its architectural history *(rental at the museum's reception-ticket desks and in the Église du Dôme - €5).*

## Musée de l'Armée★★★

*Entrance through the Cour d'honneur, on the Esplanade. ✆ 01 44 42 38 77 - www.musee-armee.fr - 10am-6pm - €14 (-28s free) - single ticket for admission to the permanent collections of the Musée de l'Armée, Église du Dôme (Napoleon I's tomb), Historial Charles-de-Gaulle, Musée des Plans-Reliefs, and Musée de l'Ordre de la Libération.*

Its exceptional collections are devoted to military art, technology, and history. The visitor journey is essentially chronological. The **armor and weapons department** presents pieces from the 13th to the 17th centuries (France, Europe, Asia, Middle East), including the sword and armor of Francis I of France.

The modern department covers the period from **Louis XIV to Napoleon III** (1643-1870). **The contemporary period** begins in 1871 and ends in 1945. The **"cabinets insolites"** show figurines, artillery pieces, and musical instruments of yesteryear. The audiovisual experience at the **Historial Charles-de-Gaulle★** takes visitors

through the public life and political career of General de Gaulle.
A veritable journey through bygone France, the **Musée des Plans-Reliefs★★** presents extraordinary models of cities, ports, and fortresses, the oldest of which were commissioned by Louis XIV.

## Musée Rodin ★★

**C5** Ⓜ *Varenne. Hôtel Biron - 77 r. de Varenne - ✆ 01 44 18 61 10 - www.musee-rodin.fr - daily ex. Mon 10am-6:30pm (the sculpture garden closes at dusk) - €13; combined ticket with the Musée d'Orsay - €24.* The Musée Rodin occupies the sublime **Hôtel Biron★★** and its garden, dating from the 18th century and where **Auguste Rodin** (1840-1917) lived from 1908. Completely refurbished, this peaceful establishment has been redesigned to offer visitors a chronological and thematic journey through Rodin's works, spread over almost 18 rooms graced with fine wood paneling. *The Cathedral, The Kiss, The Age of Bronze,* and many others, Rodin's masterpieces, mostly in bronze or marble, are characterized by their strength of expression and sense of restrained energy and power. The "Rodin at the Hôtel Biron" room is a testament to his life at the mansion. Assembled from period photographs, replete with the sculptor's furniture, since restored, the space is a fascinating cabinet of curiosities. The "Rodin and the Ancient" room features more than a hundred fragments of Greek, Roman, and Egyptian sculptures, acquired and collected by Rodin.
The site also boasts a superb **garden** dotted with major pieces (*The Thinker, The Burghers of Calais, The Gates of Hell, Ugolino and His Sons* to name a few) and a **chapel** with its 39-foot-tall glass ceiling. You can also admire works by **Camille Claudel**, such as *The Wave*, and three paintings by Van Gogh *(Portrait of Père Tanguy, View of the Viaduct in Arles or The Blue Train*, and *The Harvesters)*, from Rodin's personal collection.

## École Militaire ★

**B6** Ⓜ *École-Militaire.* Bookending the Champ-de-Mars to the southeast, the military academy is one of the main legacies of Louis XV's reign in Paris. The building consists of a central pavilion (designed by Ange-Jacques Gabriel) adorned with ten Corinthian columns crowned by a sculpted pediment. The two lower wings flanking the main building date from the Second Empire. The school was established to train 500 men from poor noble families to become cadet officers. Today the complex hosts the College of Warfare and the Institute of Advanced Studies in National Defense.

## Jardins du Champ-de-Mars

**B5-6** Ⓜ *École-Militaire or RER C Champ-de-Mars-Tour-Eiffel.* During the construction of the École Militaire, the market gardens that stretched between the new buildings and the Seine were transformed into drilling and marching grounds, or "Campus Martius", hence the name Champ-de-Mars. It was also a venue for patriotic gatherings: on July 14, 1790, "Federation Day" (attended by Louis

XVI) and the first anniversary of the storming of the Bastille prison took place there. Napoleon distributed imperial eagles and badges at the site. The Champ-de-Mars, which later became a fairground, then hosted the Paris Exposition world fairs. Nowadays, this large green space continues to draw the crowds, notably for the Bastille Day (July 14) fireworks. During fine weather, tourists and Parisians flock to the lawns for picnics or relaxation while admiring the view of the Eiffel Tower and Palais de Chaillot. At the southernmost end of the Champ-de-Mars stands the **Grand Palais Éphémère**, an immense timber-framed temporary exhibition hall (designed by architect Jean-Michel Wilmotte) built to host major shows and Olympic events while the Grand Palais (*p. 83*) is closed for renovations.



## Eiffel Tower ★★★

**AB5** *RER C Champ-de-Mars-Tour-Eiffel. Champ-de-Mars - 0 892 70 12 39 - www.toureiffel.paris - mid-Jun-late Aug: 9am-12:45am; rest of year: 9:30am-10:45pm - €11.30 (12-24s €5.60) stair access to 2nd floor, €21.50 (12-24s €10.70) stairs + elevator to top; €18.10 (12-24s €9) 2nd floor elevator, €28.30 (12-24s €14.10) elevator to top.*

### Tips for Visiting

Buy your tickets online to save time. Otherwise, if you can, arrive 15 or 30 minutes before the site opens. For the rest of the day, there's no rule: the wait time varies wildly from day to day. Tickets give access to the 2nd floor (via the stairs with 674 steps or the elevators) or to the top (3rd floor), although in this case, you have to pass by the 2nd floor and take another elevator, where the wait can be anywhere from 5 to 45 minutes. Between October and April, remember to wrap up as the line is in a windy area and it can get chilly.
The glass wall built in 2018 to protect the Eiffel Tower has made the visit somewhat more challenging.

### About the Tower

Looming over the capital, the Eiffel Tower is undoubtedly one of the most recognizable monuments in

### The Tower Saved by Radio

When the project was launched in 1884 for the 1889 Paris Exposition, Gustave Eiffel sparked controversy. He was granted a 20-year concession contract, but artists and other luminaries wrote a public protest, called "of the 300" (echoing the height of the tower). Signatories included: Maupassant, Gounod, Charles Garnier, François Coppée, Leconte de Lisle... Fortunately, to other artists' minds, the tower was a symbol of modernity, speed, and the art of the new century. Cocteau and Apollinaire celebrated the tower, which also featured in works by Pissarro, Dufy, Utrillo, Seurat, and Delaunay. In 1909, the tower was very nearly dismantled! The tower was only saved due to the fact it served as a giant antenna for wireless telegraphy: it was the site of the first radiotelephony tests in the early 20th century, before television took over.

the world. Its mass of metal girders and its elevators are the handiwork of engineer **Gustave Eiffel** (1832-1923). Between 1887 and 1889, 300 acrobatic engineers fitted 2.5 million rivets. Overall height: 984 ft; weight: 7,300 tons, and 60 tons of paint, refreshed every seven years.

On the **ground floor**, visitors can check out the elevator machinery.

The **1st floor**, 187 feet up, has been given a glass floor which you can walk on–breathtaking to say the least! The exterior gallery features a fascinating photography exhibit.

On the **2nd floor** (377 ft), windows let you glimpse every Paris monument, and animated displays present how the tower was built. There are also bars, restaurants, and shops on this floor.

On the **3rd floor**, 906 feet up, the sweeping **panorama★★★** stretches up to 37 miles all around on a clear day. Panoramic restaurants on each floor.



## At the Foot of the Eiffel Tower

After your visit to the Eiffel Tower, go admire the **Pont de Bir-Hakeim** *(**A5**)*, the bridge also unveiled for the 1900 Paris Exposition. This metal structure, its top level used by the métro, is an iconic landmark in lots of movies. Fans of Japanese culture should head to the **Maison de la Culture du Japon à Paris** *(**A5** 101 bis quai Branly - ✆ 01 44 37 95 01 - www.mcjp.fr - Tue-Sat 11am-7pm)*, a short stroll away.

On the opposite side of Quai Branly stands the **Cathédrale de la Sainte-Trinité** *(**B4** 1 quai Branly - ✆ 07 67 09 81 01 - www.cathedrale-sainte-trinite.fr - 2pm-7pm - free)*, consecrated in 2016 and topped by gleaming gold onion domes. It is home to the **Centre Spirituel et Culturel Orthodoxe Russe**—Russian Orthodox Spiritual and Cultural Center.

## Musée du Quai-Branly-Jacques-Chirac ★★

**B4-5** *RER C Pont-de-l'Alma. 37 quai Branly - ✆ 01 56 61 70 00 - www.quaibranly.fr - daily ex. Mon 10:30am-7pm - €12.*

The brainchild of Jacques Chirac and designed by Jean Nouvel (2006) merges the collections of the Musée de l'Homme and the Musée National des Arts d'Afrique et d'Océanie. The pieces are divided into four geographical areas (Oceania, Asia, Africa, America). The soft lighting and relatively dark, large halls, devoid of interior walls and rooms, superbly **showcase★★★** the collections, contextualized by countless visual and audio documents. The number of masterpieces is staggering.

The beautiful savannah garden that surrounds the museum, created by Gilles Clément, hosts various cultural activities in summer *(see website)*. The museum's northern facade is taken up by an 8,611-sq.ft **green wall★** designed by botanist Patrick Blanc. It consists of 15,000 plants from 150 species from all over the world.

# Musée d'Orsay★★★

**Millet, Degas, Renoir, Monet, Van Gogh, Gauguin, Cézanne... no Impressionist has been left behind! One of the most visited museums in Paris, the Musée d'Orsay is home to the world's finest collection of Impressionist artworks. And what a magnificent setting! A former train station from 1900, right on the Seine, affording sumptuous views of the city that saw so many pictorial innovations emerge at the end of the 19th century.**

▶**Getting there:** RER Musée-d'Orsay (Line C), M Solférino or Assemblée Nationale (Line 12).

**Detachable Map D5.**

▶**Practical information:** 01 40 49 48 14 - www.musee-orsay.fr - daily ex. Mon 9:30am-6pm (Thu 9:45pm) - €16 (-26s free).

▶**Tip:** Thursday's late-night opening attracts fewer people, so make the most of it. After your visit, stroll along the pedestrianized banks of the Seine to the Musée du Quai-Branly (*p. 72*). In front of the museum, the Passerelle Léopold-Sédar-Senghor (formerly Passerelle Solférino) is a footbridge that connects to the Jardin des Tuileries over on the Right Bank (*p. 82*).



From academic art to Post-Impressionism, the museum illustrates every artistic movement from **1848 to 1914**, thereby serving as a sensational transition between the collections of the Louvre and those held at the Centre Georges-Pompidou. The works are presented chronologically, by artist and/or by movement, and the museum is constantly evolving to provide

## Palace, Train Station, then Museum

In 1810, the Palais d'Orsay was destined to be a government administrative building. After the fire that destroyed it in 1871 during the period of the Paris Commune, the site was acquired by the Compagnie des Chemins de Fer d'Orléans. As the 1900 Paris Exposition approached, the railway company wished to build a prestigious train station whose architecture met the high esthetic standards of this elegant neighborhood close to the Louvre and the Tuileries. They chose the project submitted by Victor Laloux (1850-1937): the industrial features (glass and metal) would be concealed on the outside by a monumental facade inspired by the Louvre and inside by a coffered ceiling with stuccowork. The building was officially opened on July 14, 1900. However, when the electrification of the railway network meant longer trains, the Orsay's platforms fell short. From 1939, the station's services were confined to the Paris suburbs. In 1973, plans emerged to establish a museum dedicated to the 19th century. An architecture competition was held in 1979.

more artistic insight, light, and color. Ambitious temporary exhibitions complete the journey.

## The Major Masterpieces

### Painting and Sculpture

The collections admirably bring together official art with the innovative trends of the 19th century. The large-scale **history paintings**, which demonstrate extraordinary technical skill (works by Gérôme, Couture, etc.), and the canvasses reflecting the idealized perfection of **academic art** (*The Source* by Ingres, *The Birth of Venus* by Cabanel) are juxtaposed with the feverish touch of the **Romantic** painters (*The Lion Hunt* by Delacroix) and the intentional crudeness of the **Realists** (*A Burial at Ornans* and *The Origin of the World* by Courbet). Then the **Barbizon School** created a revolution, abandoning the historic landscapes in favor of a more sincere depiction of nature. For example, the works of Corot and Millet (including the must-see *The Angelus*). The years 1850 to 1870 heralded **Impressionism**: the new generation of artists sought to translate the fleeting nature of light. Boudin, Degas, Caillebotte (*The Floor Scrapers*), Renoir (*Ball at the Moulin de la Galette*), Manet (*The Luncheon on the Grass*, *Olympia*, etc.) and, of course, Monet (*Rouen Cathedral* series) shattered conventions. In their wake, the proponents of **Neo- and Post-Impressionnism** stepped up the artistic innovations: exploration of geometric forms for Cézanne (*Apples and Oranges*), documentary for Toulouse-Lautrec (*La Toilette*), Japonism for Vuillard (*Nannies*) and Gauguin (*Self-Portrait with the Yellow Christ*), not to mention the tormented visions of Van Gogh (*The Church at Auvers, The Starry Night, Self-Portrait*). **Sculptures** include *The Dance* by Carpeaux, *Honoré de Balzac* by Rodin, *The Small Dancer* by Degas, and *Maturity* by Camille Claudel.



### Decorative Arts

The exhibits show the eclecticism of this era marked by colonization, travel, and world fairs. The naturalist inspiration culminated in Art Nouveau: the *Dragonfly Cabinet* by Gallé, the water lily lamp by Majorelle and Daum Frères...

### Photography

Consisting of works by renowned—Le Gray, Bayard, Nègre, Nadar—or anonymous artists (around 50,000 prints in total), the collection traces the history of photography from Nicéphore Niépce in 1839 to the 1920s.

### Graphic Arts

The museum holds a collection of more than 10,000 drawings, some exceptional, such as *The Black Knot* by Seurat and *Self-Portrait with Masks* by Spilliaert.

### Architecture

This section is confined to the Second Empire (1852-1870) and Haussmann's transformations. You can see a terrific model, to a scale of 1:100, of the Opéra district in 1914, under a glass floor.

# Trocadéro - Chaillot★★ - Alma

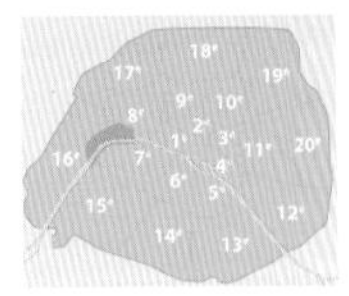


**On the Chaillot Hill, in the heart of this serene and elegant neighborhood affording tremendous views of the Eiffel Tower, everyone will find a museum to suit their interest, from ethnography, architecture, and Asian arts to modern and contemporary art, fashion, and more.**

▶**Getting there:** M Trocadéro (Lines 6 and 9), Alma-Marceau, or Iéna (Line 9). RER Champ-de-Mars-Tour-Eiffel (Line C).

**Detachable Map AC3-4.**

▶**Tip:** Sip a sundowner on the outside terrace at the Musée d'Art Moderne or at the Café Lucy on the second floor of the Musée de l'Homme to soak up superlative views of the Eiffel Tower and the Champ-de-Mars. The Palais de Tokyo doesn't close until midnight, so you can easily leave this attraction until much later in the day.



## Palais de Chaillot ★★

**A4** M *Trocadéro.* This palace, like every building in the Trocadéro complex, was erected for the 1937 Paris Exposition—or the "International Exposition of Art and Technology in Modern Life". At its center, the Parvis des Droits de l'Homme leads to a **terrace**★★★ granting unblemished views of the Eiffel Tower. Below are the **Jardins du Trocadéro**, gardens also created for the Paris Exposition. The square is flanked by two buildings.

### Musée de l'Homme★★

*17 pl. du Trocadéro - ✆ 01 44 05 72 72 - www.museedelhomme.fr - daily ex. Tue 11am-7pm - €10/13 (-25s free) - resource center open to all. Ethnographic film festival. Bookstore. Café Lucy and Café de l'Homme.*

At the juncture of scientific disciplines as diverse as they are complementary—biology, philosophy, anthropology, and history—this museum, boasting stunning displays and innovative museumography, strives to answer the three fundamental questions: who are we, where do we come from, and where are we going? From the Cro-Magnon skull to the skull of Descartes by way of the Venus of Lespugue sculpted in mammoth ivory more than 20,000 years ago, and the surprisingly large-scale (62 feet long by 36 feet tall) busts made of plaster and bronze in the 19th century, human nature is presented here in all its rich diversity. Don't miss the giant wall map where the visitor is invited to "pull" on tongues to listen to about thirty languages from around the world. In addition, virtually transform your face from *homo sapiens* to Neanderthal.

Next to the Musée de l'Homme, the **Musée National de la Marine** presents the history of the French navy from the 17th century through some 350 ship models plus a collection of naval sculptures and multiple paintings *(17 pl. du Trocadéro-et-du-11-Novembre - ✆ 01 53 65 69 69 - www.musee-marine.fr).*

### Chaillot - Théâtre National de la Danse

*1 pl. du Trocadéro-et-du-11-Novembre - ✆ 01 53 65 31 00 - theatre-chaillot.fr - ticket prices vary by production.*
Beneath the palace terrace is a vast performance auditorium. Firmin Gémier founded the TNP (Théâtre National Populaire) there in 1920, which Jean Vilar directed from 1951 to 1963. This venue puts on a sublime program of contemporary dance and theater.



### Cité de l'Architecture et du Patrimoine★★

*1 pl. du Trocadéro-et-du-11-Novembre - ✆ 01 58 51 52 00 - www.citedelarchitecture.fr - daily ex. Tue 11am-7pm (Thu 9pm) - €9 (-18s free) - €12, combined ticket with temporary exhibitions.*
This engaging complex is the result of the merger of several institutions, including the Musée des Monuments Français initiated by Viollet-le-Duc in 1879. Its grandiose main gallery presents models, wall paintings, stained glass, and, the star attractions, life-size moldings and reproductions of architectural details of France's key monuments from the Middle Ages to the 18th century. A real treat for architecture buffs! In an effort to raise public awareness of the art of construction, the institution also offers an interesting panorama of modern and contemporary architecture, and programs temporary exhibitions on a wide variety of themes.

## Musée National des Arts Asiatiques - Guimet ★★★

**A4** Ⓜ *Iéna. 6 pl. d'Iéna - ✆ 01 56 52 54 33 - www.guimet.fr - daily ex. Tue 10am-6pm - €11.50 (-25s free).*
This temple to Asian culture built in 1889 by the Lyon-born collector Émile Guimet (1836-1919) presents, in its luminous interior, renovated in the 1990s by architects Henri and Bruno Gaudin, a collection of Asian art reputed to be the largest in the world: **treasures of Cambodian art★★**, majestic gilt-bronze Buddhas, Nepalese miniatures, Tibetan statuettes and ritual objects, **burial goods★★** sourced from provinces in Northern China, and pieces of **Ming porcelain★** (1368-1644) in multicolored enamel or sumptuous blue-and-white decoration.
In addition, absolutely stunning lacquered, gilt, mother-of-pearl-inlaid furniture, and remarkable prints produced by Utamaro (18th c.), Sharaku (late 18th c.), Hiroshige (19th c.), and Hokusai, including the iconic **The Great Wave off Kanagawa★★**.
Temporary exhibitions take place in the **neoclassical Hôtel Heidelbach-Guimet** *(19 av. d'Iéna)*, an annex to the museum bordered by a Japanese garden featuring an authentic tea pavilion *(garden open to visitors during special events and conferences).*

chrisdorney/Getty Images Plus

The exterior of the Palais de Tokyo.



## Palais de Tokyo ★

**B4** Ⓜ *Iéna. 13 av. du Prés.-Wilson - ☎ 01 81 97 35 88 - www.palaisdetokyo.com - daily ex. Tue 12pm-10pm (Thu midnight) - €12 (-18s free).*
*Hip café for a bite to eat and specialist art bookstore.*
Opened in 2002 and reorganized in 2012, this fully modular space over 236,000 sq.ft is intended to be a center for all artistic practices and persuasions, regardless of the form of expression: art, design, fashion, photography, video, cinema, literature, dance... you name it. Through the year, it hosts exhibitions, performances, conferences, screenings, concerts, children's workshops, and more.

## Musée d'Art Moderne de la Ville de Paris ★★

**B4** Ⓜ *Iéna. 11 av. du Prés.-Wilson - ☎ 01 53 67 40 00 - www.mam.paris.fr - daily ex. Mon 10am-6pm - free.*
All the painting movements of the 20th century are on show in this wing of the Palais de Tokyo, built along with it for the 1937 Paris Exposition and whose original Art Deco architecture is back to its former splendor following the 2019 renovation. Presented chronologically, the permanent collection, enriched with various donations, covers the 20th-century **avant-gardes** from Fauvism (Cubism, Paris School, Surrealism, Expressionism) to the most recent movements, with works produced by

the likes of Hartung, Modigliani, Léger, Soulages, Soutine, Kupka, Bourgeois, Delaunay, Buren, Boltanski, Messager, Spoerri, Wool, Gordon, and Tinguely. Not to be missed: the first two versions of **The Dance★** by Matisse (1931 and 1932) and **The Electricity Fairy★** (1937) by Raoul Dufy, one of the world's largest paintings (almost 6,500 sq.ft, composed of 250 panels side by side). The temporary **contemporary art** exhibitions are monographic.

## Palais Galliera - Musée de la Mode de la Ville de Paris ★

**B4** Ⓜ *Iéna or Alma-Marceau. 10 av. Pierre-1er-de-Serbie - ✆ 01 56 52 86 00 - www.palaisgalliera.paris.fr - daily ex. Mon 10am-6pm (Thu-Fri 9pm) - €15 (-18s free).*



Designed by Léon Ginain, between 1878 and 1894, at the behest of Marie Brignole-Sale, Duchess of Galliera, to house her extensive art collection, this striking private mansion hosts the **Musée de la Mode de la Ville de Paris**. The fashion museum puts on a regularly updated program of themed exhibitions. The galleries at garden level hold the permanent collection, presenting the history of fashion from the 18th century to today.

## Musée Yves-Saint-Laurent

**B4** Ⓜ *Alma-Marceau. 5 av. Marceau - ✆ 01 44 31 64 00 - www.museeyslparis.com - daily ex. Mon 11am-6pm (Sat 9pm) - €10 (-10s free).*

In 2002, Yves Saint Laurent (1936-2008) announced the end of his 40-plus-year career as a fashion designer in this *hôtel particulier*, the historic headquarters where he created his most iconic looks. Now, the collection of drawings, textiles, and accessories is split between the YSL museums in Marrakech and Paris. In addition to temporary exhibitions, you can see the famous designer's office with his book shelves and desk, his unmistakable glasses on display.

### A Trip Out West

The **Musée Marmottan-Monet★★** is likely the largest collection of Claude Monet works in the world: some 94 canvasses from the master of Impressionism are on display, including the famous *Impression, Sunrise* (1872), which gave the Impressionist movement its name. You will also see the artist's drawings, notebooks, letters, and personal effects. Exhibited around works by Monet are pieces by artists and friends of his time: Renoir, Caillebotte, and Berthe Morisot. The museum also puts on temporary exhibitions, often related to Impressionism.
**Off map by A5** Ⓜ La Muette (Line 9 from Alma-Marceau) - 2 r. Louis-Boilly - ✆ 01 44 96 50 33 - www.marmottan.fr - daily ex. Mon 10am-6pm (Thu 9pm) - €14 (-18s €8.50) - €23 combined ticket with the Fondation Monet in Giverny.

# Champs-Élysées★★★ and Western Paris★

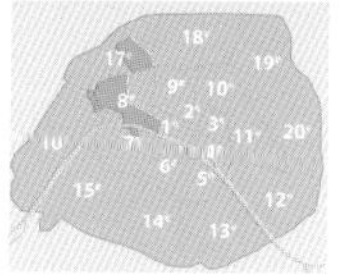

**Stretching for over four miles, this "Triumphal Way" forms the major thoroughfare in Paris. From the Louvre to the Arche de La Défense, its architecture recounts 900 years of history. Along this prestigious axis, you'll find a high concentration of top-tier government institutions, sublime palaces built for the 1900 Paris Exposition, major museums, gorgeous gardens but also, around Avenue Montaigne, all the stores of luxury ready-to-wear labels which make Paris the capital of fashion: Chanel, Dior, Vuitton, Givenchy to name a few.**

▶**Getting there:** Ⓜ Tuileries (Line 1), Concorde (Lines 1, 8, and 12), Champs-Élysées-Clemenceau (Lines 1 and 13), Franklin-D.-Roosevelt (Lines 1 and 9), George-V (Line 1), and Charles-de-Gaulle-Étoile (Lines 1, 2, and 6). RER Charles-de-Gaulle-Étoile (Line A). Batobus Champs-Élysées station.

**Detachable Map AD1-4.**

▶**Tip:** For a break, head to the Jardins des Tuileries garden or make your way down the Port des Champs-Élysées (right bank, between the Passerelle Leopold-Sédar-Senghor bridge and the Pont des Invalides), a tranquil riverside village in the center of Paris.



## Place de la Concorde ★★

**CD4** Ⓜ *Concorde.* Developed under Louis XV, since 1836 it has been dominated by the **Obélisque★**, an obelisk gifted to France by Muhammad Ali, the ruler of Egypt. Made of pink granite marked with hieroglyphics, capped with a gold pyramid, it measures 75 feet tall and weighs almost 220 tons. The island surrounding the Obélisque is the best spot to admire the views leading off from the square: the *Marly Horses* (by Coustou—the originals are at the Louvre) guide the gaze towards the Champs-Élysées; the *Winged Horses* by Coysevox (originals at the Louvre) towards the Tuileries and the Louvre. At the end of **Rue Royale★**, you can make out the huge pediment and soaring columns of **La Madeleine★** which match those of **Palais-Bourbon★** (France's National Assembly), on the other side of the **Pont de la Concorde**. On both sides of Rue Royale are classical facades: on the left, the **Hôtel de Crillon** (the famous palace) and, on the right, the **Hôtel de la Marine** *(see below)*.

## Hôtel de la Marine ★★

**D4** *2 pl. de la Concorde - www.hotel-de-la-marine.paris - 10:30am-7pm (Fri 9:30pm) - €13 salons and loggia, €17 main tour (-25s free).*

A veritable Versailles in miniature on the majestic Place de la Concorde! Built between 1758 and 1774 by Ange-Jacques Gabriel to house the royal Garde-Meuble, the office in charge of furnishing all the royal properties, the building then became the Ministry of the French Navy, until 2015. It opened its doors to the public in 2021. The first time since 1789! After four years of major renovation works, the mansion has reclaimed its former glory, from its old private apartments from the late 18th century—which appear still lived in—to the vast 19th-century ceremonial salons, looking over Place de la Concorde from the loggia on the facade. In addition, part of the building exhibits the Al Thani collection (named after the Qatari royal family), dedicated to decorative arts. Sumptuous doesn't even cut it. It was on this site that Victor Schœlcher signed the decree to abolish slavery, in 1848.



## Jardin des Tuileries ★

**D4** M *Concorde or Tuileries. R. de Rivoli - ✆ 01 40 20 53 17 - Jun-Aug: 7am-11pm; Apr-May and Sept: 7am-9pm; rest of year: 7:30am-7:30pm*

*On certain weekends, the Musée du Louvre (p. 26) puts on free guided tours so visitors can learn all about various aspects of its gardens and many sculptures.*

To embellish the Palais des Tuileries, which she started building in 1564, Catherine de' Medici planned an Italian garden. Features included fountains, a maze, a menagerie, and even a cave. Henry IV added an orangery and a greenhouse. The park became a fashionable promenade spot. In 1664, Colbert commissioned Le Nôtre to completely redesign it.

To rectify the sloping terrain, he added two terraces running lengthwise. He created the magnificent **perspective** along the central path—the start of the future Champs-Élysée—, dug out the large ponds, and lay flower beds, quinconces (clusters of five trees), and ramps. The Orangerie was built in 1853 and the Jeu de Paume court in 1861. The **Terrasse du Bord-de-l'eau**, the waterside terrace adorned with statues and planted with chestnut and plane trees, affords a beautiful view of the Seine and the gardens.

### Musée de l'Orangerie★★

*Jardin des Tuileries (Seine side) - ✆ 01 44 50 43 00 - www.musee-orangerie.fr - daily ex. Tue 9am-6pm (Fri 9pm) - €12.50 (-26s free).* The famous **Water Lilies series★★★** by Claude Monet has been shown here since 1927. This Impressionist masterwork is exhibited in natural light (as Monet requested). The Orangerie also presents the Walter-Guillaume collection: paintings by Cézanne, Sisley, Monet, Renoir, Gauguin, Marie Laurencin, Picasso, Modigliani, Utrillo, Matisse, and Soutine.

### Jeu de Paume★★

*1 pl. de la Concorde - ✆ 01 47 03 12 50 - www.jeudepaume.org - daily ex. Mon 11am-7pm (Tue 9pm) - €12 (-12s free).*

Hosts excellent temporary exhibitions dedicated to the visual image through various media: photography (from its origins to today), video, and multimedia.

alxpin/Getty Images Plus

Avenue des Champs-Élysées, seen from the Arc de Triomphe.



## The Champs-Élysées ★★

**BC3-4** Ⓜ *Condorde, Champs-Élysées-Clemenceau, Charles-de-Gaulle-Étoile.* The longest avenue in Paris (230 feet wide and 1.2 miles long, linking Place de la Concorde and the Arc de Triomphe) is also a symbol: the site of a military parade on July 14, the conclusion of the Tour de France, New Year's Eve celebrations... Walking along it from Place de la Concorde, you will pass through the English gardens, then the roundabout of the Champs-Élysées, from where you can make out, to the south, on the axis of the Invalides, the sumptuous Grand and Petit Palais *(see below)* and, to the north, the gates of the **Palais de l'Éysée**, the seat of the President of France.

At the corner of Avenue George-V, the iconic **Fouquet's**, classified as a historic monument, attracted the cream of Parisian society through the 20th century.

## Grand Palais ★

**C4** Ⓜ *Champs-Élysées-Clemenceau. 3 av. du Gén.-Eisenhower - ✆ 01 44 13 17 17 - www.grandpalais.fr - closed for renovations, partial reopening in 2024 for the Olympics, fully in spring 2025.* Built for the 1900 Paris Exposition, this is one of the most distinguished legacies from the Belle Époque: its monumental facade conceals the largest **apse** in Europe, crowned by a **glass roof**★★ measuring over 188,000 sq.ft! A commanding setting for fairs, sports competitions, and

other famous events (Art Paris, Saut Hermès, fashion shows, etc.), temporarily moved until 2024 to the **Grand Palais Éphémère** *(p. 70)*, erected on the Champ-de-Mars while the Grand Palais is given a major facelift.
The western side of the building houses the **Galeries Nationales du Grand Palais**, the regular stage for monumental art exhibitions, as well as the **Palais de la Découverte★★**, a science museum *(Av. Franklin-Roosevelt - 01 56 43 20 20 - www.palais-decouverte.fr - closed for renovations, reopening planned in 2025. Until then, science workshops are running at a temporary venue on the edge of the Parc André-Citroën—Les Étincelles du Palais de la Découverte—in the 15e arr.).*



## Petit Palais ★★

**C4** Ⓜ *Champs-Élysées-Clemenceau. Av. Winston-Churchill - 01 53 43 40 00 - www.petitpalais.paris.fr - daily ex. Mon 10am-6pm - free.*
Designed, as was the Grand Palais, for the occasion of the 1900 Paris Exposition, by Charles Girault, this architectural gem dazzles visitors with its richly ornate decoration: sumptuous entrance way, frescoes, mosaic floors... A delightful little garden, bordered by a peristyle and featuring a café, makes a lovely spot for afternoon tea. The building shelters the rich collection of the **Musée des Beaux-Arts de la Ville de Paris**, presenting French art movements between 1880 and 1914. The temporary exhibitions are usually very engaging.

## Avenue Montaigne

**BC4** Ⓜ *Alma-Marceau or Franklin-D.-Roosevelt.* An icon of luxury, this is the epicenter of Parisian Haute Couture, where the biggest names in high-end fashion have stores: Dior (at no. 30 since 1946), Chanel, Saint Laurent, Vuitton, Balenciaga, Céline, Nina Ricci, and so on. The former "Allée des Veuves" (Widows' Alley) has changed since the time when Eugène Sue serialized its bad reputation in *The Mysteries of Paris*.
At no. 15, the **Théâtre des Champs-Élysées★**, made of reinforced concrete — an innovation in its day—, is the work of the Perret brothers (1912). Antoine Bourdelle designed the facade while Maurice Denis crafted the ceiling decor in the main auditorium where Diaghilev's Ballets Russes, Josephine Baker, and Rudolf Nureyev used to dance. In May 1913, Igor Stravinsky's premiere of the *Rite of Spring* scandalized the audience, so shocked were they by the ballet's modernist style.
At no. 25, the **Hôtel Plaza Athénée** welcomes heads of state, princes, and ambassadors, as well as celebrities from all over the world.

## Galerie Dior ★★

**B4** Ⓜ *Franklin-D.-Roosevelt. 11 r. François Ier - 01 82 20 22 00 - www.galeriedior.com - daily ex. Tue 11am-7pm - €12.*
Opened in spring 2022, the museum of the mythical Christian Dior fashion house immerses visitors in the glitz and glamor of Parisian Haute Couture. From exquisite fabrics and perfect cuts to the extravagant luxury of certain

models, decades of women's fashion have been released from the archives: from the first "Corolle" gown by the house's founder, Christian Dior, in 1946, to the most iconic creations of his successors, including Yves Saint-Laurent, John Galliano, and Maria Grazia Chiuri. All staged in the most sublime surroundings–so chic!

## Arc de Triomphe ★★★

**B3** *RER A and* Ⓜ *Charles-de-Gaulle-Étoile. Pl. Charles-de-Gaulle - ✆ 01 55 37 73 77 – www.paris-arc-de-triomphe.fr – Apr-Sept: 10am-11pm; rest of year: 10am-10:30pm - €13 (-25s free) - admission not guaranteed if high influx of visitors.*

At the top of the Champs-Élysées, the Arc de Triomphe, inspired by the triumphal arches of ancient times, is colossal in size, standing 162 feet tall and 150 feet wide. Commemorating the achievements of the French armies, it has pride of place in the center of the former Place de l'Étoile—renamed Place Charles-de-Gaulle in 1970–the meeting point of 12 straight avenues, hence its former name of "Star Square". Commissioned in 1806 by Napoleon from Jean-François Chalgrin (1739-1811), the monument, at the architect's death, was barely five meters tall. The work was completed under Louis Philippe I in 1836. Since 1921, it has housed the **Tomb of the Unknown Soldier**. Since November 11, 1923, the flame of remembrance has been reignited every evening at 6:30pm. The **view★★★** from the observation deck is spectacular.



## Fondation Louis-Vuitton ★★★

**Off map by A2** Ⓜ *Les Sablons, then 10 min. walk (or shuttle from Charles-de-Gaulle-Étoile €1) - 8 av. du Mahatma-Gandhi - ✆ 01 40 69 96 00 - www.fondationlouisvuitton.fr - daily ex. Tue 10am-8pm (Fri 9pm), Wed-Thu 11am-8pm (times vary, inquire) - €16, -26s €10 (admission to the Fondation includes entry to the Jardin d'Acclimatation).*

In the northern part of the **Bois de Boulogne★**, the Fondation Louis-Vuitton is devoted to contemporary art and design. Playing with gravity and finesse, fragility and strength, the structure designed by Frank Gehry ruptures visual perspectives to blend into its environment. The Fondation holds large-scale temporary exhibitions and multidisciplinary events accessible to everybody.

A short stroll away, the attractions, playgrounds, animals, and trails of the **Jardin d'Acclimatation** won't fail to keep children entertained *(Bois de Boulogne - carrefour des Sablons - ✆ 01 40 67 90 85 - www.jardindacclimatation.fr - 11am-6pm, Wed, weekends, and school vacations. 10am-6pm - admission €7, book 15 tickets for attractions €50, 1-day pass €33).*

## AUTEUIL ★

**Off map by A6** Ⓜ *Église-d'Auteuil or Michel-Ange-Auteuil.* At the far southeastern end of the Bois de Boulogne is the old village of Auteuil, a chic and leafy neighborhood where you can make out, behind their high fences, sumptuous houses and villas (on private roads). The architect

**Hector Guimard** (1867-1942), to whom we owe the first generation of iconic Parisian métro entrances, built stunning Art Nouveau buildings here; **Rue Jean-de-La Fontaine** is a prime example.

## MONCEAU DISTRICT ★

**C1-2** The former "Monceau Plain" was, in the 19th century, taken up by opulent hôtels particuliers. Some are now museums. Streets lined with ornate Haussmannian facades converge to a delightful park. It is still a quiet, family-friendly, and genteel neighborhood.

### Parc Monceau ★

**BC2** Ⓜ *Monceau.* This garden of one-of-a-kind charm contains rare and diverse species, including sycamore maples, oriental planes, and ginkgo bilobas. At the entrance, the Ledoux Rotunda was one of the 47 booths along the city's perimeter wall for collecting taxes (p. 176).

### Musée Nissim-de-Camondo ★★

**C2** Ⓜ *Monceau. 63 r. de Monceau - ✆ 01 53 89 06 50 - www.madparis.fr - daily ex. Mon-Tue 10am-5:30pm - €12 (-26s free), €20 combined ticket with the Musée des Arts Décoratifs (**p. 30**).*
This sublime private mansion from 1914 is the quintessence of the Belle Époque period. The museum displays the sumptuous decor and furniture chosen by the former owner, the Count of Camondo.

### Musée Cernuschi ★

**C2** Ⓜ *Monceau. 7 av. Vélasquez - ✆ 01 53 96 21 50 - www.cernuschi.paris.fr - daily ex. Mon 10am 6pm - free.*
This museum harbors collections of Asian art compiled in the late 19th century by banker Henri Cernuschi.

### Musée Jacquemart-André ★★

**C2** Ⓜ *Miromesnil - 158 bd Haussmann - ✆ 01 45 62 11 59 - www.musee-jacquemart-andre.com - 10am-6pm (late nights until 8:30pm certain Mondays) - €16 (7-25s €9.50).*
*Tea room in a stunning salon and in the garden (walk-in only, the line can be off-putting).*
Inside a handsome private mansion in the Second Empire style (1869), find prestigious collections of decorative arts from the 18th century and paintings (French, Northern and Italian Renaissance schools). The non-exhaustive list includes Boucher, Chardin, Canaletto, Fragonard, David, Rembrandt, Hals, Van Dyck, and Tiepolo.

## LES BATIGNOLLES ★

**C1** Ⓜ *Rome or Porte de Clichy.*
Paris' Bohemian community has found a home in this country-style neighborhood, which extends around the village church of **Saint-Marie-des-Batignolles** (1851) and its English-style square, with a cluster of quaint bistros and quirky boutiques. To the north of the square, railway wasteland has given way to the extensive sustainable urban development project **Clichy-Batignolles**. It unfolds around the **Parc Martin-Luther-King** and the iconic tower by Renzo Piano, 525 feet tall, that hosts the new **Tribunal de Paris** *(Paris Courthouse).*

# Montmartre★★★ - Pigalle

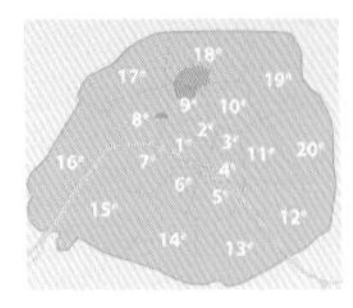


**With its iconic basilica atop the hill and its glorious art history, Montmartre continues to attract visitors in their droves. Despite the gentrification and crowds, it has retained the charming feel of a village with its cobbled streets, quaint dwellings, tucked-away passages, and vineyards. Below, south of Pigalle and around Rue des Martyrs, a cool and hip neighborhood is developing with bars and restaurants opening non-stop.**

▶**Getting there:** M Abbesses (Line 12), Blanche (Line 2), Anvers (Line 2) or Pigalle (Lines 2 and 12), Sacré-Cœur funicular, Montmartrobus.

**Local Map p. 90-91. Detachable Map E1.**

▶**Tip:** In Montmartre, the crowds tend to gather around Place du Tertre, Rue Norvins, and Rue des Abbesses. For more peace and quiet, come early in the morning or stroll along the less busy streets on the hill's northern slope. For a taste of the architecture and atmosphere of the hill, climb the steep stairs that are a big part of the area's charm. If your energy is flagging, the Montmartrobus, a small electric bus that zigzags through the narrow streets, takes a pleasantly scenic route (between Pigalle and the town hall in the 18e arr.). On the second weekend of October, don't miss the Fête des Vendanges (Grape Harvest Festival) (www.fetedesvendangesdemontmartre.com).



## WALKING TOUR OF THE BUTTE MONTMARTRE ★★★

**E1** M *Blanche.*

This walking trail will guide you around the iconic sites on Montmartre's hill and some gems off the beaten track. From Blanche métro station*(Line 2)*, take **Rue Lepic★**, which will take you past the Café des Deux-Moulins, made famous by Amélie Poulain. Continue climbing to the **Moulin de la Galette**, which has been turning in the wind for six centuries. The site of a dance hall popular in the 19th century, it inspired Renoir (see his painting at the Musée d'Orsay), Van Gogh, and Willette. Its actual name is *Blute-Fin*. At **Place Marcel-Aymé**, you can't miss the unexpected figure walking through the wall, a tribute to the author of *Passe-Muraille*, after whom the square is named. Take the quiet **Avenue Junot** to return up the Butte. Potter around the artist studios and pavilions in the **Hameau des Artistes** *(11 av. Junot)* or **Villa Léandre★**.

Turn around and cross Square Suzanne-Buisson where in the center you can see, overlooking a pond, a striking **statue of Saint Denis**, his severed head in his hands: the first bishop and celebrated martyr of Paris is said to have been beheaded

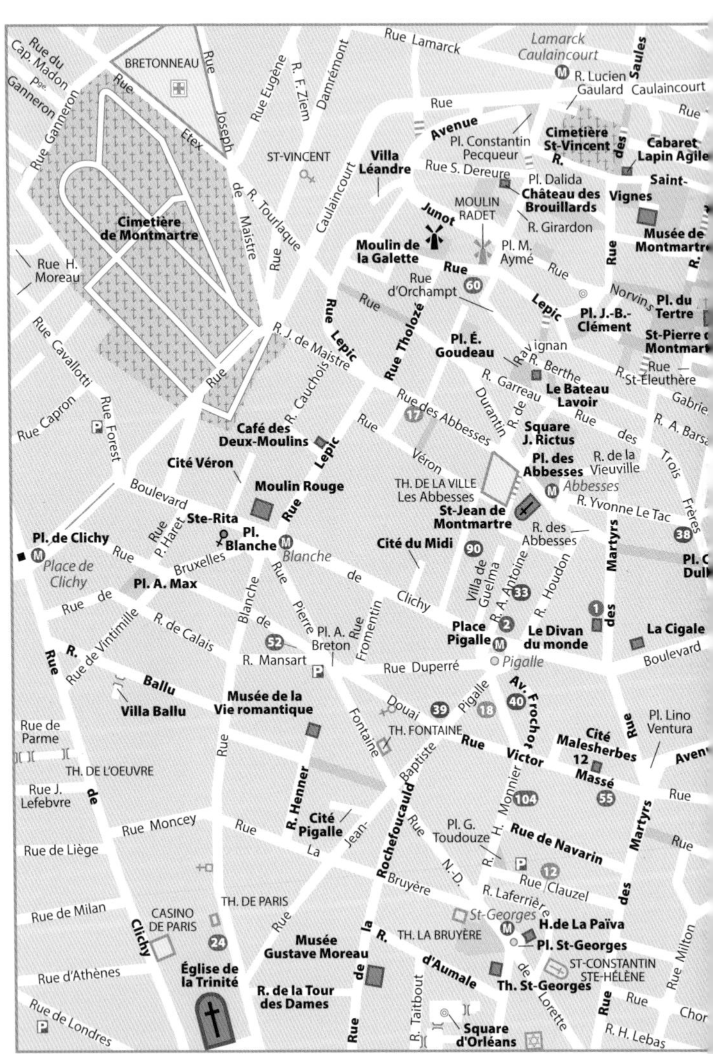
Cimetière de Montmartre
BRETONNEAU
ST-VINCENT
Villa Léandre
Moulin de la Galette
MOULIN RADET
Château des Brouillards
Cimetière St-Vincent
Cabaret Lapin Agile
Musée de Montmartre
Pl. du Tertre
Pl. J.-B.-Clément
Pl. É. Goudeau
Le Bateau Lavoir
Square J. Rictus
Pl. des Abbesses
St-Jean de Montmartre
TH. DE LA VILLE Les Abbesses
Café des Deux-Moulins
Cité Véron
Moulin Rouge
Ste-Rita
Pl. Blanche
Pl. de Clichy
Pl. A. Max
Cité du Midi
Place Pigalle
Le Divan du monde
La Cigale
Villa Ballu
Musée de la Vie romantique
TH. FONTAINE
Cité Malesherbes
TH. DE L'OEUVRE
Cité Pigalle
Pl. G. Toudouze
TH. DE PARIS
CASINO DE PARIS
Église de la Trinité
Musée Gustave Moreau
TH. LA BRUYÈRE
H.de La Païva
Pl. St-Georges
ST-CONSTANTIN STE-HÉLÈNE
Th. St-Georges
Square d'Orléans
Rue Lamarck
Rue Caulaincourt
Rue Lepic
Rue Tholozé
Rue des Abbesses
Boulevard de Clichy
Rue Blanche
Rue de Clichy
Rue Pigalle
Rue des Martyrs
Rue Victor Massé
Rue de Navarin
Rue de la Rochefoucauld
Rue de Londres

## WHERE TO EAT



## WHERE TO DRINK



## NIGHTLIFE



## WHERE TO STAY

around 250 on this very hill. To the northeast of the square, between Rue Girardon and Allée des Brouillards, there is a magnificent 18th-century country house turned dance hall: the **Château des Brouillards**. As you exit the square, in the direction of the Cimetière Saint-Vincent, greet the singer **Dalida** who lived in the neighborhood for 25 years (at 11B Rue d'Orchampt) and whose bust adorns the square bearing her name.
At the intersection of Rue des Saules and **Rue Saint-Vincent**, narrow flights of stairs, a steep slope, vegetation, and the famous **Cabaret Lapin Agile** hidden by an old acacia tree make possibly the most rustic pocket of Paris. In the **Cimetière St-Vincent** lie French luminaries the likes of Émile Goudeau, Maurice Utrillo, Dorgelès, Gabrielo, and Marcel Carné.
Pop into the small **vineyard** (Rue des Saules), planted in the early 20th century, where the harvests have earned their own festival.



## Musée de Montmartre ★

**E1** *12 r. Cortot - ✆ 01 49 25 89 39 - museedemontmartre.fr - 10am-7pm - €15 (18-25s €10).*
*Cozy tea room looking out to the garden.*
Surrounded by three delightful gardens, the museum is set in the Maison du Bel Air, which hosted celebrated artists such as Auguste Renoir, Suzanne Valadon, Émile Bernard, Émile Othon Friesz, and Raoul Dufy. Montmartre's Bohemian past is richly brought to life through posters, paintings, drawings, and recreations of the Café de l'Abreuvoir and the studio-apartment of Suzanne Valadon and her son Maurice Utrillo. It's a wonderful immersion into the history of the Butte: its spirit of freedom, Communards, and thriving art scene... Next to the Maison du Bel Air, the **Hôtel Demarne** puts on temporary exhibitions in connection with Montmartre.

## Église Saint-Pierre-de-Montmartre ★

**E1** *2 r. du Mont-Cenis - ✆ 01 46 06 57 63 - www.saintpierredemontmartre.net - 9:30am-7pm.*
The only remnant of the great Abbey of Montmartre is one of the oldest churches in Paris (11th c.), built on the site of a basilica dedicated to Saint Denis. The vaults above the nave were rebuilt in the 15th century, while the western facade dates from the 18th century. The simple grace of the church bell tower makes a striking contrast against the monumental cupolas and dome of Sacré-Cœur in the background.
The **Cimetière du Calvaire**, north of the church, is the smallest and oldest cemetery in Paris and can be glimpsed through a beautiful bronze door.

## Place du Tertre ★

**E1** Quaint buildings and trees should give this square a village feel. Yet thronged by tourists and the hundreds of artists clamoring to sketch you, it falls short of bucolic, unless you come at the break of dawn.

## Place Émile-Goudeau ★

**E1** The square graced by painters (Picasso, Braque, Juan Gris gradually established Cubism there) and poets (Max Jacob, Apollinaire, Marc Orlan). All these creative minds could be found at the **Bateau-Lavoir** (no. 13).

## Place des Abbesses ★

**E1** The Abbesses métro canopy, the handiwork of **Hector Guimard**, is one of only two remaining in Paris (the other is at Porte Dauphine). Hemmed by countless cafés and restaurants, designer shops, and various retailers, the square and the adjacent streets are bustling at all hours.
It is dominated in the south by the **Église Saint-Jean-de-Montmartre**, the first religious building made of reinforced concrete (1904), shocking at the time. Montmartre's locals nicknamed it Saint Jean "of the Bricks" owing to its exterior cladding. To the north of the square, Square Jehan-Rictus serves as the backdrop for the **Mur des "Je t'aime"**, a 430-sq.ft fresco of enameled tiles covered with "I love you" written in dozens of languages.

## Basilique du Sacré-Cœur ★★

**E1** Ⓜ *Anvers and Montmartre Funicular. Pl. du Parvis-du-Sacré-Cœur - ✆ 01 53 41 89 00 - www.sacre-coeur-montmartre.fr - 6:30am-10:30am - access pers. reduced mobility 35 r. du Chevalier-de-la-Barre (9:30am-5:30pm).*
This Roman-Byzantine-style **basilica** (1876-1914) is the work of architect Paul Abadie (1812-1884). Since its consecration in 1919, worshippers have ensured Adoration is uninterrupted around the clock. The **dome** can be accessed via the crypt *(left aisle) - ✆ 01 53 41 89 00 - www.sacre-coeur-montmartre.com - 10:30am-5:30pm - closed early Jan - €7 (-16s €4) - the dome may be closed or times changed depending on the day's weather conditions.* After 300 fairly steep steps, enjoy plunging views of Paris from the outdoor gallery: the 360-degree **panorama**★★★ reaches almost 20 miles on a clear day. The crypt holds relics and ornaments, and an audiovisual exhibit presents the history of the basilica and the devotion to the Sacred Heart of Jesus.

## Halle Saint-Pierre ★

**E1** Ⓜ *Anvers. 2 r. Ronsard - ✆ 01 42 58 72 89 - www.hallesaintpierre.org - 11am-6pm, Sat 11am-7pm, Sun 12pm-6pm - closed weekends in Aug - €9 (-15s €6) - nice café and bookstore.*
Built by a pupil of French architect Victor Baltard in 1868, this former indoor market made of wrought and cast iron and flooded with light has been beautifully preserved. For almost 30 years, the structure has been a center for **primitive,** naive, and folk art, shown in large-scale temporary exhibitions which are a welcome far cry from the academic art and major movements of contemporary art.
The area has become one big haberdashery with the **Marché Saint-Pierre**, the world's largest fabric market that is popular with both amateur seamstresses and designers from the worlds of fashion and entertainment.

## AROUND PIGALLE

**DE1-2** Ⓜ *Blanche or Pigalle.*
A nightlife hotspot packed with hip bars and boutique hotels, Pigalle has its own unique vibe that manages to be fashionable and edgy. Between Place Blanche and Place **Pigalle**, **Boulevard**

**de Clichy** draws a crowd of folk curious to see Paris after dark. In amongst the sex shops, look out for the **Cité Véron** (no. 94), a pretty alleyway of houses with well-tended gardens, whose former residents include polymath Boris Vian and poet Jacques Prévert, and the **Cité du Midi** (no. 48), where the beautiful ceramic facade of the old bathhouse is still intact.
**Place Blanche** (White Square) is named for the old plaster quarries that once surrounded it. This is where you'll find the legendary **Moulin Rouge**. Founded in 1889, it started out as a "singing café" where the bourgeois and Bohemian folk of Montmartre would come to applaud cabaret stars the likes of Yvette Guilbert, Valentin le Désossé, and La Goulue, kicking their legs to the can-can, and immortalized by Toulouse-Lautrec.



A super-cool neighborhood has developed to the **south of Pigalle** (around **Rue des Martyrs**, from Rue Henri-Monnier to Rue Rochechouart), with dozens of bars, restaurants, and organic and vintage stores drawing in the hipster crowd. Parisians now call it **SoPi** —for "South of Pigalle"—, inspired by New York's SoHo, which tells you all you need to know!
At the heart of this area is the très chic enclave of **Nouvelle-Athènes** with its neoclassical architecture and *hôtels particuliers*. The lovely **Place Saint-Georges** is the heart and soul of this area frequented by artists—Chopin, George Sand, and the like—in the mid-1800s. At no. 28, Rue Notre-Dame-de-Lorette, the **Hôtel de la Païva** is an unexpected example of Renaissance Revival architecture, from 1840, the one-time home of one of the most famous courtesans of the time, Esther Lachmann, known as "La Païva". The extravagant facade is decorated with cherubs, busts of Diane and Apollo, and other flourishes.

### Musée Gustave-Moreau ★

**E2** Ⓜ *Saint-Georges. 14 r. de la Rochefoucauld - ✆ 01 83 62 78 72 - www.musee-moreau.fr - daily ex. Tue 10am-6pm - €7.*
In 1895, Gustave Moreau (1826-1898) turned his family home into a shrine to his work. From his living quarters to the spacious, high-ceilinged studios on the second and third floors, more than 6,000 of his artistic endeavors (paintings, cartons, drawings, sculptures) are on show, unbridled imagination the hallmark of his Symbolist oeuvre.

### Musée de la Vie Romantique ★

**D2** Ⓜ *Pigalle. 16 r. Chaptal - ✆ 01 55 31 95 67 - www.museevieromantique.paris.fr - daily ex. Mon 10am-6pm - free.*
*Lovely tea room in the garden.*
The quaint leafy lane leading to this charming country house sets the tone of the place. The Dutch-French Romantic painter **Ary Scheffer** (1795-1858), a favorite of Louis Philippe I, used to entertain his learned friends there: Delacroix, Liszt, Renan. The museum presents personal effects of **George Sand** and works by Ary Scheffer.

ISSANCE DE VÉNUS

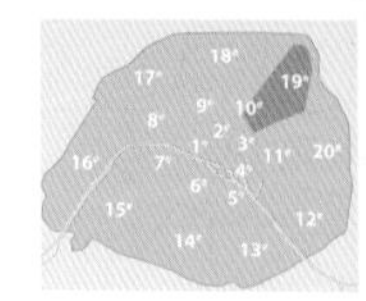


# From the Canal Saint-Martin★ to La Villette★★

**A souvenir from Paris' industrial days in the 19th century, the canal makes for a pleasant stroll, stretching all the way to Parc de la Villette. The regentrified neighborhood is particularly buzzing on sunny days, when students and a fairly young crowd congregate at the water's edge to catch some rays and have a picnic as the bistros behind set out their tables along the sidewalk. A green space and cultural hub, La Villette is a center for science and technology, the performing arts, and music of every genre. A walk in the Parc des Buttes-Chaumont is a relaxing way to end the day.**

▶**Getting there:** Ⓜ République (Lines 3, 5, 8, 9, and 11), Jacques-Bonsergent (Line 5), Goncourt (Line 11), and Jaurès (Lines 2, 5, and 7b).



**La Villette:** Ⓜ Porte-de-la-Villette (Line 7 - for Cité des Sciences et de l'Industrie), Porte-de-Pantin (Ⓜ Lines 5 and T3b - for La Philharmonie).

**Local Map p. 99. Detachable Map GH1-3.**

▶**Tip:** On Sundays and public holidays, the canal is closed to traffic, from Quai de Jemmapes, at the swing bridge, to Place Stalingrad: on foot or by bike—cycle paths along the Canal Saint-Martin, the Bassin de la Villette, and the Canal de l'Ourcq—, it's the best time to go! In summer, find a patch of grass and watch a movie during La Villette's open-air film festival.

## CANAL WALK

**G1-3** A stone's throw from Place de la République, the Canal Saint-Martin, with its hip boutiques and trendy cafés, is where cool Parisians come to hang out. A stroll along the quayside offers a moment of escape in the city.

### Canal Saint-Martin ★

*Boat Tours, p. 166.*

G1-3 With its nine **locks**, iron footbridges, cobblestones, and rows of trees, the Canal Saint-Martin—the old haunt of Arletty, Balzac, and Simenon—is charmingly scenic. At 102, Quai de Jemmapes, the facade of the **Hôtel du Nord** evokes the famous line of Arletty to Louis Jouvet: "Atmosphere, atmosphere, do I look like an atmosphere?", in the eponymous film directed by Marcel Carné (1938). Today, fashionable boutiques and vintage stores, restaurants, and cafés breathe new life into the canal's environs. Down from the street, before

Canal Saint-Martin

Stalingrad, the **Point Éphémère** is a multidisciplinary arts space (*p. 136*).

## Rotonde de La Villette ★

**G1** M *Jaurès or Stalingrad. Pl. de la Bataille-de-Stalingrad.* It was effectively one of the toll booths in a city wall of Paris controlled by tax collectors (*p. 176*). La Rotonde is now a restaurant and bar.

## Bassin de la Villette ★

**GH1** M *Jaurès or Stalingrad.*
The artificial lake extends the canal to the north. It's a pleasant spot in which to relax, with something always happening from sunrise, and popular with cyclists, runners, and folks gathering for a picnic, a coffee on a terrace, or a game of pétanque. Occupying the indoor market's former cattle warehouses, blending brick and Eiffel girders from the 1878 Paris Exposition, the MK2 Quai-de-Loire cinema stands across from its big brother, on the other side of the lake. At the other end of the lake, don't miss the spectacle of the **swing bridge** in operation on Rue de Crimée. Take Rue Riquet to get to the CENTQUATRE *(see below)*.

## CENTQUATRE-PARIS

**Off map by G1** M *Riquet. 5 r. Curial - ✆ 01 53 35 50 00 - www.104.fr - Tue-Fri 12pm-7pm, wknd 11am-7pm - price varies by event.*
Located in the colossal building formerly occupied by the city undertakers for Paris, the

### From the Nile to the Ourcq

The construction of the Canal Saint-Martin was commissioned in 1802 by Napoleon I to connect the Ourcq and Seine rivers. Pierre-Simon Girard, an engineer back from the French campaign in Egypt who had studied the level of the Nile over there, was tasked with the project, although it took until 1825 to complete it! However, a first section of the canal was inaugurated in 1808. Excavated with the aim of supplying the capital with water and adorned with Roman-style fountains, the Canal Saint-Martin with its basins and nine locks stretches for almost three miles. Achieving a height difference of 82 feet, the canal is about 10 feet deep in most places. It disappears underground between Bastille and Rue du Faubourg-du-Temple.

CENTQUATRE (#104) is a public cultural center whose primary vocation is to make contemporary art accessible to the wider public by inviting artists in residence. It's done a grand job, engaging the diverse and working-class local community in its activities. Young people bring their paraphernalia to show off their street dancing, families come to walk and visit the exhibitions, which are often free; there's always something to see or do.



## PARC DE LA VILLETTE ★

**Local Map opposite (Off detachable map by H1)**

Ⓜ *Porte-de-la-Villette or Porte-de-Pantin, Tram 3B, same stations.*

Between the Canal Saint-Denis and the Canal de l'Ourcq, on the site of the **old Paris slaughterhouses**, this vast contemporary park, dotted with playing fields, is home to the **Cité des Sciences et de l'Industrie**, the **Philharmonie de Paris**, the **Grande Halle** and the **Zénith** concert hall. With its modern architecture in a lush surrounding, it's a vibrant hub for culture and leisure.

### Cité des sciences et de l'industrie ★★

Ⓜ *Porte-de-la-Villette and T3b. 30 av. Corentin-Cariou - ✆ 01 85 53 99 74 - www.cite-sciences.fr - Tue-Sat 9:30am-6pm (Sun 7pm) - €12 (-25s €9).*

The mission of Europe's biggest science museum is to promote science culture to the widest possible audience. The exhibits drawing on latest-generation technologies really put visitors in the driving seat.

**Explora and the Planetarium** - Interactive exhibitions, with models and things to touch and engage with, explore the world of today and tomorrow. The Planetarium takes spectators on a tour of the Milky Way and the clusters of galaxies beyond.

### Cité des Enfants★★

*Inquire for times - €12 – booking recommended.*

Two spaces (for ages 2-7 years and 5-12) are filled with fun and educational experiments in the field of science and technology.

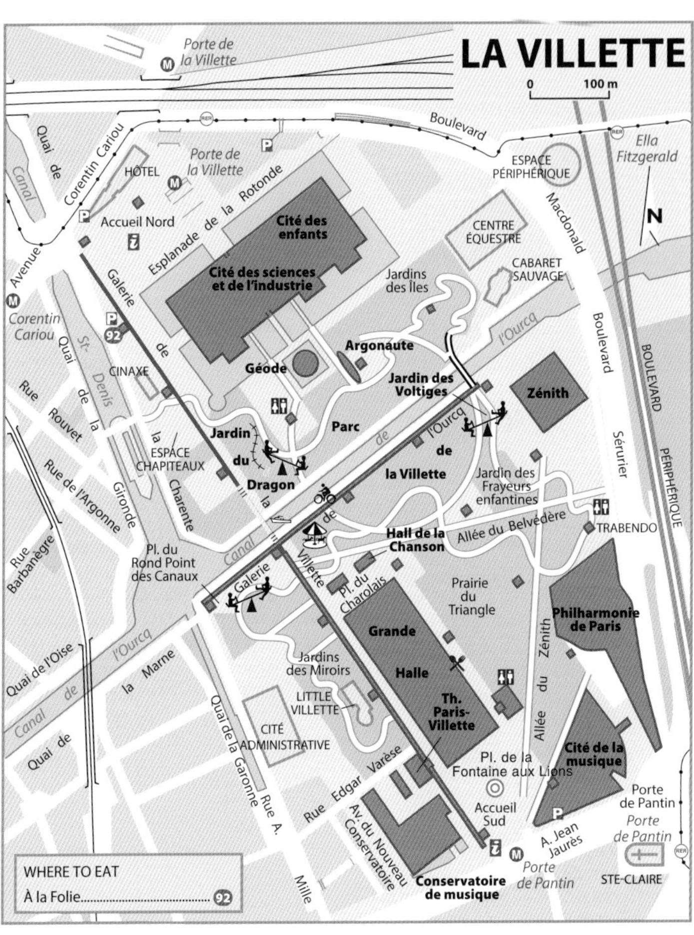
LA VILLETTE
0
100 m
Porte de la Villette
Boulevard
Ella Fitzgerald
Quai de Canal
Corentin Cariou
HÔTEL
Porte de la Villette
Esplanade de la Rotonde
Accueil Nord
Avenue
Cité des enfants
Cité des sciences et de l'industrie
ESPACE PÉRIPHÉRIQUE
Macdonald
CENTRE ÉQUESTRE
CABARET SAUVAGE
Jardins des Îles
N
Galerie de la Villette
Corentin Cariou
Quai de la Gironde
St-Denis
CINAXE
Géode
Argonaute
Jardin des Voltiges
l'Ourcq
Zénith
Boulevard Sérurier
BOULEVARD PÉRIPHÉRIQUE
Rue Rouvet
ESPACE CHAPITEAUX
Jardin du Dragon
Parc de la Villette
Canal de l'Ourcq
Jardin des Frayeurs enfantines
Rue de l'Argonne
Charente
Hall de la Chanson
Allée du Belvédère
TRABENDO
Rue Barbanègre
Pl. du Rond Point des Canaux
Galerie
Pl. du Charolais
Prairie du Triangle
Philharmonie de Paris
Grande Halle
Quai de l'Oise
Canal de l'Ourcq
la Marne
Jardins des Miroirs
Allée du Zénith
LITTLE VILLETTE
Th. Paris-Villette
Quai de
CITÉ ADMINISTRATIVE
Quai de la Garonne
Rue Edgar Varèse
Pl. de la Fontaine aux Lions
Cité de la musique
Rue A. Mille
Av. du Nouveau Conservatoire
Accueil Sud
A. Jean Jaurès
Porte de Pantin
Porte de Pantin
Porte de Pantin
STE-CLAIRE
Conservatoire de musique
WHERE TO EAT
À la Folie........ 92

## La Géode ★★

M *Porte-de-la-Villette et T3b. www.lageode.fr - closed for renovation, no reopening date announced.*
This gigantic steel ball, which has become the symbol of La Villette, contains a hemispherical cinema screen with a diameter of 88.5 ft and a surface area of over 10,000 sq.ft. Since it was acquired by Gaumont-Pathé in 2018, its future is still in limbo.

## Philharmonie de Paris-Cité de la Musique ★

M *Porte-de-Pantin et T3b - 221 av. Jean-Jaurès - ✆ 01 44 84 44 84 - www.philharmoniedeparis.fr - Tue-Fri 12pm-6pm, wknd 10am-6pm - Musée de la Musique, free.*
The new **Philharmonie de Paris** (2015), a mirror-clad complex of concert halls, was designed by Jean Nouvel. The 2,400-seat **auditorium** hosts symphonic orchestras as well as family-friendly concerts. The institution also puts on temporary exhibitions on themes related to music, its artists, and its history.
Next to it, the **Cité de la Musique**, a building designed by Christian de Portzamparc (1995), houses the **Musée de la Musique**. Through audiovisual exhibits, it presents a thousand instruments from the 16th century to the present day, along with artworks and models of major European opera houses that recreate the premieres of *L'Orfeo* by Monteverdi or *The Rite of Spring* by Stravinski.



# LES BUTTES-CHAUMONT

**H1-2** This peaceful neighborhood that feels like a village within the city developed around its famous park. From the elegant period apartment blocks on Rue Manin to the charming cobbled lanes of Mouzaïa, this is a side of Paris few tourists come to see.

## Parc des Buttes-Chaumont ★

**H1-2** M *Buttes-Chaumont, Botzaris, Pyrénées, Place des Fêtes, or Laumière. Enter the park via Rue Botzaris, Rue Manin, Avenue Simon-Bolivar, Rue de Crimée. ✆ 01 48 03 83 10 - www.paris.fr - May-Aug: 7am-10pm; Apr and Sept: 7am-9pm; rest of year: 7am-8pm - playgrounds, puppet theater, pony rides, bandstand.*
Inside the park, the Pavillon du Lac (p. 122) serves a delicious daily set lunch menu, which you can enjoy al fresco on warmer days. This bar in a former guinguette (suburban tavern), Le Rosa Bonheur, is the perfect spot for a coffee or drink in the evening (p. 136).
The Parc des Buttes-Chaumont covers an ancient bare hill, about a hundred meters high, which used to be known as "Mont Chauve" (Mount Bald, hence the park's name). In the 14th century, King Philip IV ordered every new home built in Paris to be covered in plaster, for its excellent insulation as well as fire-retardant properties. The quarries around Montmartre and Buttes-Chaumont were therefore mined for their gypsum. Over time, the hill became a refuse dump and refuge for Paris' criminal

©nickzArtworks/Getty Images Plus

Parc de la Villette.



underworld. In the 19th century, Haussmann transformed the Buttes into a park with the help of Jean-Charles Alphand, who abandoned the harmonious architectural order of the French garden style in favor of the Romantic appeal of the country garden style. Lush with native and exotic species, the park spread over undulating terrain makes for a pleasant place to walk with its lake, streams, waterfalls, and caves. Plane, poplar, maple, chestnut, locust, ash, and princess trees planted in the late 19th century are still thriving today.

## Amérique or Mouzaïa District ★

**Off map by H1** Ⓜ *Danube*

Tucked away behind towering apartment blocks, between Place du Rhine-et-Danube and Place des Fêtes, this unexpected and picturesque neighborhood is a cluster of 250 terraced houses with pretty gardens built in the 1890s, set along cobblestone lanes lit by 19th-century-style streetlamps. Back in the day, these were home to eastern Paris' blue-collar workers. An enchanting and secluded patch of bucolic Paris to discover.

# Bastille and Eastern Paris★

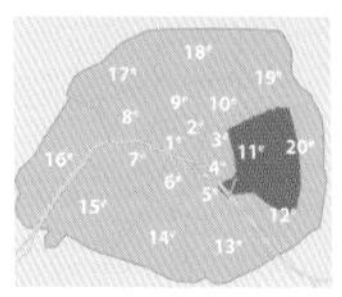


**Ethnically diverse and architecturally eclectic, awash with communal gardens, artist studios, and trendy bistros, Eastern Paris, along with the ancient and hilly villages of Belleville and Ménilmontant, will appeal to anyone seeking a more authentic Paris beyond the capital's grand monuments.**

▶**Getting there:** Ⓜ Bastille (Lines 1, 5, and 8). **Père-Lachaise:** Ⓜ Père-Lachaise (Lines 2 and 3) or Philippe-Auguste (Line 2). **Belleville:** Ⓜ Belleville (Lines 2 and 11) or Pyrénées (Line 11). **Ménilmontant:** Ⓜ Ménilmontant (Line 2), bus 96 goes up and down Rue de Ménilmontant.

**Detachable Map G6 and H3-4.**

▶**Tip:** In May, Belleville's artist studios open their doors to the public to showcase their flourishing creativity (ateliers-artistes-belleville.fr).



## BASTILLE

**G6** Ⓜ *Bastille*. For Parisians, **Place de la Bastille** is a time-honored stage for political demos and free big-headline music concerts for the masses. On the ground, lines of cobblestones trace the footprint of the former fortress of Bastille, a state prison since the 17th century and symbol of the arbitrary power of the king who only had to sign and seal a letter to send meddlesome characters such as Voltaire, Diderot, or Mirabeau to the cells. On July 14, 1789, the prison was attacked by revolutionaries, some 800 insurgents set about destroying it, stone by stone. The **Colonne de Juillet** (1831-1840), which stands at its center, was erected in memory of the Parisians killed during the revolutions of 1830 and 1848. At the top, the Spirit of Freedom holds the torch of civilization and the broken chains of tyranny. Recently refurbished, the square has become almost completely pedestrianized and now offers direct access to the Port de l'Arsenal via a wide flight of steps.

### Opéra Bastille ★

**G6** *120 r. de Lyon - ✆ 0 892 89 90 90 - www.operadeparis.fr - guided tours, booking req. (1hr30) - €17.*

Standing on the site of the former Bastille train station, it was built by the Uruguayan-Canadian architect Carlos Ott between 1983 and 1989. It houses a 2,700-seat auditorium, which shares the Paris opera program with the Opéra Garnier (☛ *p. 29*). The building's immense size can be explained by the fact that all the craftspeople required to put on an opera share the space: 51 professions, from the wig makers to the technicians, work under one roof.

## Port de l'Arsenal

**G6** Between Place de la Bastille and the Seine, below street level, the Port de Plaisance de l'Arsenal is a city harbor and, in fact, the mouth of the **Canal St-Martin** (*p. 96*) before it flows into the Seine. Bordered by terraced gardens and boats, it makes a pleasant spot for a picnic.

## Coulée Verte ★ and the Viaduc des Arts ★

**G6-H7** Running along Avenue Daumesnil *(follow it towards Gare de Lyon)*, the Viaduc des Arts harbors various craft workshops and contemporary furniture stores beneath its vaults. The huge picture windows add a touch of grandeur to the stone and pink brick arches. Above, the Coulée Verte offers an original perspective over the neighboring buildings *(access via elevators and stairs at the start of Ave. Daumesnil)*. For more than a century (1859 to 1969), this former railway line linked the Bastille to the eastern suburbs, offering Parisians the opportunity to escape the smog in the leafy Bois de Vincennes or on the banks of the Marne River. Today, it is a pedestrian path, almost three miles long, lined with silver linden and hazelnut trees, rose bushes, climbing plants, and herbs.



## Rue du Faubourg-St-Antoine

**GH6** Courtyards, cul-de-sacs, narrow streets, and pedestrian passages from olden-day Paris form the artisanal heart of this ancient faubourg, or suburb. Rare cabinetmakers and furniture producers still have their workshops and warehouses here, against a delightful backdrop of **cobblestone courtyards filled with flowers**. The quaintest of the bunch are Cour de l'Étoile-d'Or (no. 75), Cour des Trois-Frères (no. 81-83), Cour de la Maison-Brûlée (no. 89), and Passage de la Boule-Blanche (no. 50). In the vicinity, the **Marché d'Aligre** *(closed Mon)* on the eponymous square is one of Paris' prettiest markets (food, secondhand clothing and goods).

## Atelier des Lumières ★

**H4** Ⓜ *Rue-Saint-Maur. 38 r. St-Maur - ✆ 01 80 98 46 00 - www.atelier-lumieres.com - 10am-6pm (Fri-Sat 10pm, Sun 7pm) - €16 (5-25s €11).*
This digital art center in a former steel foundry from the 19th century opened its doors in 2018. Equipped with 140 projectors, the establishment has created an immersive exhibition based around classic works of art. A spectacular experience to discover the works of Picasso, Chagall, Klimt, and others like you've never seen them before.

## Cimetière du Père-Lachaise ★★

**Off map by H4** Ⓜ *Père-Lachaise. 8 bd de Ménilmontant - ✆ 01 55 25 82 10 - www.pere-lachaise.com - 8am-5:30pm, Sat 8:30am-5:30pm, Sun 9am-5:30pm (from mid-Mar to late Oct, closes at 6pm).*
This cemetery, planted with over 3,000 trees, is one of a kind for the number of its notable residents and the Romantic style of many of its graves. Built during the First Empire by Brongniart, it is a true open-air museum for funeral statuary, at times intriguing, at others

poignant. Just follow the crowds to find the graves of Jim Morrison, Chopin, Balzac, Marcel Proust, and Oscar Wilde, to name a few. There is also a monument in memory of victims deported to the WWII concentration and extermination camps, and the **Mur des Fédérés**. This, the Communards' Wall, is where, on May 28, 1871, the last bloody episode of the suppression of the Paris Commune took place. The insurgents, after shooting their prisoners, took refuge in the cemetery where they fought against the Versailles government forces. The next day, at dawn, the survivors were shot against the perimeter wall. A wide trench was dug at the foot of the wall as a common grave.

## BELLEVILLE

**H3 and off map by H3** 🅜 *Belleville.* In this working class neighborhood, climb up the lively and commercial Rue de Belleville. Legend has it that Édith Piaf was born at no. 72 when in actual fact she came into the world at the Hôpital Tenon, Porte de Bagnolet. Next take Rue des Pyrénées (on the right) as far as no. 371 where stairs lead to **Place Henri-Krasucki** and the heart of historic Belleville. From there, **Rue des Envierges** runs uphill towards the **Parc de Belleville★** which grants superb **views★★** over Paris as far as Fort Mont-Valérien in the west. Place Henri-Krasuki also leads to the picturesque streets of Rue de la Mare and **Rue des Cascades**. This long, narrow cobbled street, lined by small bars and relatively low-rise buildings, oozes provincial charm. Look out for the "regards" (manholes), small stone huts that provided access to the ancient springs under the street. At no. 42, the **Regard Saint-Martin** belonged to the Saint-Martin-des-Champs priory: on the left-hand sculpted crest, St. Martin the knight is recognizable by his steed. At no. 17 (down the stairs) is the **Regard des Messiers**, named for the guards who kept watch over the vines and fields. Finally, at the corner of the stairs on Rue Fernand-Raynaud, the rooftops of Paris stretch out before you.

## MÉNILMONTANT

**Off map by H4** 🅜 *Ménilmontant. After your tour of Belleville (above), at the bottom of Rue des Cascades, turn left on to Rue de Ménilmontant then left on to Rue de l'Ermitage.* The narrow lane **Villa de l'Ermitage** is worth a look for its artist studios and lovely gardens well tended by residents. At the end on the left, you'll also see the **Cité Leroy**, with its walls blanketed in climbing plants and traditional wooden frontage. At the corner of Rue des Pyrénées and Rue de Ménilmontant, the **Pavillon Carré de Baudouin**, a superb country house built in the 18th century as a summer home, is now an important cultural hub in the arrondissement *(www.carredebaudouin.fr)*. Next, walk down Rue de Ménilmontant as far as the **Église Notre-Dame-de-la-Croix★** (1880) which has one of the longest naves in Paris, supported by the iron ribs of its vaults. At the foot of its monumental staircase, **Place Maurice-Chevalier**, in the leafy shade of chestnut trees, sits at the heart of old Ménilmontant.

Centre de tri
Ici nous valorisons
nos déchets
JUILLET

# ADDRESSES

La REcyclerie (Porte de Clignancourt).
Adrien Roux/La REcyclerie

# Where to Eat

Find the addresses on our maps using the numbers on the listing (e.g. 1). The coordinates in red (e.g. C2) refer to the detachable map (inside the cover).

## Île de la Cité and Île Saint-Louis

**Local Map p. 20-21**

**Picnic Spot** - Square du Vert-Galant, at the tip of Île de la Cité, for a break in the heart of Paris.

### From €30

3 **Maison Maison** – **E5** - *63 voie Georges-Pompidou - 1er - M Pont-Neuf - ☎ 09 67 82 07 32 - www.maisonmaison.fr - closed Mon lunch (and Mon-Tue Nov-Mar) - tapas €9-23.* This "maison" has taken over the banks of the Seine; the dining room is even set in an old sewer worker's lodge on the quayside! Facing Pont-Neuf and Île de la Cité, the view from the terrace is magical. The menu, a selection of freshly prepared small dishes with contemporary influences, is made for sharing.



1 **Les Fous de l'Île** – **F6** - *33 r. des Deux-Ponts - 4e - M Pont-Marie - ☎ 01 43 25 76 67 - www.lesfousdelile.com - daily lunch and eve - dishes €22-28.* In the heart of Île Saint-Louis, this "neo-bistrot" blends great flavors and great vibes. Hats off to the interior, too, with its wood cabinets and collection of chickens. But you won't find these ones on your plate!

## The Louvre

**Local Map p. 31**

**Picnic Spot** - The Jardin des Tuileries welcomes you with open arms. NB: The museum houses several cafés and restaurants, some reasonably priced.

### From €25

5 **Zen** – **E4** - *8 r. de l'Échelle - 1er - M Palais-Royal - ☎ 01 42 61 93 99 - www.restaurantzenparis.fr - closed Sun and Mon eve - dishes €22-42.* Japanese canteen, with authentic cuisine and a refreshing green-and-white interior.

## Opéra-Palais-Royal

**Local Map p. 31**

**Picnic Spot** - The Jardins du Palais-Royal make a peaceful setting for a rest stop, amidst classical architecture and contemporary art (Buren's columns).

### From €10

16 **Le Stube** – **E4** - *31 r. de Richelieu - 1er - M Palais-Royal-Musée du Louvre - ☎ 01 42 60 09 85- www.lestube.fr - closed Sun and Mon eve - dishes under €20.* German snack bar, savory and sweet options, non-stop service. Savory tarts, sandwiches, currywurst, sauerkraut, Black Forest gateau, cheese tart, and, of course, Strudel.

### From €15

6 **Eats Thyme** – **E4** - *44 r. Coquillière - 1er - M Les Halles - ☎ 01 42 33 21 15 - eatsthyme.com - closed Sun eve - dishes under €20.* A great spot along a quiet street yet still close to the

**Still Nice at Twice the Price**
Our price ranges are established on the basis of the prices of the lunch set menus and deals charged at the time of our visit. However, prices may vary in the same establishment depending on whether you go there at lunchtime or in the evening. Some excellent restaurants offer set menus for less than €25 at lunchtime, while the evening menu can start at €40.

Louvre and the Bourse de Commerce. Honors Lebanese cuisine, especially the famous *man'oushe*, a pizza-style flatbread garnished with wild thyme, spicy beef, shawarma chicken, or other toppings, and the must-have mezze, like hummus and baba ganoush. Food as fresh as it is fast! Eat on the go or snag a table on the sunny sidewalk.

18 **Gyoza Bar** – **E3** - *56 passage des Panoramas - 2e - M Grands-Boulevards - 01 44 82 00 62 - closed Sun and Mon eve - dishes under €20.* Unique and original, gyoza, Japanese dumplings stuffed with pork, leek, and ginger, are served with a bowl of rice. The service is fast but the room is small, so expect to wait. Excellent value for money.

89 **Kotteri Ramen Naritake** – **E4** - *31 r. des Petits-Champs - 1er - M Pyramides - 01 42 86 03 83 - closed Mon-Tue - dishes €10-20.* This tiny Japanese restaurant serves delicious noodle soups (ramen) and mouthwatering gyoza. The often-long line is a testament to the affection for this renowned eatery.

45 **Bouillon Chartier** – **E3** - *7 r. du Faubourg-Montmartre - 9e - M Grands-Boulevards - 01 47 70 86 29 - www.bouillon-chartier.com - non-stop service 11:30am-12am - dishes under €20.* People flock to this institution to enjoy a good meal at a reasonable price (starter, main course, and dessert) and, above all, to discover the atmosphere of these budget restaurants that were known as "bouillon" (now the word for "stock"). The decor—vast glass ceiling, wood paneling, copper luggage racks, and lockers where regulars used to keep their napkins—has not changed since 1896. The line can be long.

### From €20

99 **Daroco** – **E4** - *6 r. Vivienne - 2e - M Bourse or Pyramides - 01 42 21 93 71 - www.daroco.fr - daily lunch and eve - pizzas €12-39 - dishes €22-29.* Daroco has set up shop in the legendary boutique of Jean-Paul Gaultier in the Galerie Vivienne, a gemstone's throw from Place des Victoires. In a pretty, modern-day interior, this boho trattoria serves delicious pizzas and *primi* or *secondi* with exquisite flavor pairings. However, reception is not its strong point, and the services run one into the other. Book online.

43 **JanTchi** – **E4** - *6 r. Thérèse - 1er - M Pyramides - 01 40 15 91 07 - closed Sun - dishes €15-40.* Simple yet original, this temple of Korean cuisine will pleasantly surprise you. The combos of tastes and colors drop flavor bombs on the palate. Temptating options include the *chapchei*, the famous spicy-pork

*bibimbap*, and then the homemade green-tea ice cream. Expect to wait up to 20 minutes for a table for dinner.

54 **À Côté** – **E3** - *16 r. La-Fayette - 9e - M Chaussée-d'Antin - 01 48 78 03 68 - acote.paris - closed Mon, Sat lunch, and Sun - dishes €14-22.* Boris and Sébastien promise the "plancha of your dreams": a fine rib of Limousin beef cooked "black and blue"—crispy on the surface—, béarnaise sauce, home fries, and a jumbo bone marrow. Excellent wine list.

### From €30

48 **L'Office** – **F3** - *3 r. Richer - 9e - M Poissonnière - 01 47 70 67 31 - www.office-resto.com - daily lunch and eve ex. wknd - dishes €24-36 - booking advised.* Aqua green tones, natural wood, lots of plants, ceramic tableware... The decor is pure neo-bistrot, and the menu, short and seasonal, is in the same vein. A contemporary classic!



## The Marais and Les Halles

**Local Map p. 38-39.**

**Picnic Spot** - The quays along the Right Bank, in front of the Hôtel de Ville (near the Batobus embarkation point). Several wooden tables on the waterside or under the weeping willows.

### From €10

9 **L'As du Fallafel** – **F5** - *34 r. des Rosiers - 4e - M Saint-Paul - 01 48 87 63 60 - www.l-as-du-fallafel.zenchef.com - closed Sat and Fri eve - dishes €8.50-24.* Its falafel and sandwiches made with pita bread, salad, hummus, and spices are simply divine. Also arguably the best shawarma in Paris. Whether eating in or taking out, there's always a line.

27 **Notre Café Marais** – **G5** - *11 allée Arnaud-Beltrame (enter via 12 r. de Béarn) - 3e - M Chemin-Vert - www.autisme-en-idf.org - Tue-Fri 8:30am-3pm - under €20.* A nonprofit, this café is staffed by young autistic people and social care professionals in training. A social enterprise nestled inside an old, recently renovated fire station that adds to its cozy appeal. Perfect for lunch (toasted sandwiches, salads, etc.) or light bites (homemade cakes), just a short walk from Place des Vosges.

### From €15

13 **Kitchen** – **F4** - *74 r. des Gravilliers - 3e - M Arts et Métiers - 09 52 55 11 66 - www.kitchenparis.com - 8am-2:30pm (wknd 3:30pm) - dishes under €20.* Café serving fruit juices, soups, salads, and maki. Veggie and organic cuisine, perfect for a healthy lunch break, popular with the neighborhood's hip young crowd.

23 **Paris New York** – **F5** - *10 r. Ste-Croix-de-la-Bretonnerie - 4e - M Hôtel de Ville - 01 42 47 06 59 - www.pnyburger.com - daily lunch and eve - dishes under €20.* Upmarket American classics. Burgers are the speciality here: beef from traditional breeds (Angus, Salers, Breton), exclusively grass-fed and reared outdoors. Served with fresh buns and home fries, everything is cooked to order. PNY has outposts in other Paris districts: 1 r. Perrée (3e), 24 r. Pierre-Fontaine (9e), 50 r. de Caumartin (9e), 50 r. du Fbg-St-Denis (10e), 96 r. Oberkampf (11e), 120 r. du Fbg-St-Antoine (12e), and 15 r. de la Gaité (14e).

(56) **Happy Nouilles – F4** - *95 r Beaubourg - 3e - Ⓜ Arts et Métiers - ✆ 01 44 59 31 22 - daily ex. Tue, non-stop service - dishes around €10-20.* Flavored with crispy chicken, dried pork, salted cabbage, or prawn dumplings, the *lamen* (noodle soup with broth) are the stars of the show here. Rich flavors, generous portions, and low prices, no wonder this place is always so rammed!

(39) **Popolare – E4** - *111 r. Réaumur - 2e - Ⓜ Bourse - ✆ 01 42 21 30 91 - www.bigmammagroup.com - daily lunch and eve - pizzas €10-20.* This one establishment of many in the Big Mamma Group has been treating its customers to authentic pizzas for a few years now. Come early to beat the mob. The products and servers are all Italian, while the pizzas, all excellent, are bigger than the plate. Try the double truffle topped with mozza *fior di latte*, AOP parmesan, truffle cream, and freshly grated truffle. You won't regret it!

❤ (35) **Bouillon République – G4** - *39 bd du Temple - 3e - Ⓜ République - ✆ 01 42 59 69 31 - www.bouillonlesite.com - non-stop service daily - dishes €10-15.* In late 2021, the team behind Bouillon Pigalle *(p. 120)* brought another of its typically Parisian eateries, serving timeless classics at rock-bottom prices, back to life, near Place de la République. Fantastic.

(15) **Eataly Paris – F5** - *37 r. Ste-Croix de la Bretonnerie - 4e - Ⓜ Hôtel-de-Ville - ✆ 01 83 65 81 00 - www.eataly.fr - non-stop service daily.* This 43,000-sq.ft concept store is dedicated to Italian cuisine. With a 27,000 sq.ft market and seven restaurants spanning every price point, this venue transports you to Italia thanks to its various counters specializing in deli meats, fresh pasta, cheese, and more. Or snack on a crisp-crust pizza upstairs. The courtyard is a suntrap and perfect for a casual bite to eat.

## From €20

(11) **Breizh Café – G5** - *109 r. Vieille-du-Temple - 3e - Ⓜ Saint-Paul - ✆ 01 42 72 13 77 - www.breizhcafe.com - non-stop service daily - dishes under €20.* After conquering Japan with his buckwheat crepes, Bertrand Larcher has brought to France his Japanese creperies that more than justify the house slogan: "Crepes, differently". What can you expect? Flavors like the Basquaise: asparagus, tomato, chorizo, basil, and melted cheese. Not to mention the lip-smackingly good sweet options: white chocolate mousse and matcha tea or poached peach and fresh mint.

❤ (12) **Marché des Enfants-Rouges – G4** - *39 r. de Bretagne - 3e - Ⓜ Saint-Sébastien-Froissart - daily ex. Mon. 8:30am–8:30pm (Thu 9:30pm, Sun 5pm).* Inside the indoor market favored by Paris' young, cool foodies, you can enjoy—on the go, standing at the counter, or sitting at a table—a Japanese bento, West Indian acras, a tagine, or Italian specialties. The Moroccan couscous counter has the most beautiful terrace (to get a place, arrive early on Sunday).

(10) **Soma – G5** - *13 r. de Saintonge - 3e - Ⓜ Saint-Sébastien Froissart - ✆ 09 81 82 53 51 - www.restaurants-soma.fr - daily Sun-Mon, lunch and eve - dishes €15-25 - set lunch menu €20.* This Japanese restaurant in the Marais is never empty. All down to the chef who cooks

vegetables, fish, and shellfish in front of his guests in the warm atmosphere of a typical *izakaya* (Japanese snack bar). The seared beef in ponzu sauce gets top-billing. Fine selection of sake.

### From €25

28 **Le Petit Marcel** – **F4** - *65 r. Rambuteau - 4e - M Châtelet or Les Halles - ✆ 01 48 87 10 20 - daily ex. Mon, non-stop service - dishes €17-32.* A proper institution in the Centre Georges-Pompidou district, this venue looks much the same as it did when it opened in the late 19th century: old-fashioned counter, ceramic wall tiles, and other original features. The menu honors classic bistro fare (eggs mayonnaise, Gers chicken) with the odd modern twist.

14 **Pirouette** – **F4** - *5 r. Mondétour - 1er - M Étienne Marcel - ✆ 01 40 26 47 81 - www.restaurantpirouette.com - daily ex. Sun-Mon, lunch and eve - dishes €17-27.* You may pirouette in, but you might not pirouette out after a generous meal here! The cuisine revisits traditional recipes with a playful twist, such as rum and lime baba. Stylish, contemporary interior and pleasant terrace on a pedestrian square.



95 **Frenchie Bar à Vins** – **F4** - *6 r. du Nil - 2e - M Sentier - ✆ 01 40 39 96 19 - www.frenchie-bav.com - eve only - dishes €18-45.* Grégory Marchand opened this casual wine bar—high tables, beams and exposed stones—at more affordable prices than in his restaurant across the way. It's known for its flavor pairings (grilled cuttlefish with carrots and pine nuts, croque madame with truffle), its English cheeses, and the surprises displayed on the wine menu. The line can be off-putting, so come early.

### From €30

❤ 86 **Elmer** – **F4** - *30 r. Notre-Dame-de-Nazareth - 3e - M Temple - ✆ 01 43 56 22 95 - www.elmer-restaurant.fr - closed Sat lunch and Sun-Mon - dishes €22-38.* This venue is a big hit with foodies. Young chef Simon Horwitz, who has worked with some of the greats, serves an elevated cuisine in which the products take center stage. Vegetables and meat are treated with sensitivity and respect, as shown by the lamb and pork cuts that leave the open kitchen deliciously golden. The decor of untreated wood, soft lighting, and South American tableware make the perfect finishing touches.

7 **Soon Grill** – **G5** - *78 r. des Tournelles - 3e - M Chemin Vert - ✆ 01 42 77 13 56 - www.soon-grill.com - daily lunch and eve - dishes €24-81 - set menus €49-59.* This restaurant is a bright and beautiful celebration of Korean cuisine. The classics are on the menu—grilled dumplings, marinated beef in soy sauce—but there are also lesser-known dishes too, such as *bibimbap* served in a hot stone bowl. Fine and fragrant: a real treat!

## Latin Quarter

**Local Map p. 48-49.**

**Picnic Spot** - The Jardin des Plantes makes a perfect lunchtime pit stop.

### From €15

21 **Strada Café** – **F7** - *24 r. Monge - 5e - M Cardinal-Lemoine - ✆ 09 83 67 83 64 - www.stradacafe.fr -*

Alban Couturier/Elmer

Elmer.



*8am-6:30pm, wknd 9:30am-6:30pm - dishes under €20.* This cozy café instantly immerses you in New York coffee shop vibes. It's the perfect place for a quick break and, above all, cup of organic coffee, one of the best in Paris. Great lunch deals, homemade pastries, fresh fruit juices, all in a cheerful ambience. Weekend brunch menu.

71 **Mexi and Co – E6** - *10 r. Dante - 5e - M Cluny-la Sorbonne - ✆ 01 46 34 14 12 - non-stop service daily - dishes around €15.* In this colorfully furnished restaurant with a South American soundtrack, the pitchers of margarita and house guacamole feel even more authentic. The classic burritos and nachos secured its place on the Paris foodie map.

## From €20

72 **Piment Thaï – E6** - *21 r. St-Jacques - 5e - M Cluny-la-Sorbonne - ✆ 01 56 24 84 88 - www.pimentthai21.com - daily ex. Mon, lunch and eve - dishes €15-25.* The chef, Too, grew up in Thailand in her grandmother's kitchen and, assisted by a single commis chef, cooks up the family recipes here. Delicate spring rolls, lightly breaded prawn fritters, beef with red curry, and, best of all, a fabulous *pad Thai* with melt-in-the-mouth noodles and a beef marinade selected by top butcher Hugo Desnoyer. Excellent value for money.

17 **Mirama – E6** - *17 r. St-Jacques - 5e - M Cluny-La Sorbonne - ✆ 01 43 54 71 77 - www.mirama.fr - closed wknd*

*eve - dishes €15-30.* Just a stone's throw from Boulevard Saint-Michel, just behind the Église Saint-Séverin, Mirama is a veritable haven for fans of authentic Chinese cuisine. Don't miss the soups and Peking duck, the house specialties.

(19) **Lhassa – F6** - *13 r. de la Montagne-Ste-Geneviève - 5e - M Maubert-Mutualité - 01 43 26 22 19 - daily ex. Mon-Tue, lunch and eve - dishes €15-25.* Tibetan restaurant with a zen atmosphere and ambient music. Steamed dishes, soups made from toasted barley flour, spinach, and meat, beef dumplings, all sensibly priced.

(97) **Les Arènes – F7** - *16 r. Linné - 5e - M Jussieu - 01 43 31 76 15 - www.lesarenes-paris.fr - non-stop service daily - dishes €16-27.* A fab spot between the Arènes de Lutèce and the Jardin des Plantes that's popular with the locals. This inviting brasserie is known as much for its smiley service as its changing planchas. Terrace. Excellent value for money.



### From €25

(69) **Les Délices d'Aphrodite – F8** - *4 r. Candolle - 5e - M Censier-Daubenton - 01 43 31 40 39 - www.mavrommatis.com - daily lunch and eve - set lunch menu €27.50 - dishes €20-30.* This was Egyptian-French singer Georges Moustaki's favorite tavern, a drop of Greek sunshine in the heart of the 5e arrondissement. With options including grilled octopus, garlic prawns, and lamb with shallots, chef Andreas Mavrommatis serves unpretentious fare to enliven the senses.

(4) **Kitchen Ter(re) – F6** - *26 bd St-Germain - 5e - M Maubert-Mutualité - 01 42 39 47 48 - daily ex. Sun-Mon, lunch and eve - dishes €23-25.* Pasta, but made from varieties of ancient grains, shaped according to tradition, and elevated in flavor, texture, and color by chef William Ledeuil, ably assisted by his team of passionate and carefully chosen producers. On the plate, you will find original compositions such as *girolette* with buckwheat-lemon butter, mushrooms and lovage or Cucugnan *dentelle* with cuttlefish and yuzu bouillabaisse jus.

## Saint-Germain-des-Prés-Montparnasse

**Local Map p. 57.**

**Picnic Spot** - In the Jardin du Luxembourg, affectionately known by locals as "Le Luco", make good use of the chairs at the edge of the lake or in the shade of a tree.

### From €15

(25) **Au Pied de Fouet – E5** - *3 r. St-Benoit - 6e - M Saint-Germain-des-Prés - 01 42 96 59 10 - www.aupieddefouet.fr - daily ex. Sun, lunch and eve - dishes €15-22.* This former post house is now an authentic bistro with 20 covers, where regulars come for the simple cuisine (gizzard salad, andouillette) at prices from another era, washed down with a good old bottle of vin de pays. Lively atmosphere.

(42) **Le Petit Josselin – D7** - *59 r. du Montparnasse - 14e - M Edgar-Quinet - 01 43 22 91 81 - www.creperielepetitjosselin.fr - closed Sat*

*and Sun - dishes under €20.* The sister address of the Crêperie Josselin, a local Breton institution, this version may be smaller, but it retains all the flavors. The famous double buckwheat or wheat pancakes will satisfy the healthiest of appetites.

## From €20

32 **Mamie Gâteaux – D6** - *66 r. du Cherche-Midi - 6e - M Saint-Placide - ✆ 01 42 22 32 15 - www.mamie-gateaux.com - 11:45am-6:45pm - closed Sun-Mon - dishes under €20*. Decked out in oilcloth and its well-used gas stove, this café evokes the kitchens of our grandmothers. The savory tarts of the day, accompanied with salad, are presented on the worktop covered with a checked tea towel. Those in the know come for the chocolate lava cake, butter-soaked French toast, and the carrot cake with homemade hot chocolate. The location has an excellent rep, so arrive early.

40 **Kodawari Ramen – E5** - *29 r. Mazarine - 6e - M Mabillon - ✆ 01 43 29 37 67 - www.kodawari-ramen.com - non-stop service daily - dishes under €20.* The buzzing atmosphere and narrow interior instantly transports you to one of old Tokyo's infamous alleyways. The ramen, produced on site and served in a delicious Landes chicken broth, will appeal not only to manga fans but foodies of every ilk. A house speciality: the Kurogowa ramen, made with a secret sauce and Basque farmhouse *chashu*. Avoid peak times unless you love to wait in line. A well-deserved success.

74 **Tsukizi – E6** - *2 bis r. des Ciseaux - 6e - M Saint-Germain-des-Prés - ✆ 01 43 54 65 19 - daily ex. Sun-Mon, lunch and eve - dishes € 25-35- set lunch menu €20.* A typical sushi bar where you can admire the chef expertly handling knives and raw fish. The *chirashi* is a delicacy, as are all the fish you can choose from: tuna, salmon, horse mackerel, octopus, sea bass... the list goes on.

## From €25

31 **Wadja – D7** - *10 r. de la Grande-Chaumière - 6e - M Vavin - ✆ 01 46 33 02 02 - www.wadja.fr - daily ex. wknd, lunch and eve - dishes €23-39.* Packed-in tables, old zinc bar, mirrors, 1930s lithograph prints: you're in a Paris bistro if you hadn't guessed! A timeless venue in the neighborhood for decades. Excellent value for money.

75 **Garçon! – D7** - *83 r. du Cherche-Midi - 6e - M Saint-Placide - ✆ 01 43 22 68 13 - www.garcon-cafe.com - daily ex. wknd, lunch and eve - dishes €19.50-28.* For her restaurant, Marion Trama, the daughter of the great chef Alain Trama, wanted to create a new-generation bistro. In an interior of wood and marble, sit at the zinc bar or in the dining room and make your choice from the huge board. Excellent cochonnaille, green asparagus and pan-fried foie gras, ceviche of mullet, roasted brill, crispy sweetbreads, or simply a soft and generously filled croque monsieur. Tip: book ahead, even for lunch!

29 **Blueberry Maki Bar – D6** - *6 r. du Sabot - 6e - M Saint-Sulpice - ✆ 01 42 22 21 56 - www.blueberrymakibar.com - daily ex. Sun-Mon, lunch and eve - dishes €15-26.* Fans of maki (and sushi), make a

beeline for the Blueberry! And not just because it rhymes, but for the rock bar vibes that this venue has in spades. Whether it's named Rackham the Red, Trublion, or Iroquois, here maki is king, and fresh is the only way it comes. Eel is paired with bonito or prawn, although avocado is still a firm favorite.

94 **L'Avant-comptoir du marché – E6** - *14 r. Lobineau - 6e - M Mabillon or Saint-Germain-des-Prés - ✆ 01 44 27 07 97 - www.camdeborde.com - daily, non-stop service - dishes under €20.* After the Avant-comptoir de la mer and the Avant-comptoir de la terre, both located at the Carrefour de l'Odéon, Yves Camdeborde has opened a third, wine-bar style venue at the Marché Saint-Germain where pork is the main ingredient. The local clientele rush under the huge red sow hanging from the ceiling to order boards brimming with Bigorre Black Pig coppa ham, ventreche from Béarn, roast pig ears, and blood sausage terrine. Stylish, friendly, and succulent.

30 **Marcello – E6** - *8 r. Mabillon - 6e - M Mabillon - ✆ 01 43 26 52 26 - www.marcello-paris.com - closed wknd eve - dishes €21-36.* This establishment stands out for its gorgeous below-street-level terrace that keeps the commotion of Saint-Germain-des-Près at bay. Egg white omelet and organic Japanese matcha for breakfast; truffle arancini, griddled calamari, and spelt spaghetti, *tramezzini* with cloud bread, later in the day. Here, the food is excellent for grazing at any hour of the day; you can also take your time with one of their stylish cocktails.

### From €35

76 **Ida – C7** - *117 r. de Vaugirard - 15e - M Falguière - ✆ 01 56 58 00 02 - www.restaurant-ida.com - daily lunch and eve - set menus €34-65.* Denny Imbroisi welcomes diners like old friends to his restaurant that's half contemporary bistro, half authentic trattoria. Raw fish, ceviche, sublime cold cuts sourced directly from the Boot, each suggestion is divinely interpreted. But if you come “chez Denny”, it's above all to taste his spaghetti *alla carbonara*, voted several times the best in Paris. Remember to book.

103 **Le Bon Saint-Pourçain – E6** - *10 bis r. Servandoni - 6e - M Mabillon - ✆ 01 42 01 78 24 - www.bonsaintpourcain.com - daily ex. Sun-Mon, lunch and eve - dishes €31-45.* Tucked away behind the Église Saint-Sulpice, this restaurant is run with care and passion. On the decorative side, think square tables, wooden chairs from the 1970s, leatherette benches. On the cuisine side, it's classic bistro fare with a modern spin based on excellent ingredients from the market. Roast Landes chicken, fondant potatoes, Swiss chard, mushrooms; duck pâté en croûte, foie gras, pear chutney... All simply delicious! The restaurant is often full: book ahead!

## Invalides-Eiffel Tower

**Picnic Spot** – The Jardin Catherine-Labouré *(29 r. de Babylone - 7e)* offers bucolic charm with its kitchen garden and fruit orchard. The banks of the Seine, the Esplanade des Invalides and the Jardins du Champ-de-Mars are equally appealing alternatives.

### From €15

51 **L'Augustine – C5** - *79 r. de Varenne (entrance fee to the Musée Rodin required) - 7e - M Varenne - ☎ 01 45 55 84 39 - daily ex. Mon 10am-6:30pm - lunch deals €16-20.* In the Musée Rodin's sublime garden is a pavilion where visitors and locals looking for a light bite (salads, quiches, pasta, etc.) can gather under the leafy canopy or on the lovely terrace. A little delight.

### From €20

78 **Marcel – D6** - *15 r. de Babylone - 7e - M Sèvres-Babylone - ☎ 01 42 22 62 62 - www.restaurantmarcel.fr - closed Sun eve - dishes €20-25.* At Marcel's, for once the specials are in English and the brunch is served continuously and à la carte. Eggs Benedict, meatball salad with baby lettuce, bulgur with spicy meatballs, their famous kale salad. It's impossible not to have a dessert with the tempting selection of key lime pie, moist carrot cake, and apple pie served with crème fraîche. Friendly staff and reasonable prices.

### From €35

100 **Radis Beurre – B7** - *51 bd Garibaldi - 15e - M Sèvres-Lecourbe or Ségur - ☎ 01 40 33 99 26 - www.restaurantleradisbeurre.com - daily ex. wknd, lunch and eve - set menus €35-55.* Jérôme Bonnet learned the culinary ropes at Pavillon Ledoyen and Relais Bernard Loiseau. Since 2015, in his no-frills bistro, he has been serving up tasty and well-conceived cooking: pan-fried pig's foot with duck foie gras and tangy meat jus, pan-fried calf's head, potato marmalade, and other delights. Terrace.

63 **L'Os à Moelle – A8** - *3 r. Vasco-de-Gama - 15e - M Lourmel - ☎ 01 45 57 27 27 - www.osamoelle-restaurant.com - closed Sat lunch and Sun-Mon - set lunch menu €33 - set dinner menus €43-60.* Under the helm of Thierry Faucher, one of the bistronomy pioneers, here you can enjoy hearty cuisine with a few daring touches. Across the way, La Cave de l'Os à Moelle is a pleasant and friendly wine bar for dinner on shared tables, a snack, or just a glass.

### From €40

❤ 77 **Plume – C6** - *24 r. Pierre-Leroux - 7e - M Vaneau - ☎ 01 43 06 79 85 - www.restaurantplume.com - closed Sat lunch and Sun-Mon. - dishes €34-48.* This Parisian address is not short on charm or flavor. A proponent of the bistronomy movement, the young chef proposes an inventive cuisine that focuses on the produce, including cheeses from his neighbor Quatrehomme. The dining room is bright and the decor modern, all the ingredients to be "in". Booking advised.

## Trocadéro-Chaillot

**Picnic Spot** - The Jardins du Trocadéro, with the Eiffel Tower in full view, is Insta worthy.

### From €20

41 **Schwartz's Deli – A4** - *7 av. d'Eylau - 16e - M Trocadéro - ☎ 01 47 04 73 61 - www.schwartzsdeli.fr - daily lunch and eve - dishes €15-36.* This American diner brings a touch of

New York to Paris, with the addition of checked tablecloths. There are no less than 14 burgers to choose from: beef, veggie, and even cod! Soups, pasta, sandwiches, and salads share the menu.

### From €25

❤ (79) **Les Marches** – **B4** - *5 r. de la Manutention - 16e - Ⓜ Iéna - ✆ 01 47 23 52 80 - www.lesmarches-restaurant.com - daily lunch and eve - dishes €20-30.* The cuisine at one of Paris' three "truck stops" is as traditional as they come: think ribeye with Béarnaise sauce, poached eggs in red wine sauce, and lemon sorbet, all served on red-checked tablecloths. The service is friendly, just like the owner who loves to tell diners how, fascinated by the truck stops of his youth, he made his dream come true!



## Champs-Elysées and Western Paris

**Picnic Spot** - Often overlooked, the Jardins des Champs-Élysées gardens (at the bottom of the avenue) offer their Belle Époque charm for a moment of calm. To the north, the Parc Monceau is a must-see.

### From €30

(22) **Le Mermoz** – **C3** - *16 r. Jean-Mermoz - 8e - Ⓜ Franklin-D.-Roosevelt - ✆ 01 45 63 65 26 - www.lemermozparis.fr - daily ex. wknd, lunch and eve - dishes €25-35 (tapas in the eve).* The young Californian chef Thomas Graham has succeeded in making his mark on this timeless bistro (zinc bar, mosaic floor, Art Deco chandeliers). Appealing to the eye and palate, his dishes invite impeccable products to the table, chiming with the organic and natural wine list. The place is always busy!

(20) **Ran** – **C3** - *8 r. d'Anjou - 8e - Ⓜ Madeleine - ✆ 01 40 17 04 77 - www.ran-paris.com - closed Sat lunch and Sun. - dishes €20-45.* Dining rooms in bronze and gold tones, mirrors… this restaurant serves Japanese cuisine with touches of French gastronomy, all in a sophisticated ambience. Don't think twice about ordering the *robata* meat grilled on lava stones, or the camembert tempura with miso sauce. Booking advised.

### From €40

(96) **Le Drugstore** – **B3** - *133 av. des Champs-Élysées - 8e - Ⓜ Charles de Gaulle-Étoile or George V - ✆ 01 44 43 75 07 - www.publicisdrugstore.com - non-stop service daily - dishes €30-56.* From morning thru evening, from sweet finger food at tea time to cocktails, Le Drugstore—decorated by Tom Dixon and helmed by chef Eric Frechon (sharing the address with L'Atelier de Joël Robuchon)—is part of the revival of the iconic Publicis Drugstore on the Champs-Élysées. Upmarket and so very now.

❤ (64) **Rooster** – **C1** - *137 r. Cardinet - 17e - Ⓜ Pont Cardinet - ✆ 01 45 79 91 48 - www.rooster-restaurant.com - daily ex. wknd, lunch and eve - dishes €38-42.* A winning return for Frédéric Duca after his spell in New York. In his base at Batignolles, the chef concocts fine cuisine with Mediterranean accents: sole with pine nuts and green asparagus, linguine with urchin and cuttlefish ink, milk-fed lamb to share.

Restaurant Plume

Plume.



## Montmartre-Pigalle

**Local Map p. 90-91.**

**Picnic Spot** - The Jardins du Sacré-Cœur afford stunning views of Paris.

### From €15

24 **Boca – D2** - *11 bis r. Blanche - 9e - M Trinité d'Estienne d'Orve - ✆ 01 44 91 95 96 - www.restaurantboca.fr - closed Sat lunch and Sun-Mon eve - under €20.* This bijou restaurant features a sun-shaped mirror, a clue to its joyous ambience and fun and cheerful service. Come nightfall, the main attraction at Boca are its delicious tapas, such as burrata with Vesuvius apricot puree, or marinated octopus with black garlic and heirloom tomatoes. Simple and equally attractive dishes are served at lunchtime, such as the salmon-and-mango Boca bowl. Booking advised.

2 **Bouillon Pigalle – E1** - *22 bd de Clichy - 18e - M Pigalle - ✆ 01 42 59 69 31 - www.bouillonlesite.com - non-stop service daily - dishes under €20.* Here you can experience the rock-bottom prices and classic French fare of Paris' "bouillons" of old: eggs mayonnaise, herring and potatoes in oil, beef bourgignon, coquillette pasta, sausage and potato puree, chocolate mousse, crème caramel... Open since 2017, its success, in this bohemian yet cool and touristy neighborhood, was immediate.

52 **Flesh – D1** - *25 r. de Douai - 9e - M Blanche - ✆ 01 42 81 21 93 - daily*

*ex. Sun-Mon, lunch and eve - set lunch menus €15.50-20 - dishes €21-36.* Meat lovers will be delighted. In industrial-style decor, they can enjoy Argentinean red meat and barbecued pork ribs, drizzled with a house sauce (bourbon, lemon honey, etc.), and accompanied by fries, zucchini marinated in goat cheese and lemon, or grilled coriander-parmesan corn.

## From €20

104 **Luz Verde** – **E2** - *24 r. Henry Monnier - 9e - M Pigalle - 01 70 23 69 60 - www.luzverde.fr - daily ex. Sun-Mon, lunch and eve - dishes €13-40 - lunch reserv. only, waiting list in the eve.* Young chef Alexis Delassaux (who earned his stripes at the Frenchie, the Royal Monceau, and on the *Top Chef* TV show) revisits Mexican cuisine: tuna ceviche, pork shoulder, *guindillas*, and guacamole, not forgetting the vegetarian tacos that you can wash down with a frozen margarita. A friendly taqueria in South Pigalle.



55 **Le Pantruche** – **E2** - *3 r. Victor-Massé - 9e - M Pigalle - 01 48 78 55 60 - www.lapantruchoise.com - daily ex. wknd, lunch and eve - dishes €22-28 - set menus €21-39.* People come as much for the relaxed atmosphere as for the inventive cuisine. The rack of pork served with roast new potatoes will stay a fond memory. Simple, tasty, irreverent.

81 **Brasserie Barbès** – **F1** - *2 bd Barbès - 18e - M Barbès - 01 42 64 52 23 - www.brasseriebarbes.com - non-stop service daily - dishes €15-19.* This multifaceted venue (bar, restaurant, club) has become the trendiest of hangouts in this working-class neighborhood. Detox juices and healthy cuisine are offered alongside more classic dishes such as burgers and steak tartare. When the sun's out, snag a table on the terrace for lunch. In the evening, head up to the second floor for a boogie.

**L'Esquisse** – **Off map by D1** - *151 bis r. Marcadet - 18e - M Lamarck-Caulaincourt - 01 53 41 63 04 - daily ex. Sun-Mon, lunch and eve - dishes €20-25.* Two young passionate chefs have teamed up to create this welcoming vintage bistro. Among the solid parquet and wooden benches, go globetrotting through their original dishes. For lunch, there's the daily special and concise menu; a wider choice in the evening.

## From €25

❤ 105 **Les Arlots** – **F2** - *136 r. du Faubourg-Poissonnière - 10e - M Barbès-Rochechouart or Poissonnière - 01 42 82 92 01 - daily ex. Sun-Mon, lunch and eve - dishes €18-36.* Laidback vibes and smiles all round! The generous bistro cuisine at Les Arlots draws strongly on France's regions and is excellently prepared: sausage with potato puree, Ajaccian-style tripe, mullet tartare, to name a few dishes. A fine list of natural and organic wines, too.

## From €35

❤ 98 **Chez Michel** – **F2** - *10 r. de Belzunce - 10e - M Poissonnière or Gare du Nord - 01 44 53 06 20 - www.restaurantchezmichel.fr - daily ex. wknd, lunch and eve - set lunch menu €36 - set dinner menu €42.* The half-rustic, half-marine setting is a world away from Paris. And the bistronomic fare will transport you to Brittany in no time. On the menu, kig ha farz (Breton stew), scallops from Saint-Brieuc, fish soup with chorizo and parmesan... The desserts, meanwhile, are more likely to transport you back in time: think rice pudding with fig jam and the legendary Paris-Brest. Well-stocked wine list.

60 **Le Coq & Fils** – **E1** - *98 r. Lepic - 18e -* M *Lamarck-Caulaincourt - ✆ 01 42 59 82 89 - www.lecoq-fils.com - daily lunch and eve - dishes €25-52.* Here, the celebrated chef Antoine Westermann (brilliantly) champions all things poultry. The result is magical, with a rotisserie area for lunch, where diners can watch the chefs at work, and a more secluded dining room for enjoying fine, artisanal variations on the theme of chicken in less frantic surroundings. Why not share a whole Racan chicken or Dombes duckling with friends? Sheer succulence.

## Canal Saint-Martin-La Villette and surroundings

**Picnic Spot** - The Canal Saint-Martin is popular with Parisians for an al fresco bite to eat and drink. The more family-friendly Parc de la Villette is an excellent alternative, as is the refreshingly bucolic Parc des Buttes-Chaumont.

### From €15

34 **Sol Semilla** – **G3** - *23 r. des Vinaigriers - 10e -* M *Jacques Bonsergent - ✆ 01 42 01 03 44 - www.sol-semilla.fr - closed Sun and Mon eve - dishes under €20.* Organic, plant-based, gluten-free cuisine based on fresh seasonal fruit and veg, herbs, and superfoods sold in bulk by the store, such as carob, maca, and raw cocoa. Tasty and varied dishes as fresh as a daisy! Booking advised.

### From €20

59 **Soya** – **G4** - *20 r. de la Pierre-Levée - 11e -* M *Goncourt - ✆ 01 48 06 33 02 - www.soya-cantine-bio.fr - closed Sun eve - dishes €16-20 .* Natural materials and lots of space at this organic canteen that champions fresh ingredients: think beet tartare, vegetable mezze, and delicious juices. Everything is homemade!

92 **À la folie** – **Map p. 99** - *26 av. Corentin-Cariou - Parc de La Villette, 19e -* M *Porte de La Villette - ✆ 07 76 79 70 66 - www.alafolie.paris - closed Mon-Tue, Sat eve and Sun lunch - dishes €18-48.* With its sprawling terrace filled with picnic benches, this bar-club-restaurant is the perfect place to hang out and bask in the leafy surrounds of Parc de la Villette. An address for meat-eaters (barbecue) but veggies too (salads and *poke* bowls).

93 **Fric-Frac** – **G3** - *79 quai de Valmy - 10e -* M *République - ✆ 01 42 85 87 34 - www.fricfrac.fr - daily lunch and eve - dishes under €20.* This is the temple of the croque monsieur, located on the bank of the Canal Saint-Martin. In a bright and modern setting, decked out in hanging lamps and plants and graphic scatter cushions, discover France's classic grilled cheese in all kinds of variations. The Winnie comes with goat cheese and dried fruit, while the Viking is flavored with salmon and apple. Of course, they've not forgotten the classic croque, generously packed

with Mornay béchamel sauce, grand cru emmental cheese, and Prince de Paris ham. Be sure to leave room for the house French toast! Ideal for anyone on a shoestring budget. Also in Montmartre (3 r. des Trois-Frères).

49 **Le Bichat** – **G3** - *11 r. Bichat - 10e - M Goncourt - ✆ 09 54 27 68 97 - www.lebichat.fr - non-stop service daily - dishes under €20.* A hip and friendly neighborhood joint where big tables encourage sharing. Vegan, meat or fish, the bowls are all made from organic, seasonal ingredients. Delicious gluten-free pastries. All reasonably priced.

### From €25

44 **Le Pavillon du Lac** - **H2** - *Parc des Buttes-Chaumont (entrance Pl. Armand Carrel) - 19e - M Laumière - ✆ 01 42 00 07 21 - www.lepavillondulac.fr - daily ex. Mon-Tue, 10am-5pm (wknd 5:30pm) - dishes €22-26.* In the heart of the Parc des Buttes-Chaumont, this country house-style restaurant promises a welcome breather from the bustle and din of the center. In the sunny months, its terrace is one of the most coveted in the city. A perle rare in Paris.



**Cheval d'Or** – **Off map by H2** - *21 r. de la Villette - 19e - M Jourdain- ✆ 09 54 12 21 77 - www.chevaldorparis.com - daily ex. Mon-Tue, eve - dishes €18-24.* The kitsch red-and-yellow frontage conceals an exposed stone and light wood interior graced with an open kitchen. The chefs busily doing what they do best is a pleasure to watch, and a clear nod to what the menu has in store. The asparagus in sesame sauce with grilled tofu, beef tartare with tamarind, and meagre with yuzu are delicious. Be sure to book at least a week in advance, or else sit at the counter if you come at opening time.

37 **Yaya Secrétan** – **H2** - *33 av. Secrétan - 19e - M Bolivar - ✆ 01 42 41 12 86 - www.yayarestaurant.com - lunch and eve daily - dishes €17-25 .* Featuring an olive tree in the center, "Yaya" written in big white lettering on the facade, and marine tones, this restaurant offers a tasty menu of Greek mezze and mains in a warm atmosphere where it's impossible not to share. Opt for the flavorful *stifado* beef pastilla with orange and cinnamon. For dessert, the *yaourtimas*, creamy yogurt on a bed of green olives and caramelized pistachios. A firm favorite!

### From €35

57 **Le Galopin** – **G3** - *34 r. Ste-Marthe - 10e - M Belleville - ✆ 01 42 06 05 03 - www.le-galopin.paris - closed Sun-Mon and Tue-Fri eve - set menu €55.* Working his way through various top kitchens in Paris (Ze Kitchen Galerie, Itinéraires, Porte 12) and Brittany, Julien Simmonet revels in turning what the market delivers that day into dishes packed with flavor. The bistro set menu at lunchtime or the more elaborate dishes in the evening won't fail to disappoint. With well-selected wines and charming hospitality, this establishment on Place Sainte-Marthe promises a positive experience.

### Over €80

58 **Le Chateaubriand** – **G3** - *129 av. Parmentier - 11e - M Goncourt - ✆ 01 43 57 45 95 - www.lechateaubriand.net - closed*

*Sat-Mon and Tue-Thu eve - set menu €85.* Hip thirty-somethings tend to worship (deservedly so) Inaki Aizpitarte, the genius behind the "bistronomy" movement. The now famous no-choice, surprise menu, exhilaratingly refined, draws a cosmopolitan clientele. For instance, the monkfish is roasted with garlic, almonds, and tomato, coffee beans lending extra crunch.

## Bastille and Eastern Paris

**Picnic Spot** - The lush banks of the Port de l'Arsenal are hard to resist. Further east, the Parc de Bercy faces the Bibliothèque François-Mitterrand, offering an altogether different ambience. The choice is yours!

### From €15

53 **Le Grand Bréguet** – **H5** - *17 r. Breguet - 11e - M Bréguet-Sabin - 01 43 55 74 92 - www.legrandbreguet.com - daily ex. Sun, non-stop service - under €20.* This popular canteen is the perfect embodiment of the pulsating vibes of the 11e arrondissement! Stand in line at the long counter and, come your turn, the team will set about making up your plate with a couple of raw ingredients, two cooked vegetables, and one protein to choose from the daily selection. Then find a seat at one of the huge communal tables in the vast dining room or on the terrace, in the rear courtyard. Everything is made on the premises, fresh, organic, and, oh-so healthy! From morning to evening, the establishment turns into a vibrant hangout for the local youth.

33 **Le Floréal Belleville** – **H3** - *43 r. des Couronnes - 20e - M Couronnes - 01 43 61 94 66 - www.florealbelleville.com - closed Mon and Sun eve - dishes under €20.* Nestled at the foot of Parc de Belleville, this establishment is at once bar, restaurant, and cultural space. Beyond the glass and copper, Art Nouveau facade, the industrial, garage-sale interior is warm and welcoming. The hearty dishes on the menu are based on ingredients sourced through short food supply chains. For afternoon tea, you can't go wrong with the ginger lemonade and one of the wonderful homemade pastries. *The shakshouka, acai bowl,* savory pancakes, and plenty other surprises make up the Sunday brunch menu.

62 **Dong Huong** – **H3** - *14 r. Louis-Bonnet - 11e - M Goncourt - 01 43 57 42 81 - www.pho-donghuong.fr - daily ex. Tue, non-stop service - dishes under €20.* Casual Vietnamese eatery in Belleville, fast service and excellent food. Pho, spring rolls, and super-fresh bun bo.

50 **Chez Ramona** – **H3** - 17 r. Ramponeau - *20e - M Belleville - 01 46 36 83 55 - 6:30pm-10:30pm - daily ex. Mon, eve only - dishes under €20.* The ambience is sheer joy in this iconic grocery store-restaurant, opened in the 1960s by Ramona after she left Spain and settled in France. The tiny dining room upstairs is pretty as a picture and is often thronged with regulars who come to tuck into the generous tapas and paella.

### From €20

26 **Chez Pradel** – **G5** - 3 *r. Pasteur - 11e - M Saint-Ambroise - 01 43 55 09 59 -*

*daily ex. Mon-Tue, lunch and eve - dishes €15-20.* Parquet on the floor, check; red-and-white gingham tablecloths, check; boards announcing the daily specials, check—you're definitely in a bistro! Classics like steak tartare and blood sausage with potato puree are there as you'd expect, and the rowdy atmosphere only adds to the authenticity. Second address in north Montmartre (168 r. Ordener - 18e).

102 **Aux Bons Crus** – **H5** - *54 r. Godefroy-Cavaignac - 11e -* M *Voltaire - ✆ 01 45 67 21 13 - www.auxbonscrus.fr - daily lunch and eve - dishes €15-25*. "Les Routiers", the famous red-and-blue macarons, is a brand popular with people who love the simple things in life—from checked tablecloths to Pyrex bowls—and living off the land. This bistro could have been made for Routiers aficionados: hearty portions, classics from the French repertoire, and the quintessential fixed lunch menu. On the vino side, expect a decent wine list at decent prices.

66 **Les Provinces** – **H6** - *20 r. d'Aligre - 12e -* M *Faidherbe-Chaligny - ✆ 01 43 43 91 64 - www.boucherie-lesprovinces.fr - closed Mon, Tue lunch and Sun eve - dishes €16-29.* It's fair to say that Les Provinces would turn the most committed vegetarian into a hardened carnivore. All thanks to the steaks, really, which hang quietly while pork chops chew the fat with a bunch of chorizos, who like their conversation spicy. Basically, everything is screaming to be eaten! Take your seat and let them grill your meat which will come served with steaming roasted new potatoes.

## From €30

68 **Le Cotte Rôti** – **H7** - *1 r. de Cotte - 12e -* M *Ledru-Rollin - ✆ 01 43 45 06 37 - www.lecotteroti.fr - closed wknd and Mon lunch - dishes €20-30 - booking advised.* With self-assured inventivness, eye for detail, and respect for the seasons, Nicolas Michel is an unnervingly confident master of his craft. The only catch: the price of wine by the bottle—better to order by the glass. The set lunch menu is a steal.

61 **Le Baratin** – **H3** - *3 r. Jouye-Rouve - 20e -* M *Pyrénées - ✆ 01 43 49 39 70 - closed Sat eve, Tue lunch and Sun-Mon - dishes €20-36.* An institution with a capital "I". Even the proprietor's foul temper seems to be part of the charm. The menu features classics like brawn and pig ears in vinaigrette. At the helm in the kitchen, the famous Raquel Carena is a culinary queen!

## From €50

101 **Pianovins** – **H6** - *46 r. Trousseau - 11e -* M *Ledru-Rollin - ✆ 01 48 06 95 85 - www.pianovins.com - daily ex. Sun-Mon, lunch and eve - set menus €55-67*. Eric Mancio and Michel Roncière, previously of Guy Savoy fame, have set up on the former premises of Les Déserteurs, one of Paris' foodie hotspots. Rest assured, with Pianovins, the bar is set just as high: neo-classical cuisine perfectly mastered, like scallops with hazelnut butter accompanied by feather-light celeriac and fennel cream.

38 **Towa** – **H6** - *75 r. Crozatier - 12e -* M *Faidherbe-Chaligny - ✆ 01 53 17 02 44 - www.towarestaurantparis.fr -*

Septime

*closed Mon-Tue and Wed lunch - set menus €65-85.* Close to the much-feted Marché Aligre, Towa is under the stewardship of Japanese chef Shin Okusa. Passionate about French traditions, he delivers the great classics (lamb stew, duck breast pie) as well as sauces, hot pastries, and Escoffier style pies!

65 **Septime – H6** - *80 r. de Charonne - 11e - M Charonne - 01 43 67 38 29 - www.septime-charonne.fr - daily ex. wknd, lunch and eve - set menus €65-110 - booking essential.* Septime symbolizes the very best of the latest generation of Parisian restaurants that are both cool and epicurean. Holder of one star from the Michelin Guide since 2014, Bertrand Grébaut is the type of chef who loves no-frills food and meat so juicy you'll want to mop the plate after. He has also created an offshoot dedicated to seafood, **Clamato**, at more reasonable prices. The coast in Charonne!

# Where to Drink

Relaxing terraces, lively bars, elegant tea rooms, and cool coffee shops: Paris is packed with venues where you can sit back and soak up the capital's famed *joie de vivre*.

For brunch, booking is strongly recommended.

**Find the addresses on our maps using the numbers on the listing (e.g. 1). The coordinates in red (e.g. C2) refer to the detachable map (inside the cover).**

## Île de la Cité and Île Saint-Louis

**Local Map p. 20-21.**

### Tea Room

2 **Berthillon** – **F6** - *29-31 r. St-Louis-en-l'Île - 4e - M Pont-Marie - 01 43 54 31 61 - www.berthillon.fr - Wed-Sun 10am-8pm.* Since 1954, Paris' most famous ice-cream parlor has kept its crown. Alongside the classics, they offer countless more unusual flavors, the likes of lychee, rhubarb, and lemon thyme sorbets and gingerbread or stem ginger ice creams. Tatin ice cream (caramelized apple), iced nougat bars, and granitas are also popular with customers. Enjoy to go or in the small tea room with around 20 covers.



## The Louvre

### Tea Rooms

16 **Smith & Son Café** – **D4** - *248 r. de Rivoli - 1er - M Concorde - 01 53 45 84 40 - www.smithandson.com - 12m-7pm, Sun 12:30pm-6:30pm.* Nestled on the upper floor of the iconic English-language bookstore Smith & Son, dear to Woody Allen's heart, this tea room is like something out of an Agatha Christie novel. It's nigh impossible to truly appreciate your smoked tea without an all-butter shortbread, carrot cake, or porridge. The afternoon tea service features savory specialties such as pork pie and salmon on toast. The view of the Jardin des Tuileries and the memory of George Washington (this is his old apartment!) add to the magic of the place.

8 **Angelina** – **D4** - *226 r. de Rivoli - 1er - M Tuileries - 01 42 60 82 00 - www.angelina-paris.fr - 8am-7pm, Fri-Sun 8:30am-7:30pm.* This gorgeous tea room, with its classic decor, across from the Tuileries, is an institution, feted for its pastries and its creamy (and nutritious) old-fashioned hot chocolate.

### Bars

6 **Le Fumoir** – **E5** - *6 r. de l'Am.-de-Coligny - 1er - M Louvre-Rivoli - 01 42 92 00 24 - www.lefumoir.com - 11am-1pm.* A cozy bar with club chairs and benches, between the Louvre and Saint-Germain-l'Auxerrois. Le Fumoir has more than one string to its bow: it's a café, tea room, library, and top-notch restaurant, too.

## Opéra-Palais-Royal

**Local Map p. 31**

### Tea Room

36 **Aki Artisan Boulanger** – **E4** - *16 r. Ste-Anne - 1er - M Pyramides - ☏ 01 40 15 63 38 - www.akiparis.fr - 7am-8:30pm - closed Sun.* Blending the best of French and Japanese traditions is this bakery's recipe for success. Choose between the matcha green tea Opera cake, bento, or baguette... The flavors will transport you to different places and the selection is as rich as the baker's imagination.

### Bars

79 **Le Café de la Comédie** – **E4** - *157 r. St-Honoré - 1er - M Palais-Royal-Musée-du-Louvre - ☏ 01 42 61 40 01 - 7am-2am.* The ideal place for a sit-down, whatever the time of day, between the Louvre and the Comédie-Française, facing the beautiful Place Colette and its Kiosque des Noctambules sculpture over the métro entrance, the work of Jean-Michel Othoniel.

3 **Hemingway Bar** – **D4** - *38 r. Cambon - 1er - M Opéra or Tuileries - ☏ 01 43 16 33 74 - www.ritzparis.com - 5:30pm-12:30am.* The English bar at the Ritz will immerse you in the hushed and intimate atmosphere that former patrons like Cole Porter, Scott Fitzgerald, and Ernest Hemingway, whose manuscripts and safari trophies adorn the walls, were so fond of. Alas, the British mixologist Colin Field, twice voted "the world's best bartender", has left, but it's in good hands.

45 **Harry's New York Bar** – **D3** - 5 r. Daunou - *2e - M Opéra - ☏ 01 42 61 71 14 - www.harrysbar.fr - 12pm-1am.* Opened in 1911, this iconic bar—the first to sell Coca-Cola in France! — is decorated with the typical wood paneling of a New York bar, transported to Paris during Prohibition. Coco Chanel, Rita Hayworth, and Humphrey Bogart have sipped the anthology of cocktails that put this legendary establishment on the map.

## The Marais and Les Halles

**Local Map p. 38-39.**

### Brunch

1 **L'Ébouillanté** – **F5** - *6 r. des Barres - 4e - M Pont-Marie - ☏ 01 42 74 70 52 - daily ex. Mon 12pm-6pm - brunch on Sun from midday.* Located behind the apse of the Église Saint-Gervais, this tiny tea room boasts one of the prettiest terraces in Paris! On the menu: salads, *brik* (North African stuffed pancakes), pastries, 30 varieties of tea, fruit cocktails, and more.

### Tea Rooms

4 **Mariage Frères** – **F5** - *30 r. du Bourg-Tibourg - 4e - M Hôtel de Ville - ☏ 01 42 72 28 11 - www.mariagefreres.com - 10:30am-7:30pm.* Renowned worldwide, this brand (est. 1854), stocks more than 500 teas sourced from around 30 countries, as well as jams, cookies, chocolate, teacups, and teapots. Entering this tea room is like stepping back to another time.

71 **Lily of the Valley** – **G4** - *12 r. Dupetit-Thouars - 3e - M Temple - ☏ 01 57 40 82 80 - www.lilyofthevalleyparis.com - daily ex. Sun-Mon 10am-6pm.* Beneath the flowery ceiling, you might not be surprised to spot a pink cat perched on a branch.

Lily's is a haven of organic tea made in France, sold loose. Teashop classics are here, although the cheesecakes are low-fat, the cookies made with granola, and the scones packed with cranberries. The friendly proprietor Pauline will steer you in the right direction. The charming tableware adds a lovely old-fashioned touch.

12 **Carette** – **G5** - *25 pl. des Vosges - 4e - M Saint-Paul, Chemin-Vert, or Bastille - ✆ 01 48 87 94 07 - 7:30am-11pm.* The famed pastry and tea room at Place du Trocadéro opened a second venue at Place des Vosges in 2010, with a superb terrace inside the arcade, just along from the Pavillon de la Reine. The hot chocolate is just as delicious and the macarons just as scrumptious.

Martin Amyot/Hoct&Loca

Chocolate fountains at Hoct&Loca.

Short savory menu for lunch, including club sandwiches, salads, and surprise bread.

14 **Comme à Lisbonne** – **F5** - *37 r. du Roi-de-Sicile - 4e - M Saint-Paul - ✆ 07 61 23 42 30 - www.commealisbonne.com - 11am-7pm.* A tea room to nibble on a nice, light *pastel de nata*, warm and sprinkled with cinnamon, just like in Belém!

15 **Hoct&Loca** – **F5** - *99 r. de la Verrerie - 4e - M Châtelet - ✆ 01 45 32 12 09 - www.hoctloca.com - 10am-8pm.* An original concept: a hot chocolate bar with six taps pouring unctuous chocolate sourced from the Caribbean, Venezuela, or Brazil, that you can taste before you choose. Sweet tooths will melt over the gourmet hot chocolate served with surprise sweet treats.

## Bars

22 **Bubar** – **G6** - *3 r. des Tournelles - 4e - M Bastille - ✆ 01 40 29 97 72 - 7pm-2am.* No French varieties on the list of this wine bar, exclusively wines from overseas, all expertly selected by Jean-Loup (the unmissable man with a beard) who runs the show. Take a seat at the bar to chat with the proprietor and tuck into the free tapas served to patrons.

13 **Bisou** – **G4** - *15 bd du Temple - 3e - M Oberkampf or Filles-du-Calvaire - ✆ 01 40 27 82 85 - www.bar-bisou.fr - 5pm-2am.* Located between Place de la République and Cirque d'hiver, this fruit-forward cocktail bar—which clearly likes to see life through rose-tinted spectacles—champions all things organic and seasonal. There's no menu to look at; the options are dictated by the preferences, mood, and imagination of the founder

Nicolas Munoz! Original cocktails decorated with edible flowers are accompanied, if you're feeling peckish, with generous portions of hummus or sardine rillettes.

26 **Le Liquorium** – **F5** - *11 r. St-Denis - 4e - Ⓜ Châtelet - ✆ 09 63 69 02 72 - liquorium.fr - Wed-Sat 6pm-2am.* A speakeasy filled with intriguing curiosities, and hidden away in the basement of The Drink Doctor, Le Liquorium serves delicious cocktails inspired by apothecary recipes of old. Try the Hocus Pocus, cognac with yuzu tea and syrup, egg white, and thyme. The "Spellbook of Homeopathic Incantations" is a chance to concoct your own cocktails, test tubes in hand.

9 **Candelaria** – **G4** - *52 r. de Saintonge - 3e - Ⓜ Filles-du-Calvaire - ✆ 09 50 84 19 67 - www.candelaria-paris.com - 6pm-2am.* This cocktail bar is one of the most feted in the capital. You can't tell from the outside: you need to walk across a bright taqueria that hardly appeals (although the tacos do) and through the door at the back: on the other side, the clientele sit in the softly lit interior to religiously sip the boldly creative cocktails.

10 **Le Mary Celeste** – **G4** - *1 r. Commines - 3e - Ⓜ Filles-du-Calvaire - www.lemaryceleste.com - 12pm-2:30pm, 6pm-2am, wknd 12pm-2am.* A super-hip bar in the top end of the Marais, so expect a throng. It's busy and pricey, but the people-watching and drinks are worth the effort! Choose from wine, draft beer, or the cocktails, some mixed with mezcal. The crowd is international, just like the menu that's served for lunch and dinner.

❤ 17 **Little Red Door** – **G4** - *60 r. Charlot - 3e - Ⓜ Filles-du-Calvaire - ✆ 01 42 71 19 32 - www.lrdparis.com - 5pm-11pm.* This cocktail bar, which ranked five in the "World's 50 Best Bars" in 2022, lies behind, as you might have guessed, a little red door. It's not a small reference. And it's easy to see why it's so successful, amidst the sounds of jazz and the solid concoctions inspired by architectural styles. For example, the "Art Deco" cocktail composed of Bulleit Rye whisky, Merlet cognac, fermented dates, and violet tea.

29 **Le Tout-Paris** – **E5** - *Hôtel Cheval Blanc Paris (7th floor). 8 quai du Louvre - 1er - Ⓜ Pont-Neuf - ✆ 01 79 35 50 22 - www.chevalblanc.com - 7am-1am - booking advised.* At the top of the La Samaritaine department store, Tout-Paris confidently draws in "All of Paris" courtesy of its cascading terraces with plunging views of the Seine and one of the capital's most iconic panoramas, from Notre-Dame to the Eiffel Tower! Open for breakfast (brunch on Sunday), dining, or cocktails. Expensive but unforgettable!

## Wine Bars

7 **Barav** – **G4** - *6 r. Charles-François-Dupuis - 3e - Ⓜ Temple - ✆ 01 48 04 57 59 - www.lebarav.fr - Tue-Sat 5pm-11:30pm.* An authentic wine bar, its wines accompanied by carefully selected market produce, all served in a room with true Parisian bistro spirit.

73 **La Belle Hortense** – **F5** - *31 r. Vieille-du-Temple - 4e - Ⓜ Saint-Paul - ✆ 01 48 04 71 60 - www.cafeine.com/belle-hortense - daily ex. Mon-Tue 5:30pm-2am.* In the mood for a finely selected glass of wine? Plus a good book? La Belle Hortense will kill two birds with one stone. This unique establishment, both wine bar and

bookstore, is perfect for lovers of fine wines, literature, and a quiet spot to enjoy them.

## Latin Quarter

**Local Map p. 48-49.**

### Tea Rooms

18 **The Tea Caddy** – **E6** - *14 r. St-Julien-le-Pauvre - 5e - M Cluny-la-Sorbonne - ✆ 01 43 54 15 56 - www.the-tea-caddy.com - 11am-7pm (wknd 7:30pm).* An institution that has remained unchanged since 1928, this cozy tea parlor keeps the English tea tradition alive. The lovely proprietor happily supplies paper and pencils to keep children entertained and ensure customers can enjoy their tea and light bites in peace and quiet. Mouthwatering pies, scones, muffins, and homemade tarts.



87 **Odette** – **E6** - *77 r. Galande - 5e - M Cluny-la-Sorbonne - ✆ 01 43 26 13 06 - www.odette-paris.com - 12pm-7:45pm (wknd 10am).* A great place to enjoy cream puffs in the small vintage dining room upstairs, or to go.

### Bars

19 **Le Castor Club** – **E6** - *14 r. Hautefeuille - 6e - M Odéon - ✆ 09 50 64 99 38 - 7pm-2am (Thu-Sat 4am - closed Sun-Mon.* Where's the forest? Beside the stuffed beaver the place is named for, the hunting lodge vibes and country music on a loop are more reminiscent of a speakeasy from the Prohibition era. For all that, the Castor Club is a stylish and laidback venue, and the cocktails are well made. The basement opens for dancing at the weekend.

20 **The Bombardier** – **F7** - *2 pl. du Panthéon - 5e - M Cardinal-Lemoine - ✆ 01 43 54 79 22 - www.bombardierpub.fr - 4pm-2am, wknd 11:30am-2am.* Fish and chips in the Latin Quarter? Well, what else do you expect at this typically English pub! Calm and collected during the week, it can get pleasantly rowdy at the weekend thanks to the good selection of beers and matches shown on the big screen. Come early, the terrace can get rammed in summer.

### Legendary Cafés

**Saint-Germain-des-Prés –** Follow in the footsteps of the existentialists of the 1950s, Sartre, and Simone de Beauvoir! Destination Café de Flore, Les Deux Magots, and Brasserie Lipp (p. 58).

**Montparnasse –** The hotspots of Montparnasse during the interwar period, where artists and intellectuals would gather, have since become high-end brasseries, and the occasional tourist trap, but nevertheless it's always a quintessentially Parisian experience to sit, if only for a coffee, amidst their Belle Époque chandeliers, gigantic mirrors, and red-leather benches. The quartet comprises La Coupole, Le Dôme, La Rotonde, and Le Sélect (p. 63).

Not forgetting: La Closerie des Lilas, 171 bd du Montparnasse - 6e - ✆ 01 40 51 34 50 - www.closeriedeslilas.fr - 12pm-2:25pm, 7pm-10:15pm.

**21 Café de la nouvelle mairie** – **E7** - *19 r. des Fossés-St-Jacques - 5e - M Luxembourg - ✆ 01 44 07 04 41 - 8am-12am - closed wknd.* A place beloved among Parisians—and it's easy to see why! Natural wines (sulfite gets bad press here) wash down copious dishes: hand-chopped Chavassieux sausage on crushed potatoes or chicken liver terrine, enjoyed at the zinc bar. When the weather warms up, the terrace draws the crowds.

### Wine Bar

**74 Les Pipos** – **F7** - *2 r. de l'École-Polytechnique - 5e - ✆ 01 43 54 11 40 - 9am-1am - closed Sun.* Vintage Paris is in full swing here! Les Pipos, in the heart of the university district, continues to attract students on the terrace flanking the delightful Place Larue. Traditional cuisine on the menu.

## Saint-Germain-des-Prés-Montparnasse

**Local Map p. 57.**

### Tea Room

**30 Bread & Roses** – **D7** - *62 r. Madame - 6e - M Rennes - ✆ 01 42 22 06 06 - www.breadandroses.fr - Tue-Fri 10am-7pm (Sat 9am, Sun 9:30am).* Tea room (with terrace), but also a bakery (delicious breads), cake shop, fine deli, and restaurant. A wide variety of baked goods: scones, muffins, cheesecake, carrot cake, rum baba, crumble, millefeuilles, and fruit cakes.

### Bars

**77 Le Bar du Marché** – **E6** - *75 r. de Seine - 6e - M Odéon or Saint-Germain-des-Prés - ✆ 01 43 26 55 15 - 8am-2am.* The "BDM" is the best place to soak up the vibrant atmosphere of Saint-German-des-Près. Take a seat on the heated terrace to enjoy your glass of vino accompanied by a hot dog smothered in grated cheese, an omelet, or a thick slice of sourdough bread topped with rillettes. Prices on the high side, but worth it for this highly Parisian experience.

❤ **25 La Palette** – **E5** - *43 r. de Seine - 6e - M Mabillon - ✆ 01 43 26 68 15 - www.lapalette-paris.com - 8am-2pm (Sun 10am).* An old-fashioned café still "overrun" by the Fine Arts students from next door. Some of them, the oldest, have even left paintings on the walls of the historic dining room, which is worth checking out! The shaded terrace, very pleasant in summer, is often busy.

**28 Chez Georges** – **D6** - *11 r. des Canettes - 6e - M Mabillon - ✆ 01 43 26 79 15 - 6pm-2am (Sun-Mon 1am).* This one of Paris' most legendary bars has its original bar and photos on the wall that are now vintage. Perfect for a glass of wine with friends.

**31 Le Smoke** – **D7** - *29 r. Delambre - 14e - M Edgar-Quinet - ✆ 01 43 20 61 73 - www.le-smoke.fr - 12pm-2am (Sat 5pm) - closed Sun.* In Montparnasse, if you're not drawn to the big, iconic cafés, head to Le Smoke where it's happy hour every day from 2:30pm to 7:30pm (Sat. 5pm-9pm). Food menu for lunch or dinner. It's always crowded, the ambience nice and jazzy.

Ker Beer.

### Beer Bar

(27) **Ker Beer** – **D8** - *10 r. Vandamme - 14e* - Ⓜ *Montparnasse* - ✆ *01 42 84 43 22* - *www.kerbeer.bzh* - *5pm-1:30am.* In the heart of a pocket of Montparnasse low on places to go, this co-op bar champions the craft of Breton microbreweries (15 draft beers and about 50 bottled varieties). Excellent charcuterie boards and delicious seafood tapas for when hunger strikes.

### Wine Bar

(76) **Freddy's** – **E6** - *54 r. de Seine - 6e* - Ⓜ *Saint-Germain-des-Prés* - *12pm-12am.* This bar, which doesn't have proper tables or even a phone number (it does have a Facebook page!), focuses on its core business: wine and its exquisite menu. A place to enjoy excellent wines and tasty tapas, the likes of crispy beef and seared white tuna.

## Invalides-Eiffel Tower

### Bars

(78) **Café Central** – **B5** - *40 r. Cler - 7e* - Ⓜ *École-Militaire* - ✆ *01 47 05 00 53* - *www.lecentral-paris.com* - *7am-1am.* Nestled along the tranquil, pedestrianized Rue Cler, Café Central looks the kind of place that might draw the well-to-do kids of the swanky 7e arr. With its New York-style interior and vast terrace, the ambience nonetheless manages to stay nice and casual.

## Grand Hotels for Afternoon Tea

5 **Le Bristol** – **C3** – *112 r. du Faubourg-St-Honoré - 8e - M Miromesnil - 01 53 43 43 00 - www.oetkercollection.com - 3pm-6pm - €60.* In the Jardin Français, the cherubs on the "Fountain of Love" are the spectators to your summer teatime that comes with savory morsels, scones, muffins, and exquisite petits fours by head pastry chef Pascal Hainigue.

11 **Le Ritz** – **D3** – *15 pl. Vendôme - 1er - M Opéra - 01 43 16 33 74 - www.ritzparis.com - 2pm-6pm - €68-103.* In the Salon Proust at the Ritz, cabinets of vintage books and the roaring fireplace make a delightful setting for afternoon tea. François Perret, honored in 2019 as the "best restaurant pastry chef in the world", excels in the craft of baking and will regale you with his sponge fingers, Florentine biscuits, and tuile cigar rolls. All presented on beautiful white Limoges porcelain.

92 **Le Shangri-La** – **A4** – *10 av. d'Iéna - 16e - M Iéna - 01 53 67 19 91 - www.shangri-la.com - afternoon tea - wknd 3pm-6pm - €68.* Almond-orange calissons, chestnut-blackcurrant Mont Blancs, chocolate tartlets, cookies, financier almond cakes, and shortbread are just some of the suggestions on the 100% vegan afternoon tea menu at restaurant La Bauhinia.

## Champs-Elysées and Western Paris

### Tea Room

❤ 35 **Le Bar @ Plaza Athénée** – **B4** - *25 av. Montaigne - 8e - M Alma-Marceau - 01 53 67 66 65 - www.dorchestercollection.com - 6pm-12:30am (Thu-Sat 2am).* In the beautifully elegant La Galerie, head pastry chef Angelo Musa, former "Best Craftsman of France" and world pastry champion, presents his creations, including the delectable "100% Vanilla".

## Montmartre-Pigalle

**Local Map p. 90-91.**

### Bars

**Comestibles et Marchands de vins** – **Off map by E1** - *65 r. du Mont-Cenis - 18e - M Jules-Joffrin - 01 73 70 56 28 - www.cmv18.com - 12pm-2pm, 6pm-10pm, wknd 12pm-10pm.* Wine cellar, tapas bar, restaurant, and fine deli, this eclectic establishment is the brainchild of Sébastien Arnaud, a foodie passionate about French produce. Ospital charcuterie, Belle-Iloise canned fish, fillet of duck, beef bourguignon, and elevated sandwiches are all on the menu.

90 **Marlusse et Lapin** – **E1** - *14 r. Germain-Pilon - 18e - M Pigalle - 01 42 59 17 97 - daily ex. Sun 6pm-2am.* The two bartenders, Marlusse and Lapin, know how to have a good time. Here, happy hour kicks off at 4pm, and fans of "real" beer are well catered for: Chouffe, Karmeliet, and other Delirium brews make up the list paired with an excellent selection of cocktails. Don't miss the room at the back, which will transport you to another time.

93 **Francis Labutte** – **Map p. 90-91** - 122 r. Caulaincourt - *18e* - Ⓜ *Lamarck-Caulaincourt* - ✆ *01 42 23 58 26* - *8am-2am (Sun 9am).* A neighborhood institution, frequented by both locals and the students of the Femis (the film and TV school) next door. From breakfast to dinner, simple fare is served with a smile in an atmosphere boasting just the right amount of cool. A staircase that is pure Montmartre leads down to a terrace that gets busy when the sun is out.

38 **Le Progrès** – **E1** - *7 r. des Trois Frères* - *18e* - Ⓜ *Anvers* - ✆ *01 42 64 07 37* - *9am-2am.* This establishment may have preserved its vintage decor, but its clientele is unmistakably up with the times. Expect cooking like grammy used to make and drinks on the terrace at one of the most attractive intersections in the neighborhood.



39 **Le Sans-Souci** – **E2** - *65 r. Jean-Baptiste-Pigalle* - *9e* - Ⓜ *Pigalle* - ✆ *01 53 16 17 04* - *daily ex. Sun-Mon 11am-2am.* This institution in South Pigalle is the HQ of the local party crowd. Its understated interior, calm during the day, attracts a hip and easy-going throng at night courtesy of the electro-rock sounds spun by the DJ. Rowdy but friendly. At the end of Rue Victor-Massé, on the right, Le Mansart is in the same group and offers similar vibes, albeit a fraction "chicer".

40 **Le Dirty Dick** – **E2** - *10 r. Frochot* - *9e* - Ⓜ *Pigalle* - ✆ *01 48 78 74 58* - *6pm-2am (Fri-Sat 3am).* This former hostess bar is now a hip venue in South Pigalle, one of Paris' newest fashionable neighborhoods. Amidst colorful, tiki vibes, Le Dirty Dick offers cocktails inspired by the tropics of Polynesia, Hawaii, or Mexico using fresh juices and made-in-house pre-mixes, some served in coconuts or shells. There's a lot going on!

❤ **La REcyclerie** – **Off map by E1** - *83 bd Ornano* - *18e* - Ⓜ *Porte de Clignancourt* - ✆ *01 42 57 58 49* - *www.larecyclerie.com* - *12pm-12am, Fri 8am-2am, Sat 11pm-2am, Sun 11am-10pm.* There's no other venue in Paris that comes anywhere close to the REcyclerie as far as originality goes! Occupying the former Ornano train station, this café-bar has taken over the main concourse and the open-air terraces that border the disused tracks of the old inner-circle railroad. Customers can even borrow tools to do repairs and upcycling. The concept is 100% eco-friendly, including a vegetable garden, a chicken coop, and beehives. It's worth dropping in, if only to support this worthy initiative!

### Beer Bar

33 **La Brasserie Fondamentale** – **E1** - *6 r. André Antoine* - *18e* - Ⓜ *Pigalle* - ✆ *09 72 14 27 63* - *www.lbf-biere.fr* - *6pm-2am (Mon 12am, Tue 1am), Fri 5pm-2am, Sat 4pm-2am (Sun 11pm).* Timber and metal barrels clearly set the tone of this Parisian brew pub. At the circular bar, 15 top-quality French craft beers are available on tap. The service is friendly and the staff take real pleasure in introducing you to their brews in this taproom where the hop is king. The more creative can join in a beer-making workshop.

## Canal St-Martin-La Villette and around

### Bars

51 **Le Floréal** – **G3** - *150 av. Parmentier and 73 r. du Fg-du-Temple* - *10e* - Ⓜ *Goncourt* - ✆ *01 40 18 46 79* - *www.*

*lefloreal.com - 8am-2am (Sun 12am).* This former bar-tobacconist's has become one of the hottest spots in the neighborhood. The decor is pure 1950-1960s, with formica tables, chairs upholstered in green or red leatherette, and, out front, a mosaic in the same vibrant tones.

52 **Le Comptoir Général** – **G3** - *84 quai de Jemmapes - 10e - M République - ✆ 01 44 88 24 48 - lecomptoirgeneral.com - 6pm-1am, Thu-Fri 6pm-2am, Sat 11am-2am, Sun 11am-1am - closed Mon* Is it a pirates' lair or treasure island? A mix of both! This immense venue, styled like a Hollywood movie set, is without contest Paris' most surprising cocktail bar. Also a seafood restaurant and fine grocery store. The place is rammed during the weekend brunch!

❤ 43 **Gravity Bar** – **G3** - *44 r. des Vinaigriers - M Château-d'Eau or Gare de l'Est - ✆ 06 98 54 92 49 - Tue-Sat 6pm-2am.* Gravity Bar combines the art of mixology and high-end snacking in a thoughtful interior where wood and concrete ooze Scandi minimalist vibes. The drinks are categorized by desired effect: Disorientation, Weightlessness, Cold Sweats... You get the picture. From the kitchen, expect duck tataki with fig and pistachio; salmon "bonbons" with carrot pancakes; poached pear with fresh goat cheese... Delightful.

❤ 54 **Le Syndicat Bar** – **F3** - *51 r. du Faubourg-St-Denis - 10e - M Château-d'Eau - www.syndicatcocktailclub.com - 6pm-2am.* Don't let the signs of civil unrest out front put you off! Inside, the marble bar and metallic curtains create a very different image. More in keeping

Cyrille George Jerusalmi/Comptoir Général

Le Comptoir Général.

with this venue that describes itself as the "Organization for the Defense of French Spirits", promoting 100% French beverages, always with style. Old school hip-hop is the soundtrack to your cocktail.

56 **Lavomatic** – **G4** - *30 r. René-Boulanger - 10e - M République - www.lavomatic.paris - 6pm-1am, Thu-Sat 6pm-2am - closed Sun-Mon.* It's one of the most secret bars in Paris, located as it is behind an inconspicuous laundromat. Once inside, look for the hidden button to discover a bar with pop decor, stylishly tatty walls, plush cushions, and even a couple of swings to sit on. Serves imaginative cocktails made with spices, fruit, and vegetables, like the "DetoxOmatic" consisting of beetroot, blackcurrant,

gin, citrus, and artichoke liqueur.

23 **L'Ours Bar** – **F2** - *8 r. de Paradis - 10e - M Château-d'Eau or Gare de l'Est - 01 45 23 40 06 - 6pm-1am, Wed-Sat 6pm-2am - closed Sun.* Located in a neighborhood that the after-dark crowd have taken by storm. The cocktails at L'Ours are classic or inventive, such as the Point Vert (Venezuelan rum, peach liqueur, lime, basil, and egg white) or the Gusano (mezcal, red Martini, Campari, agave syrup, and chocolate bitters). Special mention goes to the Jardin Anglais and its cucumber garnish! A selection of cheese or charcuterie boards to keep patrons going.

64 **25° Est** – **G1** - *10 pl. de la Bataille-de-Stalingrad - M Jaurès or Stalingrad - 09 53 27 68 16 - daily ex. Mon 3pm-2am.* One of the prettiest terraces in Paris. Set on the edges of the canal, you can sip a glass practically touching water in amidst a fun and lively crowd. Here, the "Joyful Hours" start at 3pm, and bartenders churn out Cuba Libre, Pina Colada, Long Island, and White Russian cocktails like nobody's business. Food options include salmon tartare, deep-fried goat cheese, and burgers.



55 **Point Éphémère** – **G2** - *200 quai de Valmy - 10e - M Jaurès - 01 40 34 02 48 - www.pointephemere.org - 12pm-2am, Mon-Tue 5pm-2am.* This venue puts on exhibitions, concerts, and performances, hosts artists, and runs a bar and restaurant which you can enjoy in the hall with large picture windows or on the pleasant terrace bordering the Canal Saint-Martin. The rooftop is also open on sunny days from June to September.

94 **Rosa Bonheur** – **H2** - *Parc des Buttes Chaumont, enter from Rue Botzaris - 19e - M Botzaris - 01 71 60 29 01 - www.rosabonheur.fr - Thu-Sun 12pm-1am.* Nestled in idyllic, green surrounds, this former guinguette offers a delightful spot for a breather in the heart of the Parc des Buttes-Chaumont. In the evening, electro-pop music gets the place pumping! After taking over a barge moored opposite the Pont Alexandre-III *(see "Nightlife", p. 149)*, the Rosa Bonheur family has grown even more: since 2021, its famed guinguette spirit is breathing new life into the Chalet de la Porte Jaune, in the thick of the Bois de Vincennes.

95 **Péniche Antipode** – **H1** - *across from 55 quai de Seine - 19e - M Jaurès - 01 42 03 39 07 - www.penicheantipode.fr - 5:30pm-2am, wknd 10am-2am. Between mid-July and August, the barge moves to Bobigny (shuttle provided).* Master mariner Kevin is at the helm of this barge moored in the lake at La Villette. All products are fair trade and, come sunny days, service is available on the deck. Also on the program: children's shows, concerts, and other events.

83 **Chez Jeannette** – **F3** - *47 r. du Faubourg-St-Denis - 10e - M Châteaud'Eau - 01 47 70 30 89 - 8am-2am (Sun 9am).* One of Paris' hippest hotspots. Chez Jeannette exudes easy charm, with its neon lights and old-school formica bar. For a coffee, beer, or mojito, the venue caters to every time of day. Food menu, too.

### Beer Bar

❤ 96 **Paname Brewing Company** – **H1** - *41 bis quai de la Loire - 19e - M Crimée - ✆ 01 40 36 43 55 - www.panamebrewingcompany.com - 10am-1am.* A craft beer lover's paradise on the canalside. The beers here may have funny names (a "Monkey in Winter", anyone?), but they're no less thirst-quenching, especially when you sip them right on the water. This next-generation brewery offers a sophisticated selection of craft beers in a gorgeous setting.

## Bastille and Eastern Paris

### Bars

60 **Combat** – **H3** - *63 r. de Belleville - 19e - M Pyrénées or Belleville - ✆ 09 80 84 78 60 - 6pm-2am (Sun 12am).* The three women at the helm certainly pack a punch. Front of house, Elena Schmitt and Margot Lecarpentier (previously at Experimental). Mixing the cocktails, Élise Drouet with her fiendishly original concoctions, like the 14130 (calvados, daikon leaves, gum arabic syrup, lime juice) or the Quatresse, Laphroaig mixed with Suze, lime, and sage. Served with a smile, in a bright interior in the heights of Belleville.

50 **Le Perchoir** – **H4** - *14 r. Crespin-du-Gast - 11e - M Ménilmontant - ✆ 01 83 62 64 22 - leperchoir.fr - Wed-Sat 6pm-2am.* One of Paris' most popular rooftop bars (Romain Duris is a regular). Offers amazing views of Paris, but the food is worth a visit, too: the lobster sandwich, for instance, is divine.

**Les Chaises** – **Off map by H4** - *33 r. de la Chine - 20e - M Pelleport - ✆ 09 51 65 08 24 - 12pm-2:30pm, 6pm-2am, Sat 6pm-2am - closed Sun.* No tourists at this très Parisian neighborhood bar where you can drink Gallia, a craft beer brewed in Paris. The clientele are invariably local, and come to snack on charcuterie and cheese boards while enjoying the excellent selection of wines, beers, and cocktails. You can just as easily find them catching a concert, playing cards, or attending a writing workshop.

66 **L'Alimentation Générale** – **H4** - *64 r. Jean-Pierre-Timbaud - 11e - M Parmentier - ✆ 01 43 55 42 50 - www.alimentation-generale.net - 7pm-2am (Fri-Sat 5am) - closed Sun-Tue - admission varies by what's on.* It's like being in a grocery store, except the shelves are stacked with world music! Low prices and high quality, the occasional concerts, and something to eat... it's fiesta time! Fun and eclectic crowd.

### Beer Bar

49 **La Fine Mousse** – **H4** - *6 av. Jean-Aicard - 11e - M Rue-St-Maur - ✆ 01 48 06 40 94 - www.lafinemousse.fr - from 5pm.* In the Oberkampf district, the beer flows, of course, so long as it's craft, whether brewed in France or further afield. A paradise for beer aficionados with a selection of 20 draft varieties, plus a decent wine list. Workshops are held to teach the art of beer tasting.

### Wine Bars

57 **Les Caves de Prague** - **H6** - *8 r. de Prague – 12e - M Ledru-Rollin - ✆ 01 72 68 07 36 - www.cavesdeprague.fr -*

*Tue-Sat 4pm-11pm.* The alchemy of the place is impossible to explain. Down a quiet street, this wine shop with its bright, light wood interior is a rare find. Thomas, a wine merchant interested in his patrons, will find just the right bottle for your palate, without trying to peddle the most exorbitantly priced bottles, which makes a welcome change. Excellent charcuterie boards. In summer, there's usually a wait for the few tables on the terrace. Jostle your way to the front if you have to!

### Music Bars

69 **Le Vieux Belleville – H3** - *12 r. des Envierges - 20e - M Pyrénées - ✆ 01 44 62 92 66 - www.le-vieux-belleville.com - Mon-Fri 11am-3pm, Tue and Thu-Sat 8pm-2am.* This neighborhood bistro is nice and friendly. In the evening, classic songs from old Paris do the rounds, while the ad hoc choir formed by the patrons will have you bopping and singing along in no time.

**La Maroquinerie – Off map by H3** - *23 r. Boyer - 20e - M Ménilmontant - ✆ 01 40 33 35 05 - www.lamaroquinerie.fr - rest.: concert evenings 7pm-11pm.* A bar, restaurant, and exhibition space, but above all a concert venue, La Maroquinerie puts on an eclectic lineup where contemporary music gets top-billing. Cozy terrace to unwind and enjoy a night cap.

The Parisian café, as iconic as the Eiffel Tower.

# Shopping

**Opening Hours**: Most stores are open from 10am to 7pm, and closed on Sundays, with the exception of the department stores and retail outlets in the international tourist areas (p. 158).

**Sales**: Since January 2020, the winter and summer sales officially last four weeks, with reductions of up to 70%.

*Locate the main shopping districts on the map on p. 140-141.*

## Everyday Shopping

**Les Halles and Rue de Rivoli:** this is the center of ready-to-wear where all leading international fashion brands have an outlet, on Rue de Rivoli and/or in and around the **Forum des Halles**, the underground shopping mall. Plenty of bargain souvenir shops in the vicinity, too.
On the Left Bank, **Rue de Rennes** and its neighboring streets are home to stores for fashion, interior decor, music, and books, among others. Nearby, on **Rue Saint-Placide, Rue du Cherche-Midi, and Rue d'Alésia**, you'll find big brand outlet stores and bargain basements, with discounts of up to 50%.

## Luxury Boutiques

On **Rue du Faubourg-Saint-Honoré,** luxury boutiques (haute couture, gems, and jewelry around Place Vendôme) mingle with concept stores. Top fashion designers all have a boutique on **Avenue Montaigne** (Chanel, Dior, etc.) or **Avenue George-V** (Hermès, Givenchy), and, increasingly so, in the **Marais**. On the Left Bank, Saint-Germain-des-Prés is the epicenter of luxury.

## Hip Stores

**The Marais**: the designer stores and art galleries that abound in the neighborhood draw fashion-conscious tourists and Parisians.
If you love vintage fashion, secondhand goods, and design, head to the **Abbesses** district in Montmartre, or **Rue de Charonne**, a hub of young designers and quirky independent stores.
For a timeless shopping experience, potter about the **covered passages** (Galerie Vivienne, Passage Verdeau), around the Grands Boulevards.

## Left Bank Shopping

Saint-Germain-des-Prés: luxury prêt-à-porter boutiques on Boulevard St-Germain have taken over the bookstores. Countless antique shops line Quai Voltaire and Rue du Bac, while art galleries abound along Rue de Seine, Rue Guénégaud, Rue des Beaux-Arts, and around.

## Department Stores

**Le Bon Marché**, the oldest of Paris' department stores, and today the most luxurious, is located at Sèvres-Babylone (7e). Don't leave without perusing the famous Grande Épicerie!

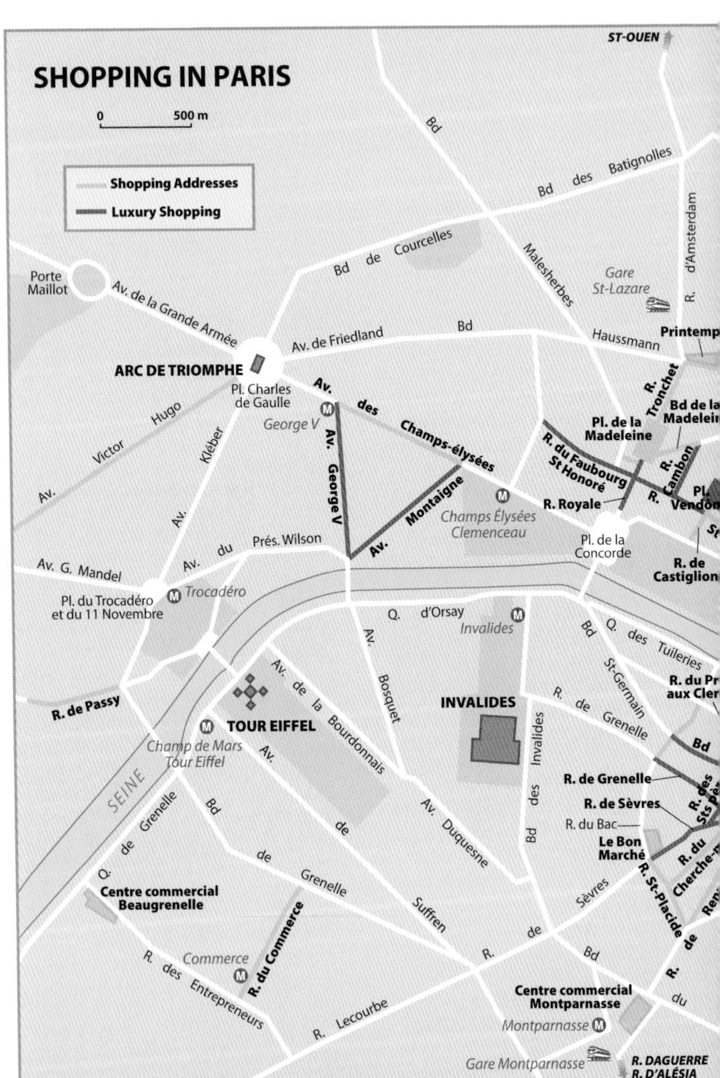
SHOPPING IN PARIS
0 500 m
Shopping Addresses
Luxury Shopping
ST-OUEN
Bd des Batignolles
Bd de Courcelles
Bd Malesherbes
R. d'Amsterdam
Gare St-Lazare
Porte Maillot
Av. de la Grande Armée
Av. de Friedland
Bd Haussmann
Printemps
ARC DE TRIOMPHE
Pl. Charles de Gaulle
Av. des Champs-élysées
George V
Av. George V
Av. Montaigne
Av. Victor Hugo
Av. Kléber
R. Tronchet
Bd de la Madeleine
Pl. de la Madeleine
R. du Faubourg St Honoré
R. Cambon
R. Royale
Champs Élysées Clemenceau
Pl. de la Concorde
R. de Castiglione
Av. du Prés. Wilson
Av. G. Mandel
Pl. du Trocadéro et du 11 Novembre
Trocadéro
Q. d'Orsay
Invalides
Av. Bosquet
Q. des Tuileries
Bd St-Germain
R. du Pré aux Clercs
R. de Passy
TOUR EIFFEL
INVALIDES
R. de Grenelle
Champ de Mars Tour Eiffel
Av. de la Bourdonnais
Bd des Invalides
R. de Grenelle
R. de Sèvres
R. du Bac
Le Bon Marché
R. des Sts Pères
R. du Cherche-Midi
SEINE
Q. de Grenelle
Bd de Grenelle
Av. de Suffren
Av. Duquesne
R. St-Placide
Centre commercial Beaugrenelle
R. du Commerce
R. de Sèvres
Bd du
Commerce
R. des Entrepreneurs
R. Lecourbe
Centre commercial Montparnasse
Montparnasse
Gare Montparnasse
R. DAGUERRE
R. D'ALÉSIA

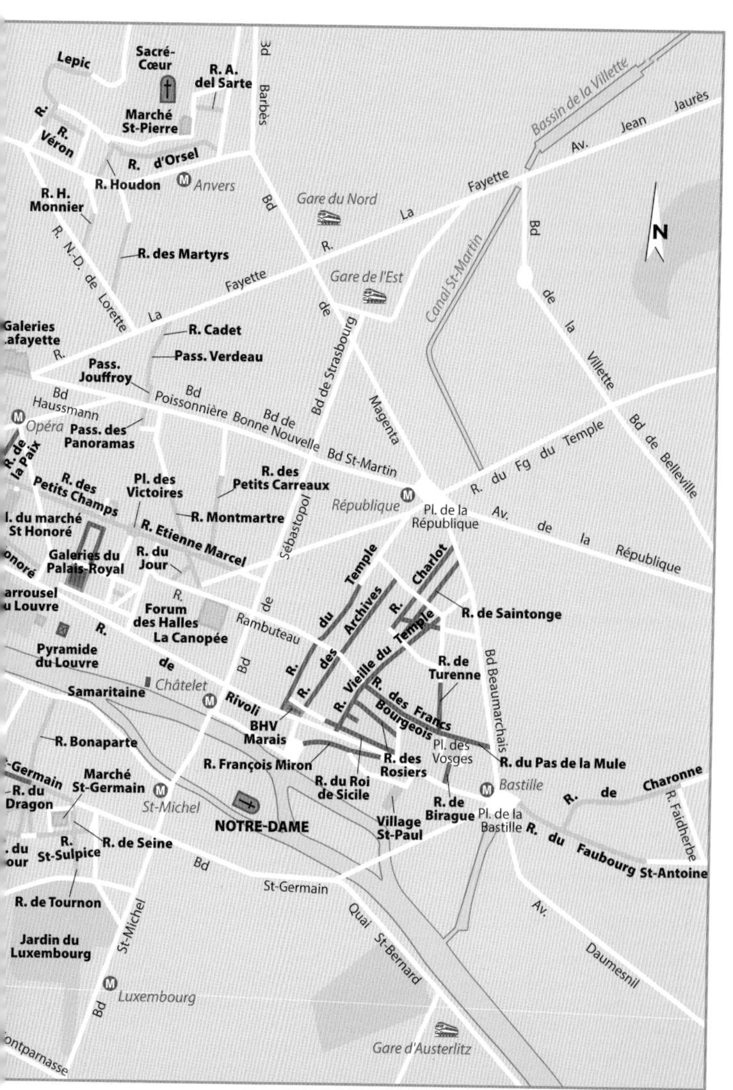

Lepic
Sacré-Cœur
R. A. del Sarte
Marché St-Pierre
R. Véron
R. d'Orsel
R. Houdon
Anvers
R. H. Monnier
R. N.-D. de Lorette
R. des Martyrs
Bd Barbès
Gare du Nord
Gare de l'Est
R. La Fayette
Av. Jean Jaurès
Bassin de la Villette
Canal St-Martin
Bd de la Villette
N
Galeries Lafayette
R. Cadet
Pass. Verdeau
Pass. Jouffroy
Bd Haussmann
Bd Poissonnière
Bd de Bonne Nouvelle
Bd St-Martin
Bd de Strasbourg
Bd Magenta
Opéra
Pass. des Panoramas
R. de la Paix
R. des Petits Champs
Pl. des Victoires
R. des Petits Carreaux
R. Montmartre
République
Pl. de la République
R. du Fg du Temple
Av. de la République
Bd de Belleville
R. Etienne Marcel
R. du Jour
Galeries du Palais-Royal
Bd de Sébastopol
R. du Temple
R. des Archives
R. Charlot
R. de Saintonge
R. Vieille du Temple
R. Rambuteau
Forum des Halles
La Canopée
Pyramide du Louvre
R. de Rivoli
Châtelet
Samaritaine
R. de Turenne
Bd Beaumarchais
R. des Francs Bourgeois
BHV Marais
Pl. des Vosges
R. du Pas de la Mule
R. Bonaparte
R. François Miron
R. des Rosiers
R. du Roi de Sicile
Marché St-Germain
St-Michel
NOTRE-DAME
Village St-Paul
R. de Birague
Pl. de la Bastille
Bastille
R. de Charonne
R. Faidherbe
R. du Faubourg St-Antoine
R. du Dragon
R. St-Sulpice
R. de Seine
Bd St-Germain
R. de Tournon
Jardin du Luxembourg
Bd St-Michel
Luxembourg
Quai St-Bernard
Av. Daumesnil
Gare d'Austerlitz

More touristy but no less enchanting, **Printemps** and **Galeries Lafayette**, on **Boulevard Haussmann** (9e), attract thousands of shoppers every day. From ready-to-wear to the stars of haute couture, you'll be spoiled for choice!
Opened in 1856, the **BHV Marais** (4e) still stocks practically everything under the sun (the basement dedicated to home improvements is legendary). Right behind it, on Rue de la Verrerie, BHV L'Homme is five floors of menswear under one roof.
Finally, La **Samaritaine** (1er) is front-page news again: the historic brand by Pont-Neuf reopened in 2021 after a staggering 15 years of renovations. The concept store is amazing!

## Favorite Addresses



**Find the addresses on our maps using the numbers on the listing (e.g. ①). The coordinates in red (e.g. C2) refer to the detachable map (inside the cover).**

### Quirky

① **Deyrolle** – **D5** - *46 r. du Bac - 7e - Ⓜ Rue du Bac - ✆ 01 42 22 30 07 - www.deyrolle.com - closed Sun.* Deyrolle is a world of its own. From stuffed prairie animals to a plethora of butterflies and other pinned insects, this place sets the benchmark for taxidermy and entomology. Established in 1831, this cabinet of curiosities will keep you entertained for hours!

### Home Decor and Stationery

② **Fleux** – **F5** - *39 and 52 r. Ste-Croix-de-la-Bretonnerie - 4e - Ⓜ Hôtel-de-Ville - ✆ 01 53 00 93 30 - www.fleux.com - daily.* A temple of stylish interiors, from kitchen gadgets to designer furniture by way of Jielde lamps and scented candles, Fleux stocks a well curated selection of the unusual and the kitsch.
⑭ **Calligrane** – **F5** - *6 r. du Pont-Louis-Philippe - 4e - Ⓜ Pont-Marie - ✆ 01 48 04 09 00 - www.calligrane.fr - closed Sun-Mon.* This art and creative stationery emporium is well known by artists for its wide selection of papers: rare, made of plant fibers, from Japan, Nepal, and much more, in lots of different sizes. Notebooks and small leather goods complete the tempting offering.

### Beauty

③ **Buly 1803** – **E5** - *6 r. Bonaparte - 6e - Ⓜ Saint-Germain-des-Prés - ✆ 01 43 29 02 50 - www.buly1803.com - closed Sun.* This boutique resembling a 17th-century pharmacy looks like an original, but you'd be wrong. In this universe of walnut, marble, and terracotta, the products are all simple and natural. From soaps to creams, from rose water to antique oil, it will be hard to leave empty handed. A second address is at the top of the Marais, at 45 Rue de Saintonge.

### Foodie Destinations

④ **Épicerie Izraël** – **F5** - *30 r. François-Miron - 4e - Ⓜ Saint-Paul - ✆ 01 42 72 66 23 - closed Sun-Mon.* Stepping inside the Épicerie Izraël is akin to entering Ali Baba's cave. For over 50 years, this store has been supplying Parisians who love food from around the world with exotic spices and products sourced from the four corners of the globe.
⑤ **Maison Plisson** – **G5** - *93 bd Beaumarchais - 3e - Ⓜ Saint-Sébastien-Froissart - ✆ 01 71 18*

**Puces de Saint-Ouen**

There aren't enough hours in the day to cover this open-air flea market! While every style and genre of secondhand or antique item imaginable is represented, the prices can be on the high side... All around, vintage clothing and bric-a-brac are touted (sometimes without a license) for a song in a fun and vibrant atmosphere.
Ⓜ Porte-de-Clignancourt (Line 4) - www.pucesdeparissaintouen.com - Fri 8am-12pm, wknd 10am-6pm, Mon 11am-5pm.

*19 09 - www.lamaisonplisson.com - daily.* This new-generation grocery store revolves around organic produce, short food supply chains, and healthy eating. From the bakery to the meat counter to the fruit and vegetables, you'll crave everything in sight. In-store restaurant.



❾ **Stohrer – E4** - *51 r. Montorgueil - 2e - Ⓜ Les Halles - ✆ 01 42 33 38 20 - www.stohrer.fr - daily.* The oldest patisserie in Paris (1730) is a must-see! This is where Nicolas Stohrer invented the desserts for the Royal Court. Beside the sandwiches for lunch, people mainly flock for the sweet specialties.

❼ **La Manufacture de Chocolat Alain Ducasse – G6** - *40 r. de la Roquette - 11e - Ⓜ Bastille - ✆ 01 48 05 82 86 - www.lechocolat- alainducasse.com - daily.* The much feted chef Alain Ducasse needs no introduction, but did you know about his passion for cocoa? At his Manafacture, he produces chocolate in the purest of tradition, which is reflected in the decor. His savoir-faire has earned the enterprise "Living Heritage Company" status—and the proof is in the pudding!

**La Laiterie de Paris – Off map by F1** - *74 r. des Poissonniers - 18e - Ⓜ Marcadet - Poissonniers - ✆ 01 42 59 44 64 - closed Sun and Thu lunch.* At the foot of the Butte Montmartre, this authentic cheese shop is run by a young team that makes its own lip-smacking cheeses and yogurts. A pioneer in the strong comeback of short food supply chains!

## Concept Stores

❻ **Merci – G5** - *111 bd Beaumarchais - 3e - Ⓜ St-Sébastien-Froissart - ✆ 01 42 77 00 33 - www.merci-merci.com - daily.* This mecca of fashion and design never fails to surprise. Constantly on the lookout for new trends, Merci offers a curated selection of objects and apparel over 16,145 sq.ft. The linen and tableware collections alone are worth a visit. Three in-store food and drink outlets offer a shopping breather.

❽ **Sergeant Paper – G3** - *26 r. du Château d'Eau - 10e - Ⓜ Jacques-Bonsergent - ✆ 01 83 89 99 55 - www.sergeantpaper.com - daily ex. Mon.* This concept store specializing in graphic arts subtly mixes in illustration, street art, and photography, highlighting a selection of young artists every month. The brand champions accessible art, and each art print is produced with the utmost care and comes with a certificate of authenticity.

**MK2 Store – Off map by H8** - *128-162 av. de France - 13e - Ⓜ Bibliothèque François Mitterrand - ✆ 01 53 61 71 70- www.mk2.com/mk2-store - daily.* With the spotlight on cinema, this wood-and-aluminum concept store, spread over 7,500 sq.ft, stocks DVDs,

CDs, and books related to your favorite indie movies. Not to mention cult movie merch like *Blade Runner* whisky glasses and Bang & Olufsen speakers designed by David Lynch. Take a selfie in the Harcourt photo booth then flip through a book at Bob's Café run by film buff Marc Grossman.

## Bookstore

⑮ **Le Piéton de Paris – F6** - *58 r. de l'Hôtel-de-Ville - 4e - Ⓜ Hôtel de Ville or Pont Marie - ☏ 01 53 69 09 16 - daily ex. Sun-Mon.* Lovers of Paris have their own bookstore: fiction, poetry, history, architecture, children's titles... anything provided the capital features in its pages!

## Photography

⑯ **Paris est une photo – E3** - *55 passage Jouffroy - 9e - Ⓜ Grands-Boulevards - ☏ 01 56 92 04 47 - www.photo.paris - daily.* - Tucked away inside the beautiful iron-and-glass Passage Jouffroy (est. 1847), this photo gallery and frame store devoted to the capital is the ideal spot to treat yourself to a souvenir print of Paris of yesteryear or today.

## Fashion

⑩ **Brand Bazar – D6** - *33 r. de Sèvres - 6e - Ⓜ Sèvres-Babylone - ☏ 01 45 44 40 02 - www.brandbazar.com - daily ex. Sun.* A haven for fashionistas, Brand Bazar is a purveyor of fashion that is both on-trend and in demand. From major labels to young French or international designers, the collection is always consummately current. The jewelry is elegant and colorful, the bags are boho chic, and the shoes all beautifully made. They don't take themselves too seriously, and the service is friendly.

F. Vielcanet/Alamy/hemis.fr

Maison Plisson.



## Souvenirs

⑬ **Paris Rendez-Vous – F5** - *29 r. de Rivoli - 4e - Ⓜ Hôtel de Ville - ☏ 01 42 76 43 43 - daily ex. Sun.* The City of Light is immortalized on anything you can imagine: mugs, tea towels, chocolate, coloring books, and more. The products, often stamped with an Eiffel Tower, are cute. The perfect address to take home souvenirs.

# Nightlife

The City of Light is also plenty fun after dark. Hurry to catch one of the capital's surprisingly eclectic shows or experience its incredibly vibrant party scene.

**Find the addresses on our maps using the numbers on the listing (e.g. 1). The coordinates in red (e.g. C2) refer to the detachable map (inside the cover).**

## Finding What's On

The go-to guide for planning your nights on the Parisian tiles, **L'Officiel des Spectacles** *(€2.20 from newsstands, www.offi.fr, or the app)* publishes, every Wednesday, the latest listings in the capital (movies, theaters, concerts, cabarets, and dinner shows), and publicizes guided tours around Paris.



The site **nuit.lebonbon.fr** posts day-by-day listings of what's on at night around Paris. Also check out the other general listings sites and apps:
- www.lylo.fr (in French)
- www.parisbouge.com (in French)
- www.sortiraparis.com/en/
- www.timeout.com/paris/en
- www.telerama.fr/sortir (in French)
- evene.lefigaro.fr (in French)

## Theater Tickets

Three kiosks around Paris sell theater tickets at up to half price, for the most expensive, for performances that same day. More than 100 shows and 120 theater productions are on offer. Bank cards not accepted. Arrive 30 minutes before they open to improve your chances of snagging seats.

**Kiosque Madeleine** – **D3** - *Pl. de la Madeleine - 8e - M Madeleine - www.kiosqueculture.com - Tue-Sat 12:30pm-2:30pm, 3pm-7:30pm, Sun 12:30pm-3:45pm.*

**Kiosque Montparnasse** – **D7** - *Pl. Raoul-Dautry - 15e - In front of Gare Montparnasse - M Montparnasse-Bienvenüe - www.kiosqueculture.com - daily ex. Mon. 12:30pm-7:30pm, Sun 12:30pm-3:45pm.*

**Office du Tourisme et des Congrès de Paris** – *29 r. de Rivoli - 4e- M Hôtel de Ville - www.kiosqueculture.com - 10am-5:50pm.*

## Tickets for Under 30s

Anyone under the age of 30 can collect invitations or buy show tickets at incredibly low prices.

**Kiosque Jeunes Canopée** – *10 passage de la Canopée – 1er - M Châtelet - kiosquejeunes.paris.fr - daily ex. Sun-Mon 11am-6pm.*

## Concerts

For "classic" concerts in large venues, such as the Philharmonie de Paris, the Auditorium de Radio France, the Salle Pleyel, or the Salle Gaveau, booking in advance is essential.

Concerts take place every evening in smaller venues (churches, bars, clubs, etc.). Visit www.lylo.fr or www.offi.fr for full listings.

## Opera & Dance

The two venues operated by the **Opéra National de Paris**, namely the

Opéra Bastille *(**G6** - Ⓜ Bastille)* and the Opéra Garnier *(**D3** - Ⓜ Opéra),* put on a packed program of operas, concerts, and recitals, as well as classical and contemporary ballets. Some productions must be booked several months in advance. Visit the website: www.operadeparis.fr/billetterie.
The **Opéra Comique Salle Favart (E3** - Ⓜ *Richelieu-Drouot)* also shows operas and recitals. Find out more at www.opera-comique.com.
For contemporary dance, see the program of the **Théâtre National de Chaillot (A4** - Ⓜ *Trocadéro)* at theater-chaillot.fr.
Fans of dance and music productions should also consult the programs of the **Théâtre de Châtelet** (www.chatelet.com) and the **Théâtre de la Ville** (www.theatredelaville-paris.com).

## Cabarets

Parisian nightlife owes much of its international renown to its sumptuous cabaret shows, some of which have been going since the 19th century: the **Moulin Rouge** *(**D1** - Ⓜ Blanche)*; the **Crazy Horse** *(**B4** - Ⓜ Alma-Marceau)*; and the **Paradis Latin** *(**F6-7** - Ⓜ Jussieu)*. Another stalwart of the cabaret scene, (1) **Madame Arthur (E1** - Ⓜ *Pigalle)* is an institution opened in 1946, slap bang in the center of Pigalle, famed for its drag shows sung in French. Nostalgic and alternative.

Rosa Bonheur sur Seine

## Cultural Centers

(16) **Maison des Métallos** – **H4** - *94 r. J.-P.-Timbaud - 11e - M Couronnes or Parmentier - ✆ 01 47 00 25 20 - www.maisondesmetallos.paris.* In 1937, this former factory became the Maison des Métallurgistes, an important trade union center for metal workers. Today a cultural establishment run by the City of Paris, the venue puts on theater, dance, digital art installations, exhibitions, gatherings, and talks. There's a bar on site, too.

**La Bellevilloise** – **Off map by H5** - *19-21 r. Boyer - 20e - M Gambetta or Ménilmontant - ✆ 01 46 36 07 07 - www.labellevilloise.com.* Established in 1877 in the wake of the Paris Commune, this Parisian co-op, the first of its kind, is now an independent and multidisciplinary cultural hub featuring concerts, movie screenings, jazz brunches, festivals, and private parties. The venue with its olive trees planted beneath the huge glass ceiling is next-level cute.

**CENTQUATRE-PARIS** – *See p. 97.*

B. Gardel/hemis.fr

La Bellevilloise.



## Clubs

Paris has a host of clubs and you can find their contact info at www.soonnight.com/category/clubbing/ (in French, flyers for free access and discounts), www.timeout.com, and www.villaschweppes.com (in French). Admission is often free for women before midnight; men will usually have to pay €10-15 depending on the venue. Sometimes booking is required. In addition, ID is often requested at the entrance to most clubs, for which the minimum age is typically 18.

### Our Club Selection

(2) **Le Duplex** – **A3** - *2 bis av. Foch - 16e - M Charles-de- Gaulle-Étoile - www.leduplex.com - 11:30pm-6am - free before 12:30am with flyer - R&B and electro.* Three rooms, three vibes. Themed nights thru the week, inquire about private events.

(10) **Rex Club** – **F3** - *5 bd Poissonnière - 2e - M Bonne-Nouvelle - ✆ 01 42 36 10 96 - Wed-Sat 11:45pm-7pm – electro.* Iconic club in Paris where international DJs get the party pumping.

(12) **Badaboum** – **H6** - *2 r. des Taillandiers - 11e - M Ledru-Rollin - ✆ 01 48 06 50 70 - badaboum.paris - times vary by what's on - electro.* Concerts followed by club nights featuring sound and visual installations.

## On the Water

### Right Bank

**Between the Louvre and Pont-Marie**, the site of the Paris Plages artificial beaches, the summer vibes are in full swing thanks to al fresco bars, dancing, and concerts. The party continues upstream as far as **Quai de la Rapée**, where floating bars on "péniches" (barges) draw a hip crowd.

### Left Bank

A cluster of bars, restaurants, péniches, and al fresco clubs can be found **between the Royal and Alexandre III bridges.**

6 **Concorde Atlantique – D4** - *in front of 23 quai Anatole-France - 7e - M Assemblée-Nationale - 01 40 56 02 82 - www.bateauconcordeatlantique.com.* With three floors overlooking the Seine, this barge is often closed for private parties, but also hosts club nights.

32 **Rosa Bonheur sur Seine – C4** - *37 quai d'Orsay - Port des Invalides - 7e - M Invalides - 01 42 00 00 45 - www.rosabonheur.fr - daily ex. Mon-Tue 6pm-1:30am (Wed 12:30am), Sat 12pm-1:30am (Sun 12:30am).* The little brother of the famed Rosa Bonheur des Buttes-Chaumont (*p. 136*), this bar-barge is just as welcoming. The boat's deck turns into a dancefloor at dusk. Tasty tapas and stunning views of the Grand Palais.

**At the foot of the Institut du Monde Arabe**, the **Jardin Tino-Rossi** turns into an open-air dance school and hall for lovers of salsa, rock, and tango. Whether you watch or take part, it's always spectacular!

### The Quaiside Takeover

Since the launch of Paris Plages in 2002 and the closure of the roads on the riverbanks—the Left Bank in 2013, the Right Bank in 2016—, the Parisians have taken back en masse the Seine's quays, as well as the banks of Paris' canals and lakes, which become one big open-air hangout spot through the sunny months. People love to bring picnics, open a bottle, play pétanque, dance on barges, or take an open-air salsa class.

**Between the bridges of Bercy and Tolbiac**, the quays house multiple entertainment venues, some more permanent than others.

**Bateau Phare – Off map by H8** - *11 quai François-Mauriac - M Bibliothèque-F.-Mitterrand - 06 89 86 35 03 - www.lebateauphare.co - 12pm-11pm (Thu 12:30 am, Fri-Sat 1:30am).* A veritable institution on the Paris nightlife scene, the former Batofar has undergone a remodel. Now the clientele comes to enjoy the excellent food or just a glass of something chilled. Terrace on the quayside from May to September.

### From the Canal Saint-Martin to La Villette

*See "Explore Paris" p. 96 and "Where to Drink" p. 134.*

# Where to Stay

Multiple districts, unique vibes, Paris can feel residential (7e, 15e, 16e), party central (3e, 10e, 11e), chic (6e, 7e, 8e), or family-friendly (12e, 13e, 14e, 15e).

**Find the addresses on our maps using the numbers on the listing (e.g. 1). The coordinates in red (e.g. E3) refer to the detachable map (inside the cover).**

*Our price ranges are based on one night in a standard double room in low/high season. Plenty of promotions to be found online.*

## Central Paris

**Local Map p. 20-21**

### From €240

2 **Hôtel Andréa** – **F5** - *3 r. St-Bon - 4e- Ⓜ Châtelet - ✆ 01 42 78 43 93 - www.hotelandrea.paris - 32 rooms, €245-580* ☕. You won't be disappointed with this hotel as central as they come: from the lobby to the rooms to the breakfast room, it's undergone a full refurb. Up-to-date decor and air-con throughout. One to bookmark for sure.



## Opéra-Palais-Royal

**Local Map p. 31**

### From €150

11 **Hôtel des Arts** – **E3** - *7 cité Bergère - 9e - Ⓜ Grands-Boulevards - ✆ 01 42 46 73 30 - www.hoteldesarts.fr - 25 rooms €150-250 - ☕ €8.* Nestled within Cité Bergère, this hotel boasts the charm and tranquility of a provincial establishment. The rooms are bright.

10 **Hôtel Chopin** – **E3** - *46 passage Jouffroy - enter at 10 bd Montmartre, 9e - Ⓜ Grands-Boulevards - ✆ 01 47 70 58 10 - 01 47 70 58 10 - www.hotelchopin-paris-opera.com - 36 rooms €150-190 - ☕ €10.* This bijou hotel is astonishingly calm in this animated neighborhood. The rooms, all with brightly colored walls, must be booked well in advance.

### From €380

❤ 14 **The Hoxton** – **E3** - *30-32 r. du Sentier - 2e - Ⓜ Bonne Nouvelle - ✆ 01 85 65 75 00 - www.thehoxton.com/paris - 172 rooms €380-530.* With its large glass roof, colorful sofas, and winter garden, this former private mansion from the 18th century has a pleasantly laidback look and feel. All four room categories are tastefully designed. On the premises, the restaurant Rivié serves French cuisine while the Jacques' Bar and Planche offer different vibes for a drink.

## The Marais and Les Halles

**Local Map p. 38-39**

### From €190

3 **Hôtel Crayon** – **E4** - *25 r. du Bouloi - 1er - Ⓜ Palais-Royal-Musée du Louvre - ✆ 01 42 36 54 19 - www.hotelcrayon.com - 26 rooms €191-327 - ☕ €16.* A colorful and welcoming hotel decorated top to bottom by artist Julie Gauthron. From the "home from home" bar area to the vintage

furnishings that make every stay unique, this hotel has a cozy, guest-house feel.

### From €260

4 **Hôtel du Petit Moulin** – **G4** - *29-31 r. de Poitou - 3e - M Saint-Sébastien-Froissart - ✆ 01 42 74 10 10 - www.hotelpetitmoulinparis.com/fr - ✕ - 17 rooms €260-460 - ☕ €13.* Christian Lacroix put his design stamp on this hotel. It's exclusive and fancy, a successful blend of traditional and modern. From clawfoot tubs to gaudy colors, every room is a gem!

## Latin Quarter

**Local Map p. 48-49**

### From €150

❤ 16 **Hôtel Henriette** – **F8** - *9 r. des Gobelins - 13e - M Les Gobelins - ✆ 01 47 07 26 90 - www.hotelhenriette.com - 32 rooms €150-250 - ☕ €14.* Just moments away from the Latin Quarter, the Hôtel Henriette oozes charm with its interiors in various shades of blue, designer lighting, and 1960s vintage furniture. The cozy atmosphere flows through to the patio which is made for quiet contemplation.

### From €200

5 **Hôtel des Grandes Écoles** – **F7** - *75 r. du Cardinal Lemoine - 5e - M Cardinal-Lemoine - ✆ 01 43 26 79 23 - www.hoteldesgrandesecoles.com - 51 rooms €200-387 - ☕ €16.* These three cottage-style houses in the buzzing Latin Quarter offer a breath of fresh air in the leafy courtyard. The main building has retained its somewhat old-fashioned charm, while the other two have been nicely renovated. Extremely popular.

S. Sonnet/hemis.fr

Hôtel Chopin.



## Saint-Germain-des-Prés-Montparnasse

**Local Map p. 57**

### From €85 to €150

1 **Hôtel de Nesle** – **E5** - *7 r. de Nesle - 6e - M Odéon - ✆ 01 43 54 62 41 - www.hoteldenesleparis.com - P - 18 rooms €85-150.* Almost too good to be true! The rooms—some without full bathrooms—are all incredibly decorated: colonial, Far Eastern, rustic, Molière… The garden is planted with Tunisian palm trees. All in the heart of Paris!

### From €100

**Solar Hotel** – **Off map by E8** - *22 r. Boulard - 14e - M Denfert-Rochereau - ✆ 01 43 21 08 20 -*

*www.solarhotel.fr* - P - *34 rooms €100-130* ☕. Clearly established by a keen environmentalist given that the food is organic, all waste is recycled, waste water is collected, energy is saved, and guests can even recharge on the flowery terrace. The first 100% eco-friendly hotel in Paris. Bikes available for guest rental.

### From €160

7 **Hôtel de Sèvres** – **D7** - *22 r. de l'Abbé-Grégoire - 6e* - M *Saint-Placide* - ✆ *01 45 48 84 07 - www.hoteldesevres.com* - P - *32 rooms €160-200* - ☕ *€14*. If you love to shop, then this hotel is right next door to Le Bon Marché! With its floral wallpaper, the establishment is nice and inviting.

### From €200

**Fabe Hotel** – **Off map by**

**C8** - *113 bis r. de l'Ouest - 14e* - M *Pernety* - ✆ *01 40 44 09 63 - www.lefabehotel.fr - 17 rooms €200-290* - ☕ *€12*. From green and chocolate tones and poetically named rooms (Mona Lisa, Rugiada, French Romance) to headboards embossed with huge prints of flowers that are echoed on the furniture, this hotel certainly catches the eye. Designer, cozy, and practical.

## Invalides-Eiffel Tower

### From €170

8 **Le Bailli de Suffren** – **C7** - *149 av. de Suffren - 15e* - M *Ségur* - ✆ *01 56 58 64 64 - www.lebailliparis.com - 25 room €170-270* - ☕ *€15*. Conveniently located between the Eiffel Tower, the Invalides, and Montparnasse, this hotel has been renovated in a minimalist style while retaining its Parisian charm. The rooms are comfortable, bright, and well soundproofed.

## Trocadéro-Chaillot

### From €200

**Hôtel Le Hameau de Passy** – **Off map by A4** - *48 r. de Passy - 16e* - M *La Muette* - ✆ *01 42 88 47 55 - www.hameaudepassy.com* - P - *32 rooms €200-250* - ☕ *€15*. A cul-de-sac leads to this tucked-away hotel and its darling interior courtyard, lush with greenery. Peaceful nights guaranteed in rooms that are small, but modern, and well kept.

## Montmartre-Pigalle

**Local Map p. 90-91**

### From €160

12 **Hôtel des 3 Poussins** – **E2** - *15 r. Clauzel - 9e* - M *Saint-Georges* - ✆ *01 53 32 81 81 - www.les3poussins.com - 40 rooms €160/270* - ☕ *€13*. Down a sleepy street, this small hotel boasts bright rooms festooned with photos of Paris. Some are equipped with a kitchenette. Small patio to relax or take breakfast.

17 **Hôtel Basss** – **E1** - *57 r. des Abbesses - 18e* - M *Abbesses* - ✆ *01 42 51 50 00 - www.hotel-basss.com - 36 rooms €180-300* - ☕ *€11*. In the heart of Montmartre, the soft shades of this renovated hotel make for a comforting stay. The pleasant lobby will encourage you to hang out, especially given that the snacks are self-serve. Simple and clean, the rooms are beautifully decorated.

### From €200

❤ 18 **Le Pigalle** – **E2** - *9 r. Frochot - 9e* - M *Pigalle* - ✆ *01 48 78*

*37 14 - www.lepigalle.paris* - ✕ - *40 rooms €200-380* - ☕ *€15.* This next-generation hotel has a distinct identity. Beyond the trendy and subtly subversive decor, this venue is a popular local hangout and fosters collabs with artists, artisans, and shopkeepers in the environs. The rooms are equipped with decks and vinyl to play, a minibar, an iPad, and a gorgeous retro bathroom. For a good night's sleep, opt for a courtyard-side room.

## Canal Saint-Martin-La Villette

### From €210

13 **Best Western Hôtel Littéraire Arthur Rimbaud – F3** - *6 r. Gustave-Goublier - 10e* - Ⓜ *Strasbourg-St-Denis* - ✆ *01 40 40 02 02 - www.hotel-litteraire-arthur-rimbaud.com - 42 rooms €210-410* - ☕ *€19.* This hotel is well situated close to the Gare de l'Est and Gare du Nord train stations. The well-appointed rooms are all themed: nature, feathers, poetry... Comfortable and cozy.

### From €260

19 **Hôtel Providence – F3** - *90 r. René-Boulanger - 10e* - Ⓜ *République* - ✆ *01 46 34 34 04 - www.hotelprovidenceparis.com* - ✕ - *18 rooms €260-550* - ☕ *for a supp.* Gorgeous moldings, Hungarian herringbone parquet, velvet curtains, and a bar in precious wood: this place takes Parisian chic seriously. The renovated Providence is a bijou of a boutique hotel, ideal as a base for exploring Eastern Paris. It has a terrace if you want to check it out over a coffee.

## Bastille and Eastern Paris

### From €100

**Mama Shelter Paris East – Off map by H4** - *109 r. de Bagnolet - 20e* - Ⓜ *Gambetta* - ✆ *01 43 48 48 48 - www.mamashelter.com* - ✕ - *170 rooms €100-270* - ☕ *€19.* The original, stripped-back but whimsical decor is the handiwork of Philippe Starck in this vast, state-of-the-art hotel. Sprawling lounge bar, restaurant flooded with natural light, long terrace overlooking the old railroad, and a popular brunch on the weekend.

### From €160

15 **Le 20 Prieuré Hôtel – G4** - *20 r. du Grand-Prieuré - 11e* - Ⓜ *Oberkampf* - ✆ *01 47 00 74 14 - www.hotel20prieure.com - 32 rooms €160-237* - ☕ *€13.* This hotel has embraced a contemporary urban style and offers small but cozy rooms, all in shades of white, with designer furniture and blown-up photos of Paris.

**Cinéma-Hôtel Paradiso – Off map by H6** - *135 bd Diderot - 12e* - Ⓜ *Nation* - ✆ *01 88 59 20 01 - www.mk2hotelparadiso.com* - ✕ - *37 rooms €160-408* - ☕ *€16.* Created by the mk2 movie theater brand in 2021, this hotel is the first to be entirely dedicated to the silver screen. Each room is equipped with a giant screen for watching movies from the hotel's huge selection from the comfort of your bed! A dream stay for movie buffs.

# PLANNING YOUR TRIP

From the Pont Alexandre-III looking out to the Invalides.
A. Serrano/hemis.fr

# Know Before You Go

## Getting There by Train

SNCF Train Information and Ticket Reservations: ✆ 3635 - www.SNCF-connect.com.

### Train Connections

All stations are very well served by public transport and cabs, and have a Vélib' bike rental station.
**Gare de Lyon** (12e arr.): trains from the southeast of France, Italy, and Switzerland. Lines 1 and 14, RER A, B, and D.
**Gare de Bercy** (12e arr.): trains from Clermont-Ferrand, Burgundy, and some stations in Lyon. Auto Train service. Lines 6 and 14.
**Gare d'Austerlitz** (13e arr.): trains from southwest France and Spain. Lines 5 and 10, RER C.
**Gare Montparnasse** (15e arr.): trains from the Grand-Ouest region. Lines 4, 6, 12, and 13.
**Gare du Nord** (10e arr.): trains from northern France, the United Kingdom, Belgium, and the Netherlands. Lines 2, 4 and 5, RER B, D, and E.
**Gare de l'Est** (10e arr.): trains from eastern France and Germany. Lines 4, 5, and 7. The RER D, B, and E can be reached from Gare du Nord, one station stop from Gare de l'Est.
**Gare Saint-Lazare** (9e arr.): trains from Normandy. Lines 3, 9, 12, 13, and 14, RER E.
*"Cabs" and "Public Transport", p. 160-161.*



## Getting There by Plane

Paris has two international airports. To check your flight status and plan getting to/from the airport: **www.parisaeroport.fr**.
**Roissy Charles-de-Gaulle** Airport is about 14 miles north of Paris, via the A1 autoroute. **Orly** Airport is about 7 miles south of Paris, via the A6 autoroute. In addition, **Beauvais** Airport, located 50 miles north of Paris, serves various low-cost airlines.
*Details of public transport connections, p. 3.*

## Getting There by Bus

Since the bus sector was liberalized, multiple bus routes have opened up between the capital and major French cities, often at competitive fares, notably with Blablacar Bus (www.blablacar.fr/bus) and Flixbus (www.flixbus.fr).

## Getting There by Car

Although traveling by car is economical for a family, there are also disadvantages: finding parking spaces, exorbitant parking costs, traffic congestion, etc.
Since 2021 and the introduction of a "Paris Low Emission Zone", the most polluting vehicles are no longer permitted to move about freely in the capital. A Crit'Air sticker must be obtained from the website www.certificat-air.gouv.fr.

| SELECT COSTS (IN EURO) TO PLAN YOUR BUDGET | |
|---|---|
| A double room in a comfortable hotel | 120-180 |
| A double room in a premium hotel | 180-250 |
| A meal in a regular restaurant | 20-30 per person |
| A meal in a good restaurant | 40-55 per person |
| A meal in a fine-dining restaurant | 75-150 per person |
| A glass of wine | 5-8 |
| A cocktail in a bar | 10-15 |
| Admission to a national museum | 8.7-17 |
| One métro ticket/book of 10 tickets | 2.10/16.90 |

## When To Go

Paris draws visitors all year round. Christmas/New Year, Easter, and summer are the busiest periods, as well as during major trade fairs. If you plan to come at these times, make any reservations and bookings you need way in advance. Some hotels offer special rates during the **low season** (November to March, excluding Christmas holidays and major events).

## Further Travel Advice

**Office de Tourisme et des Congrès de Paris** – Paris Tourist Office - www.parisjetaime.com
Everything you need to know about events, museums, guided walks, hotels, restaurants, and more. Online hotel booking and ticketing for sites and museums, cruises, Paris Visite pass (transportation), etc.

**Comité Régional du Tourisme Paris Île-de-France** – Regional Tourist Office - www.visitparisregion.com
**Mairie de Paris** – Paris City Hall - www.paris.fr
**What's On in Paris** – quefaire.paris.fr
This site, run by Paris' City Hall, updates its listings of excursions, exhibitions, and activities every week.

## Vacation Budgeting

To help plan your budget, use the table above.

**Don't Panic!**

**EU-wide Emergency Number** – ✆ 112
**Urgent Medical Aid** - ✆ 15
**Police** – ✆ 17
**Fire** – ✆ 18
**Emergency Doctors** - ✆ 01 47 07 77 77
**Poison Center** - ✆ 01 40 05 48 48
**Stolen Bank Card** – ✆ 0 892 705 705 (€0.35/min.)

# Your Stay A-Z

## Alternative Travel Ideas

### Find Out More

**www.parisjetaime.com** – The Paris Tourist Office lists eco-addresses in its "Sustainable Paris" section: accommodation, restaurants, shops, organic markets, etc.

### Alternative Accommodation

**www.hotels-insolites.com** – A selection of dream places to stay, either for their quirky interiors or amazing location, or both. Priced accordingly.



**www.paristay.com** – This agency lists luxury apartments for short-term rentals.

### Dine with a Local

**www.eatwith.com** – This platform connects visitors to Paris with hosts who want to share their cooking.

## Cabs

### Finding a Cab

You can easily find one in the vicinity of train stations and along the main thoroughfares. If you see one, wave to hail it. If a taxi is free, the green light will be on. You can also book by phone or online. In this case, the pick-up charge will be added to the fare.
Minimum Fare: €7.30.
Initial Charge: €4.18.
Maximum Price per Kilometer Driven: €1.21.

### Booking

**www.g7.fr** – ✆ 3607 (€0.45/min.) - phone app. G7 Van provides minivans for 5-7 passengers plus luggage, while G7 Access offers vehicles for people with mobility needs.
**Ride-Hailing Services** – www.lecab.fr or www.uber.com.

## Children

Paris is a very child-friendly city. They'll love the Eiffel Tower, Bateaux-Mouches river cruises, and, of course, the capital's big parks. But don't forget these places designed to keep children entertained:
- the Jardin des Plantes, with its natural history museum, evolution exhibit, and zoo (*p. 54*)
- Parc de la Villette, with the Cité des Enfants (science museum) and Géode (Omnimax theater) (*p. 98*)
- Museum of Hunting and Nature (*p. 42*)
- CENTQUATRE-PARIS (*p. 97*)
- Jardin d'Acclimatation (amusement park) (*p. 86*)
- the Grévin waxworks (*p. 34*)

## Disabilities

**www.parisjetaime.com** – On the official website of the Paris Tourist Office, visit the "Accessible Paris" page, where you will find the *Paris for People with Disabilities* guide with lots of useful information (transport, restaurants, adapted tourist amenities, etc.).

**Museums** – Most museums and tourist attractions are wheelchair accessible. The museums of the City of Paris (www.parismusees.paris.fr) organize various activities for the disabled public: workshops, tactile tours, talks in sign language and/or lip reading, and special visits for people who are neurodivergent.

**Restrooms** – All public restrooms around the city are accessible (*p. 161*).

**Transportation** – All bus lines are wheelchair accessible thanks to a retractable ramp at the back of the bus. However, only métro Line 14 and certain RER stations are accessible. The website **www.iledefrance-mobilites.fr** will help you find the most accessible public transport routes.

The cycle lane on Rue de Rivoli.

**G7 Access** (01 47 39 00 91 - www.g7.fr - phone app) is a cab service that runs a fleet of adapted vehicles to transport people with mobility needs.

**Guided Tours** – The nonprofit Parisien d'un jour - Paris Greeters (www.greeters.paris) organizes tours catering specifically to people with disabilities (*p. 165*).

The organization AICV rents out **bicycles** (handbikes, tricycles, etc.) designed for people with disabilities (*p. 164*).

## Cycling

Cycling has become an easy and practical mode of transport in and around Paris: over 600 miles of bike lanes crisscross the capital, and new lanes are constantly being added to improve safety for cyclists. Paris City Hall has made cycling one of its priority issues to make the capital more peaceful and less polluted. More and more Parisians are therefore taking up cycling, especially considering that since the 2019 winter strikes, which included transport workers, and the Covid-19 pandemic, the bike is the most reliable way to reach your destination on time! A *Paris à vélo* (Paris by Bike) map is distributed at city halls and at branches of the Paris Tourist Office.

**Requirements** – Bell, reflectors, lighting at night; use of reserved bike parking spaces (it is illegal to chain bikes to street furniture).

Sidewalks are also banned to cyclists.

**Info** – www.paris.fr/a-velo

### Self-Service Bikes

**Vélib'Métropole** – This simple system gives you complete freedom: collect a bike wherever you want, return it wherever you want, at any of the many stations around the capital and neighboring suburbs. Mechanical (green) or electric (blue) bikes.
Price – 24-hour pass (mechanical): €5 (allows 30-minute trips on a mechanical Vélib', after that charged €1/30 min.); 24-hour pass (electric): €10 (includes six 45-min, trips by electric Vélib', after that charged €1/30 min.); 3 days: €20 (same conditions).
Info – www.velib-metropole.fr
"Vélib'" – Phone app available on App Store and Google Play.



**Lime** – This app gives you access to these self-serve e-bikes using your phone (€0.25/min. + €1 unlocking fee).
Info – www.li.me

### Rental

You'll need to bring your ID for any rental. Helmet, basket, or child seat may be charged extra to the daily rental fee.

**Paris à Vélo** – 22 r. Alphonse-Baudin - 11e - Ⓜ Saint-Sébastien-Froissart - ✆ 01 48 87 60 01 - parisavelo.fr - Apr-Oct: 9:30am-1pm, 2pm-5:30pm (Wed-Fri 6pm, wknd 7pm); Nov-Mar: 9:30am-1pm, 2-5pm (Wed-Fri 5:30pm, wknd 6pm) - city bike: €17/½ d., €20/1 d.; e-bike: €35/½ d., €42/1 d. - security deposit (€100-€2,000) - themed guided tours (3 hr): €34 (min. 12 participants).

**AICV (Animation Insertion Culture et Vélo)** – 38 bis quai de la Marne - 19e - Ⓜ Ourcq - ✆ 01 43 43 40 74 - www.aicv.net - Wed-Sun 9:30am-12:30pm, 1:30pm-5pm (Nov-Mar: Tue-Sat) - €10/3hr, €15/1 d. (adult), €8/3hr, €10/1 d. (child) - plus security deposit of €200. Ideally located on the lake at La Villette, this organization will also provide you with cycling routes.

## Emergency Numbers

*"Don't Panic", p. 157.*

## Evening Entertainment

Paris more than lives up to its reputation as a city to have fun in. There are plenty of things to do at night and entertainment venues, from theaters to legendary cabaret shows.
*"Nightlife", p. 146.*

## Free Admission

Most national monuments and museums are free for EU nationals under the age of 26. For those aged 26 or over, national museums are free on the first Sunday of the month. Access to the permanent collections of the **museums operated by the City of Paris** is free for everyone, excluding the Catacombes and the Crypte Archéologique de Notre-Dame.
**Info** – www.parismusees.paris.fr

## Gardens & Parks

The capital has almost 500 green spaces. They open between 8am and 9:30am on weekdays and at 9am at the weekend. Closing times are seasonal: from mid-Apr to end Aug, 9 or 10pm; Sep-Oct, 8pm; early Mar to mid-Apr,

7pm; Feb and end Oct to mid-Nov, 6pm; rest of year: 5:30pm. **Info** - www.paris.fr

Most of Paris' parks and gardens have lawns and some have designated picnic areas.

Guided tours are a great way to discover Paris' main gardens (*p. 165*).

## Guided Tours

Guided tours of monuments, neighborhoods, and exhibitions are available daily in Paris. They are advertised in some of the big national newspapers, in the event press (check **L'Officiel des Spectacles**), and at the entrance to monuments. Programs are also available from branches of the Paris Tourist Office and, of course, on the websites of museums and monuments. To ensure a place, your best bet is to book before you arrive at the meeting place.

A good source of tour ideas is the website of the Paris Tourist Office, **www.parisjetaime.com**, which lists numerous service providers offering tours on original forms of transport, including classic 2CVs and rickshaws.

### Walking Tours

**Association pour la Sauvegarde et la Mise en Valeur du Paris Historique** – 44-46 r. François-Miron - M Saint-Paul - 01 48 87 74 31 - www.paris-historique.org - Mon-Fri 1pm-6pm, Sat 12pm-7pm, Sun 2pm-6pm. Guided tours of monuments and select neighborhoods of Paris on the theme of architecture (€15, €7 for -25s). Guided tour of Maison d'Ourscamp (organization's headquarters), upon reservation (€5), to discover 800 years of Parisian history.

**Office de Tourisme et des Congrès de Paris** – Paris Toutist Office - www.parisjetaime.com. Its website lists qualified guides offering tours of the capital.

**Guided Tours of Parks and Gardens** - Paris City Hall offers guided tours of the capital's gardens and parks. Program on the City of Paris website: www.paris.fr/jardins.

**Parisien d'un jour - Paris Greeters** – www.greeters.paris - These "Paris" ambassadors lead, free of charge (donations to the organization welcome) and on request, groups of one to six people for an alternative way to discover Paris.

**Ça se visite** – 06 72 20 27 11 - www.ca-se-visite.fr - €16 by foot, €19 by scooter (€14-17, free for -10s). Urban walks (2-2½ hr), on foot or scooter, to meet the everyday folk and artists living in Paris' more authentic neighborhoods. Check out the program on the website.

**Paris par Rues Méconnues** – 06 62 98 96 64 - www.paris-prm.com - groups of 1-20 people. A variety of tours, peppered with stories recounted by enthusiastic guides, based on original themes for an alternative approach to tourism and to go out and meet real Parisians.

**Montmartre en Chansons** – montmartreenchansons.com. Tour guide and seasoned singer Anne-Sophie Guerrier leads groups around Montmartre, and performs French classics along the way! Discover the Butte's history of song.

## Bus Tours

Paris through a window or from a panoramic rooftop, on board a vehicle that leads the way: another great way to discover the city, with or without commentary. There are various options: **tourist buses and coaches**, of course, but also the buses in the RATP network (*☞ 160*), some of which pass through historic districts for the price of a bus fare, and you get to ride with Parisian folk.

**Montmartrobus** – Circular service around the Butte Montmartre between the city hall of the 18e arr. and Place Pigalle (t+ ticket).

**Big Bus Paris** – www.bigbustours.com/en/paris - guided tours on a double-decker bus - stops: Eiffel Tower, Champ-de-Mars, Opéra Garnier, Louvre-Pyramide, Louvre-Pont des Arts, Notre-Dame, Musée d'Orsay, Champs-Élysées, Grand Palais, Trocadéro - tour takes approx. 2 hr but you can hop on and off during the ride - day fare €45 (-12s €25), buy tickets on the bus, or online (cheaper). For days and times, please check the website.



**Tootbus** – www.tootbus.com/en - Guided tours on a double-decker panoramic bus. The 24-hour Paris Discovery package (€42, child €22) includes hop-on and hop-off at all 10 stops: Haussmann-Department Stores, Opéra Garnier, Louvre, Notre-Dame, Musée d'Orsay, Concorde, Champs-Élysées, Trocadéro, Eiffel Tower, Pont Alexandre III. Other packages: including river cruise, children's special, late night, express, etc. Tickets available on board the bus or online.

**Paris City Vision** – www.pariscityvision.com – Tours on a double-decker bus to discover the capital's most prestigious monuments. Day pass €45, audio-guided city tour (1hr30) €29.

## Boat Tours

**Bateaux-Mouches** – Port de la Conférence - Pont de l'Alma (Right Bank) - ☎ 01 42 25 96 10 - www.bateaux-mouches.fr - guided river sightseeing cruises (1hr10) €15 (-12s €6), lunch cruise €80, dinner cruise €85-155.

**Bateaux Parisiens** – Port de la Bourdonnais (foot of the Eiffel Tower) - ☎ 0 825 01 01 01 - www.bateauxparisiens.com - guided sightseeing cruise (1hr) €18 (-12s €9). Lunch and dinner cruises, too.

**Vedettes de Paris** – Port de Suffren (foot of the Eiffel Tower) - ☎ 01 44 18 19 50 - www.vedettesdeparis.com - selection of cruise packages: guided cruise (1hr) €20 (-11s €9); with kids (1hr) €20 (-11s €9); apéritif cruise (1hr) €20-29 (-11s €9), and more.

**Paris Canal** – ☎ 01 42 40 96 97 - www.pariscanal.com - booking required - cruise on the Seine and Canal St-Martin between the Musée d'Orsay (Ⓜ Solférino) and Parc de la Villette (Ⓜ Porte de Pantin) - duration 5hr - €23 (-14s €15).

**Canauxrama** – 13 quai de la Loire - ☎ 01 42 39 15 00 - www.canauxrama.com - cruise on the Canal Saint-Martin between the Port de Plaisance de

Paris-Arsenal, across from 50 bd de la Bastille (M Bastille), and the Bassin de la Villette, 13 quai de la Loire (M Jaurès) - duration 2hr30 - €22 (-14s €10) - for other cruises, inquire.

## Lost & Found

Before do you anything else, if possible go back to the place where you think you likely lost the item in question. Then: **Lost Property** – www.ppbot.fr. You must report lost property before you can run a search.

## Opening Hours and Public Holidays

**Stores**: generally 10am-7pm, daily ex. Sun.
**Food Venues**: often open Sun morning and closed Mon.
**Neighborhood Grocery Stores**: many remain open late in the evening.
**Supermarkets**: 9am-8pm, daily ex. Sun (some big brands such as Monoprix are open until 10pm and on Sunday morning).
**Department Stores**: 10am-8pm.
**Museums and Monuments**: ticket offices generally close 30 minutes before the site closes.
**Churches**: no entry during services and most close between 12pm and 2pm.
Some tourist sites and stores may close on the following **public holidays**: January 1, Easter Monday, May 1 and 8, Ascension Day, Whit Monday, July 14, August 15, November 1 and 11, December 25.
Museum and monument openings on public holidays vary greatly. Best to check in advance.

## Pharmacies

The pharmacies below are open 24/7.
**Pharmacie internationale** – 5 pl. Pigalle - 9e - M Pigalle - ✆ 01 48 78 38 12.
**Pharmacie Européenne** – 6 pl. de Clichy - 9e - M Place de Clichy - ✆ 01 48 74 65 18.
**La Pharma de Répu** – 5 pl. de la République - 3e - M République - ✆ 01 47 00 18 08.
**Pharmacie Opéra Bastille** – 6 bd Richard-Lenoir - 11e - M Bastille - ✆ 01 47 00 49 44.
**Aprium Pharmacie centrale Paris 15** – 52 r. du Commerce - 15e - M Avenue-Émile-Zola - ✆ 01 45 79 75 01.
Other pharmacies are open late in the evening (www.parisinfo.com).



## Post Office

**Opening Hours**: Mon-Fri 8am-7pm, Sat 8am-12pm - closed Sun and public holidays.
One post office in Paris has extended opening hours.
**Poste Centrale du Louvre** – 50 r. du Louvre - 1er - M Louvre-Rivoli or Étienne-Marcel - www.laposte.fr - 8am-12am (Sun 10am-12am).

## Public Restrooms

The 435 Parisian "Sanisettes" (self-contained public toilets) are open from 6am to 10pm, some 24/7. They are free of charge and self clean after each use (3-minute wait between each user). Free toilets can also be found in department stores, shopping malls, and airports. However, train station toilets charge.

There are several free phone apps to locate restrooms around Paris.

## Public Transport

### Métro

The simplest, fastest, and most economical way to get around. Just one downside: the crowds at peak hours (8am-9:30am, 5pm-7:30pm). Fourteen lines crisscross the capital, with an average frequency of one train every 2 to 4 minutes (6 to 8 minutes after 8:30pm and on weekends). They run from 5:30am to 1:15am (2:15am on Fridays, Saturdays, and the night before public holidays.
To estimate your travel time, factor in 2 min. per station and 3 min. for every connection (e.g. for a 15-station trip, with two connections, expect a 35-minute journey).
**Theft** – To reduce the risk of theft, keep your bags closed and in sight at all times.
**Info** – www.ratp.fr



### Buses

Arguably the most pleasant mode of transport. The only cons are the traffic and the occasionally erratic service, especially on Sundays.
The network has around 60 intra-city routes. Board at the front of the bus, except for articulated buses on which you can use any door. Always validate your ticket in the yellow machine. If you have a magnetic pass, use the purple machine.
**Noctilien Bus** – 47 routes run all night (from 12:30am to 5:30pm), between Paris and the suburbs: these are the Noctilien buses, their route number preceded by the letter N. In Paris, they leave from five main stations: Gare de Lyon, Gare de l'Est, Gare Saint-Lazare, Gare Montparnasse, and Châtelet. Among them, the highly practical circular lines N01 (inner circular) and N02 (outer circular) pass through Paris' most frequented night spots. N01-N02 service frequency: every 17 min. (10 min. Fri-Sat).
**Info** – www.ratp.fr

### RER

Perfect for traveling to the outskirts of Paris (La Défense, Versailles, Disneyland, Roissy and Orly airports), but less practical for "inner" Paris, because even though it is faster than the métro, the RER ("Regional Express Network") always calls for additional effort to get to its platforms, which are deeper underground than those of the métro.
The network consists of five lines, three of which serve Châtelet-Les-Halles central station (Lines A, B, and D).
**Line A**, running west to east, goes out to Disneyland Park.
**Line B**, north to south, goes to Roissy Charles-de-Gaulle Airport in the north, and Antony in the south (to take the Orlyval).
**Line C**, running west to east, serves Versailles-Rive-Gauche (for the Palace).
**Line D** runs from north to southeast.
**Line E** runs from west to east.
Never throw your ticket away after disembarking a train because you'll need it to exit the station.
**Info** – www.ratp.fr

### Tramway

Eleven tram lines serve the Paris suburbs. This mode of transport does not really concern "tourist" journeys, apart from the T3a and T3b routes that operate along the Boulevards des Maréchaux, connecting with bus, métro, and RER services, the tram providing a means to travel around the outskirts of Paris. In the south, the T3a line connects Porte de Versailles (exhibition park) to Porte de Vincennes (and its forest), via the Parc Montsouris and the Bibliothèque François-Mitterrand (library). In the north-east, line T3b can be convenient for reaching Parc de la Villette (Porte de la Villette or Porte de Pantin stops).
**Info** - www.ratp.fr

### Batobus

An original—but expensive!—way to explore Paris by boat on the Seine and cruise to the most popular neighborhoods and monuments.
**Batobus** - www.batobus.com - 10am-7pm (5pm from Mon to Thu mid-Nov to end Mar), every 25 min. - €20/1 d. (-16s €9), €23/2 d. (-16s €14). Stops (indicated by a red symbol on our detachable plan): Eiffel Tower, Invalides, Musée d'Orsay, Saint-Germain-des-Prés, Notre-Dame, Jardin des Plantes, Hôtel de Ville, Louvre, Place de la Concorde.

### Journey Planning

Visit **www.ratp.fr**. The RATP's free phone app **Bonjour RATP** (App Store and Google Play) is handy for deciding the best mode of transport to take. Another useful tool is **www.citymapper.com/paris** or download the app. Like RATP, it's free and works in offline mode.
*Public transport map on the back of the detachable map.*

### Transport Tickets

**The t+ ticket** - In the métro and the RER, the t+ ticket, available in paper or digital format, allows passengers to travel around Paris and change lines. It's valid for 90 minutes provided you don't exit the network. However, ticket prices for the RER outside Paris vary depending on the distance; a t+ ticket lets you travel the entire line and make bus-to-bus, bus-to-tram, and tram-to-tram connections throughout a 90-min. journey between the first and last ticket validations.
**The Navigo Easy pass** - A contactless, non-personalized pass that acts as a digital ticket. You can lend the pass to a friend, but for any journey, each passenger must possess and validate a pass (two passengers cannot share one pass). On sale (€2) at métro, RER, and other network stations.
**The Bonjour RATP app** - Lets you buy and upload tickets on your smartphone.
**Bus tickets by text message** - Option to purchase your bus tickets by text: when the bus is approaching, send a text "Bus+Route no." to 93100 (e.g. "Bus29"). The text reply message acts as the ticket (valid for 1 hour, no changes permitted).
**Fares** - In métro and RER stations, the paper t+ ticket can only be purchased individually; to benefit from the preferential fares of a book of 10 t+

tickets, you'll have to go digital (Navigo Easy pass).
One ticket: €2.10; digital book (10 tickets): €16.90, conc. (ages 4-9): €8.45.
On the bus, purchased individually from the driver or via text message: €2.50 (ticket valid for one trip and no connections).

### Paris Visite Pass

This pass gives holders unlimited travel by métro, bus, tram, RER, and Transilien. Two options: zones 1 to 3 for Paris only; zones 1 to 5 which includes, for example, Roissy-CDG and Orly airports, Disneyland Paris, and the Château de Versailles. It also offers discounts for select attractions and activities.



Valid for 1, 2, 3, or 5 days. Adult price:
- **zones 1-3**: €13.55/1 d.; €22.05/2 d.; €30.10/3 d., and €43.30/5 d.
- **zones 1-5**: €28.50/1 d.; €43.30/2 d.; €60.70/3 d., and €74.30/5 d.

**Info** – www.ratp.fr

## Sundays

In Paris, stores in tourist areas are permitted to open on Sundays.
All stores are open in the **Marais**, especially around Rue du Temple/ Rue des Francs-Bourgeois, and in the vicinity of **Les Halles**, around the **Champs-Élysées**, and in the **Carrousel du Louvre**. Select **department stores** – Galeries Lafayette at Opéra, Le Bon Marché Rive Gauche, Le BHV Marais –, the **shopping malls** of Beaugrenelle, Bercy Village, Les 4 Temps at La Défense, and in the main **train stations** are also open on Sunday.
*"Shopping", p. 139.*

## Tourist Passes

**Paris Museum Pass** – Valid for 2, 4, or 6 consecutive days, it offers free, direct, and unlimited access to more than 50 museums (permanent collections) and monuments in Paris and the Paris region. On sale at www.parismuseumpass.com, in museums, tobacconists ("tabacs"), and branches of the Paris Tourist Office. Price: €55/2 d., €70/4 d., €85/6 d. Good value for anyone planning on fitting in lots of museums, especially as it includes skip-the-line access.
**Paris Passlib'** – The Paris Tourist Office launched a new version of its Passlib' in 2021. Fully digital and with a dedicated app, this pass is now valid for one year and, depending on the package you choose (from €45), lets you choose between 3 to 7 activities from a wide selection of cruises, bus tours, museum tours, etc. Available at www.parisjetaime.com
*"Paris Visite" Pass, p. 163.*

## Vigipirate

The "Vigipirate" (anti-terrorist security) plan has been stepped up since the Paris terrorist attacks in 2015. Bag searches are widespread at the entrances to large stores, museums, and concert venues. Helmets, backpacks, and umbrellas are often required to be stored in museum lockers. Tip: travel light!

pawel.gaul/Getty Images Plus

Cruise on the Seine.



## Visitor Information

### Office de Tourisme et des Congrès de Paris

**Permanent Visitor Information Points**

**Hôtel de Ville** (main office) – 29 r. de Rivoli - 4e - Ⓜ Hôtel-de-Ville - www.parisjetaime.com - daily 10am-7pm (Sun and pub. holidays 6pm).

**Gare du Nord** – 18 r. de Dunkerque - 10e - Ⓜ Gare du Nord - Mon-Sat 9am-5pm - closed Sun and pub. holidays.

### Comité Régional du Tourisme Paris Île-de-France

**www.visitparisregion.com** - Greeters, information, and sale of tourist products. Information points at the airports, Galeries Lafayette, and Disneyland Paris.

# Festivals and Events 2023-2024

## Temporary Exhibitions

▶**Amedeo Modigliani. A Painter and His Art Dealer** – From Sep 2023 to Jan 2024 - www.musee-orangerie.fr
▶**Chagall, Paris-New York** – Until Jan 2024 - www.atelier-lumieres.com
▶**Gertrude Stein and Pablo Picasso** – Sep 2023 to Jan 2024 - museeduluxembourg.fr
▶**Iris van Herpen** – Nov 2023 to Apr 2024 - madparis.fr
▶**Julia Margaret Cameron, Arresting Beauty** – From Oct to Jan 2024 - jeudepaume.org
▶**Gustave Eiffel's Paris (1832–1923)** – From Jul 2023 to Jan 2024 - www.citedelarchitecture.fr



▶**Modern Paris, 1905-1925** – From Nov 2023 to Apr 2024 - www.petitpalais.paris.fr
▶**The Treasury of Notre-Dame Cathedral**– From Oct 2023 to Feb 2024 - www.louvre.fr
▶**Naples in Paris. The Louvre Hosts the Museo di Capodimonte** – Jun 2023 to Jan 2024 - www.louvre.fr
▶**Louis Janmot, The Poem of the Soul** – From Sep 2023 to Jan 2024 - www.musee-orsay.fr
▶**Metal** - From Apr to Sep 2024 - philharmoniedeparis.fr
▶**Métro! Grand Paris in Motion** – From Nov 2023 to Apr 2024 - www.citedelarchitecture.fr
▶**Fashion and Sports, from One Podium to Another** – Sep 2023 to Apr 2024 - madparis.fr
▶**Notre-Dame de Paris. From Builders to Restorers** – Until Apr 2024 - www.citedelarchitecture.fr

For a full list of current events, visit **www.75.agendaculturel.fr** or **quefaire.paris.fr**.

▶**Paul Klee: Painting Music** – Until Jan 2024 - www.atelier-lumieres.com
▶**Picasso, Drawing to Infinity** – Oct 2023 to Jan 2024 - www.centrepompidou.fr
▶**Women and Surrealism** – Until Mar 2024 - museedemontmartre.fr
▶**Treasures in Black & White** – From Sep 2023 to Jan 2024 - www.petitpalais.paris.fr
▶**Van Gogh in Auvers-sur-Oise. The Final Months** – Sep 2023 to Jan 2024 - www.musee-orsay.fr
▶**Viva Varda!** – From Oct 2023 to Feb 2024 - www.cinematheque.fr

## Highlights by Month

### October

▶**Nuit Blanche** – Early Oct, late-night installations and artistic performances around the city - quefaire.paris.fr/nuitblanche
▶**Fête de la Science** – Science-related workshops and talks at La Villette and Palais de la Découverte - www.fetedelascience.fr
▶**Fête des Vendanges** – Grape harvest festival on the Butte Montmartre - one wknd in mid-Oct - www.fetedesvendangesdemontmartre.com
▶**Paris+** – International contemporary art fair in and outside the Grand Palais Éphémère - 4 d. mid-Oct - www.artbasel.com

▶**Paris Motor Show** – Porte de Versailles - mid-Oct (even-numbered years) - mondial.paris

## November

▶**Paris Photo** – Grand Palais Éphémère- 4 d. early Nov - www.parisphoto.com

▶**MIF Expo** – The "Made in France" fair at Paris Expo Porte de Versailles - 4 d. mid-Nov - www.mifexpo.fr

## December

▶**Salon du Livre et de la Presse Yeunesse** – Children's book and press fair, Espace Paris-Est-Montreuil - 7 d. late Nov to early Dec - slpjplus.fr

▶**Open-Air Ice Rinks** – At the Tuileries Christmas Market, Forum des Halles, Champ-de-Mars Christmas Village, and other sites - www.paris.fr

## January

▶**Festival Mondial du Cirque de Demain** – Circus of Tomorrow, Bois de Vincennes, Pelouse de Reuilly - 4 d. late Jan - www.cirquededemain.paris

## February

▶**Chinese New Year** – Huge parades in the Asian neighborhoods of the 13e arr. and Belleville - www.chine-informations.com

▶**Art Capital** – Grand Palais Éphémère - 4 d. mid-Feb - artcapital.fr

▶**Paris Carnival** – From Place Gambetta to République – www.carnaval-paris.org

▶**Paris International Agricultural Show** – Porte de Versailles - 9 d. from late Feb to early Mar - www.salon-agriculture.com

Sarah Bastin/Fnac Live

The Fnac Live Festival outside the Hôtel de Ville.

## April

▶**Foire du Trône** – Giant funfair, Bois de Vincennes, Pelouse de Reuilly - until late May - www.foiredutrone.com

▶**Art Paris** – Grand Palais Éphémère - 4 d. early Apr - www.artparis.com

▶**Festival du Livre de Paris** – Paris book fair, Grand Palais Ephémère - 3 d. mid-Apr - www.festivaldulivredeparis.fr

▶**Paris Marathon** – www.schneiderelectricparismarathon.com

## May

▶**Foire de Paris** – Major retail fair, Porte de Versailles - early May - www.foiredeparis.fr

▶**Kiosques en Fête** – Free concerts at Paris' bandstands until end of year - www.parisjetaime.com

▶**Jazz in Saint-Germain-des-Prés** - mid-May - www.festivaljazzsaintgermainparis.com



▶**Taste of Paris** – Grand Palais Éphémère - 4 d. mid-May - paris.tastefestivals.com

▶**Long Night of Museums** – mid-May - www.nuitdesmusees.culturecommunication.gouv.fr

▶**Roland-Garros** – Porte d'Auteuil - 15 d. late May, the French tennis open - www.rolandgarros.com

## June

▶**Marché de la Poésie** – poetry festival - Pl. Saint-Sulpice, 5 d. early Jun – www.marche-poesie.com

▶**Fête de la Musique** – city-wide music festival - 21 June - www.fetedelamusique.culturecommunication.gouv.fr

▶**Marche des Fiertés Lesbiennes, Gays, Bi et Trans** – Paris' LGBTQ+ pride festival - www.gaypride.fr

▶**Solidays** – Hippodrome de Longchamp - last wknd in Jun, music festival supporting the fight against AIDS - www.solidays.org

▶**Fête Foraine des Tuileries** – Funfair in the Jardin des Tuileries until late Aug.

▶**Festival Fnac Live** – Music festival outside the Hôtel de Ville - 3 d. late Jun, free concerts - www.fnac.com

▶**Festivals du Parc Floral** – From late Jun to late Aug at the Parc floral - festivalsduparcfloral.paris - Paris Jazz Festival/Pestacles/Classique au Vert/Les Nocturnes.

## July-August

▶**Paris 2024 Olympic and Paralympic Games** – From Jul 26 to Aug 11, 2024, then Aug 28 to Sep 8 - www.paris2024.org

▶**Japan Expo** – Parc des Expositions de Paris-Nord Villepinte - mid-Jul - www.japan-expo-paris.com

▶**Fête nationale du 14 Juillet** – Firemen's balls, fireworks, and military parade for Bastille Day.

▶**Paris l'été** – 2nd fortnight in Jul - www.parislete.fr

▶**Paris Plages** – From mid-Jul to mid-Aug on the Seine quays and in lake at La Villette – quefaire.paris.fr

▶**Open-Air Cinema** – From mid-Jul to mid-Aug, Parc de la Villette – lavillette.com

▶**Fête de Ganesh** – Parades in the 10e and 18 arr. - late Aug - www.templeganesh.fr

## September

▶**Jazz à La Villette** – From late Aug to mid-Sep - www.jazzalavillette.com

▶**Heritage Days** – mid-Sep - www.journeesdupatrimoine.culturecommunication.gouv.fr

▶**Techno Parade** – Mid-Sep.

▶**Festival d'automne à Paris** – Mid-Sep to mid-Jan - www.festival-automne.com.

# FIND OUT MORE

La Bourse de Commerce-Pinault Collection.
Patrick Tourneboeuf/Bourse de Commerce – Pinault Collection

# Paris Through the Ages

## A Compact Capital

Encircled since 1973 by its Boulevard Périphérique—a ring road that can be seen as well as heard!—and bookended east and west by two green lungs (Bois de Boulogne and Bois de Vincennes), the capital is roughly circular in shape, wider (11 miles east to west) than it is tall (six miles north to south), and bisected by the River Seine. As a capital, it's rather *petit*—40.54 square miles compared with Madrid's 233—, where its citizens are packed in like the proverbial sardines: over 53,000 residents per square mile (compared with 9,200 in Marseille).



This small, enclosed patch of land, home to a population of two million people, is the beating heart of France, a veritable crucible shaped over two millennia.

## Significant Milestones

The first defensive system protecting Lutetia, a Gallic settlement founded by the Parisii in the 3rd century BCE on Île de la Cité, was the Seine and its marshland. Through the centuries, the city's sustained population growth, expanding political role, and need to defend the city militarily and collect taxes to finance its sprawl prompted the construction of six walls or boundaries, the capital gradually subsuming its suburbs.

### The Gallo-Roman Wall

*See box* **1** *on the map on p. 177.*

Conquered by Julius Caesar's armies in 52 BCE, Lutetia took advantage of the Pax Romana to develop beyond the Seine. Thus a brand new, entirely Roman, city emerged during the 1st and 2nd centuries on the hill looming over the left bank, facing Île de la Cité (the present-day 5e arrondissement). Its population is estimated to have reached 6,000 at its peak.

But around 276-285, the Barbarian invasions forced the Parisii to retreat to Île de la Cité which they surrounded

### Paris, the Snail

Administratively speaking, Paris resembles a snail's shell: in the center, you have the 1e arrondissement and, wrapping around it, the 2e, 3e, 4e, and 5e arrondissements that encapsulate the historic heart of the city (ancient and medieval). Close together, and continuing the helical loop, the 6e to 11e arrondissements encompass the suburbs of the Ancien Régime while the remaining arrondissements close the loop, occupying the territory of the formerly independent villages united within Paris in 1860. Since April 2020, the first four arrondissements have been grouped into a single administrative division, Paris Centre, managed by the same city hall. However, the old postcodes have been retained.

*See the map inside the cover, at the beginning of the guide.*

with a wall, repurposing stones from Roman monuments. This would have confined an area of around 20 acres. During the 4th and 5th centuries, Paris—Lutetia was named after its inhabitants from 360—remained enclosed within its tight, stone boundary.

## From Clovis to Suger

Clovis, King of the Francs, established his capital in Paris in 508 owing to its strategic location. He settled on the island, which became henceforth known as Île de la Cité.

From the 6th to the 10th century, the marshes were dried out and turned into farmland, while the port and commercial activity developed around Place de Grève (today Place de l'Hôtel-de-Ville).

Several sanctuaries were built during the Merovingian period, now all gone aside from a few remains in the Chapelle Saint-Symphorien inside the Église Saint-Germain-des-Prés.

Under the reign of Hugues Capet, the city expanded outwards onto both sides of the river, the right bank taking off faster than the left bank. The king made the Palais de la Cité (today's Palais de Justice) his residence.

Important sanctuaries appeared, principally on Île de la Cité, thanks to the adviser to Louis VI and Louis VII, Suger, Abbot of Saint-Denis.

## Philip Augustus' Wall

*See wall* **2** *on the map on p. 177.*

From 1180 to 1210, a sturdy wall was built on the order of King Philip II, who wanted to protect Paris and its people before he left for the Third Crusade. Extending more than three miles, it was reinforced, upstream, by a chain dam across the Seine and, downstream, by the Fortresse du Louvre and the Tour de Nesle (on the site of the current Institut de France). City life was concentrated on the right bank around Châtelet and the Grand Pont (which connected Île de la Cité with the right bank), west of Place de Grève.

The streets were paved, helping to ease traffic and improve sanitation. More and more fountains were erected, and the management and distribution of water improved thanks to the regular drawing of water from local springs, like those in Belleville.

It was also during this period that Paris assumed its standing as an important capital: the construction of Notre-Dame began in 1163 (it would take over a century to complete), and the Université de Paris was founded in 1215.

## Charles V's Wall

*See wall* **3** *on the map on p. 177.*

It was Étienne Marcel, the provost of the merchants, who, having taken power, started the building of a new wall in 1356. Completed under Charles V, hence its name, this fortification was bolstered in the east by the Forteresse de la Bastille, and surrounded by ditches.

By then, Paris spanned over 1,000 acres and had a population of more than 150,000 inhabitants.

Roads led to the village of Montmartre, the Basilique Saint-Denis, the commandery of the Temple (to the north of the current Marais), and the

Fort de Vincennes, further driving the city's development on the right bank. This right bank became the center of the city's commercial activities, as opposed to Île de la Cité, the heart of Paris' political and religious power, and the left bank, mostly given over to schools and the university (hence its future name of "Latin Quarter").

## Louis XIII's Wall

*See wall* **4** *on the map on p. 177.*

In the 16th century, neither the League nor the religious wars succeeded in slowing down the urban expansion and proliferation of civil and religious buildings, which actually experienced fresh impetus under Henry IV, with the creation of Place Royale (now Place des Vosges) and the Hôpital Saint-Louis. Charles IX, between 1560 and 1574, and then Louis XIII expanded the Philip Augustus' Wall westwards, in order to make room for the Palais du Louvre they had extended as well as the suburb of Montmartre and the first suburb of Saint-Honoré. Built from 1633 to 1636, Louis XIII's Wall survived until 1754.



During the reign of Louis XIII, Paris became a major capital: Richelieu built the Palais-Royal (1629), founded the Académie Française (1635), and the Marais, on the heels of Place Royale, was sumptuously spruced up.

## Louis XIV and Paris

On the verge of defeating the Fronde civil wars, the young Louis XIV made a triumphant entry into the capital in October 1652. Nevertheless, still wary of the Parisians, he decided to settle in Versailles in 1682. Although the city was no longer the capital, the king did not neglect it, as evidenced by the numerous additions he made, from Place Vendôme to Place des Victoires by way of the Invalides and the reconstruction of the Louvre.

In the late 1660s, when he returned from Vincennes by carriage, Louis XIV was struck by the ugly sight of Charles V's fortifications, now in ruins and all but useless since his last victories. He ordered them to be demolished and a courtyard planted with four rows of trees to be built in its place. The ditches were filled and a raised terrace, from where one could look out to the countryside, was erected. The ensemble formed a splendid promenade, wide enough for four carriages. The development of these "grands boulevards" (the word "boulevard" originally referring to the flat surface of a rampart) kick-started the expansion of the city out to the suburbs: Saint-Germain and Saint-Marcel were brought into the fold of the city while Saint-Antoine was being built. It was also during this period that Le Nôtre designed a grandiose east-west axis: it cut through the Allée des Tuileries, forming the beginnings of the Champs-Élysées.

## The Fermiers Généraux's Wall

*See wall* **5** *on the map on p. 177.*

From 1784, the borders of Paris were embodied by the wall of the *fermiers généraux*—tax collectors of the "tax farming" system established during the Ancien Régime. It was no longer a defense wall, but a "fiscal wall" set up to prevent fraud on the duties received at the city's barriers.

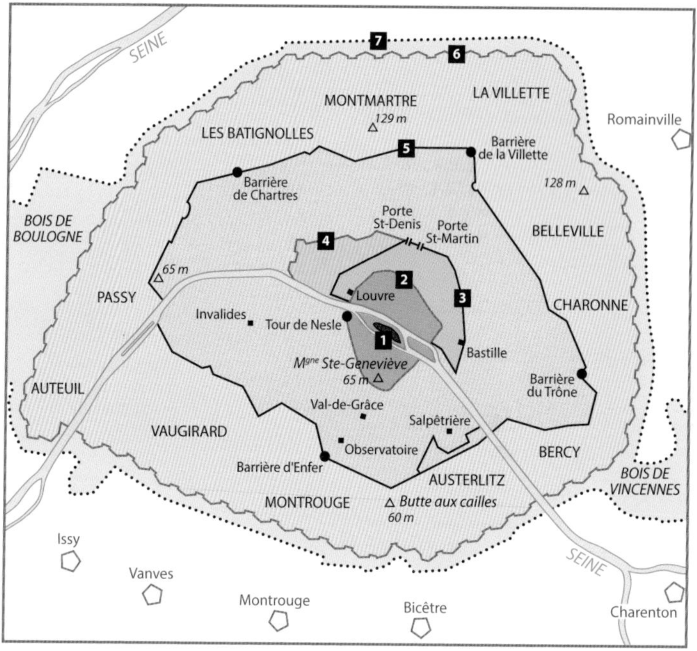

Built from 1784 to 1797, it traced the path of the current exterior boulevards, used by the aerial métro (Lines 2 and 6). This 14-mile-long and 10-foot-high wall was punctuated by 57 "toll booths" that subjected goods entering Paris, such as wine, coal, or timber, to taxes and duties. Four of these toll booths, their design entrusted to the architect Ledoux, the father of Neoclassicism, have survived: the rotundas at Monceau and La Villette and the square pavilions at Denfert-Rochereau and Nation. Highly unpopular, the fermiers généraux's wall was abolished during the French Revolution.

From the revolutionary period and then through the Empire, Paris stayed on brand with its grandiose Neoclassical monuments, designed to extol public virtues, such as the Panthéon and the Arc de Triomphe.

## The Thiers Fortifications

*See wall 6 on the map on p. 177.*

These fortifications served a military purpose. The invasion of France and then Paris by the Russian army in 1814 and 1815 demonstrated the need to protect the capital. Thiers proposed a fortified enclosure at a distance of between half a mile to two miles from the fermiers généraux's wall, capable of withstanding enemy strikes. The proposal was adopted on August 1, 1841. Some 29 miles of wall composed of dressed stone and gritstone were built, protected inside by a 50-foot-wide ditch (the current Boulevards des Marechaux) and outside by a military zone over 650 feet wide, punctuated by 94 bastions.

Although Thiers' fortifications never had to defend Paris from enemy troops, they still played a major role when, 18 years after their construction, a bill was enacted to move the city's boundaries out to the inner ditch that ran around them.



**The annexation of 1860** - From 1860, all the land situated between the fermiers généraux's wall and Thiers' wall was annexed to Paris. Four municipalities were completely abolished and integrated into the capital: Vaugirard, Grenelle, La Villette, and Belleville. Seven others partially so, such as Passy and Auteuil. Finally, 13 others only gave up a small portion of their territory, including Vanves, Issy, Neuilly, and Saint-Ouen.

From these new 19,274 acres, which resulted in the creation of 20 arrondissements (up from 12 previously), and the epic urban planning works orchestrated by prefect Haussmann *(see p. 185)*, modern Paris was born. In every neighborhood, wide avenues were laid to improve traffic circulation through the city, while railways were breaking ground (the first line, connecting Paris to Saint-Germain, opened in 1837).

## From the Paris Commune to 1900

The fires that blazed during the Paris Commune in 1871 resulted in the reconstruction of major public buildings: the Hôtel de Ville, the Richelieu wing of the Palais du Louvre, and the Légion d'Honneur. The Palais-Royal and Palais de Justice were also restored. The Opéra Garnier was completed in 1875 and the construction of Sacré-Cœur was started. Finally, in 1889, for the occasion of the Paris Exposition, the Eiffel Tower appeared in the sky over Paris, an icon of modern Paris. 1900 was another year of sweeping urban changes: the Pont Alexandre-III and the Grand Palais were opened between the Champs-Élysées and Invalides, the Orsay train station stood across from the Louvre, on the right bank, and perhaps most excitingly of all, the underground world beneath the metropolis opened up with the first line of the métro, between Porte de Vincennes and Porte Maillot. The entrances to the stations designed by Hector Guimard, a proponent of the Art Nouveau movement, added colorful flourishes to the urban landscape.

## Today's Boundary

*See boundary* **7** *on the map on p. 177.*

The Third Republic razed Thiers' fortifications (1919) and established, from 1925 to 1930, the final boundaries of Paris: the forests on both sides—Bois de Boulogne and Bois de Vincennes—and a narrow circular strip of land increased its area to just over 26,000 acres. During the Second World War,

Paris lost its status as the capital. The city was bombarded, then declared an "open city" and occupied. The government was moved to Vichy.
On August 26, 1945, General de Gaulle triumphantly paraded down the liberated Champs-Élysées, to the rapturous applause of the Parisians. The population of Paris reached 2,700,000.

## The Post-War Period

To recover, Paris launched massive real-estate rebuilding projects and large-scale developments led by the presidents of the Republic, as in the time of kings. In the early 1950s, the government sought to establish a business district capable of competing with the world's largest markets, planting the seed for La Défense, established west of the grand historical perspective of the Louvre and Étoile.
After the construction of Maison de Radio-France (1963) and the Front de Seine development (the first skyscraper was completed in 1970) under de Gaulle, Paris welcomed a building that unleased a tumult of differing opinions: the "Centre d'art contemporain de Beaubourg", opened in 1977 on the initiative of President Georges Pompidou, hence its name of Centre Pompidou.
During the seven-year term of Valéry Giscard d'Estaing, it was decided that the Gare d'Orsay would become a museum and the slaughterhouses at La Villette a science museum (these two museums would be opened under Mitterrand in 1986).

## The Mitterrand Years

President Mitterrand has a global reputation for major architectural projects. In actual fact, among all the projects decreed, only one of them, the Grand Louvre and its pyramid, opened in April 1989, was the result of a direct commission placed by the president with an architect. All other monuments were the subject of national competitions, such as the Ministry of Finance complex, the Institut du Monde Arabe, and the Cité de la Musique, or international competitions such as the Opéra de la Bastille, the Bibliothèque Nationale de France, and the Arche de La Défense.

## A New Direction

While a legacy of Jacques Chirac's presidency was the Musée du Quai-Branly (2006), it seems that the age of great monuments has ended in favor of consideration for the **"ordinary city"**, the priority now being to improve the everyday environment of Paris' residents and to safeguard the existing built heritage.
Since the early 2000s, driven by a broader strategy to improve the "sharing of public space", the focus has been on the development of "soft mobility" (increasing cycle lanes, launch of the self-service bicycle service, Vélib', in 2007) and public transport (creation of a tramway around Paris). The aim is to drastically reduce the space given to cars.
With land becoming increasingly scarce, the repurposing of old railroad and industrial sites and the conversion of existing buildings has presented an opportunity to develop new districts, like the "ZAC" (urban development zones) of **Paris Rive Gauche**, around the new Bibliothèque Nationale de France,

L. De Simone/AGF RM/age fotostock

The CENTQUATRE-PARIS, an arts center installed in the old funeral house.

and **Pajol**, in the 18e arrondissement. The three branches of the armed forces and all the services of the Ministry of Defense were brought together in 2015 at the new site of **Balard**, France's answer to the Pentagon, in the 15e arrondissement.

**And tomorrow?** - Among the major projects underway, other railway sites are being redeveloped: the new Clichy-Batignolles eco-district, with housing, public amenities, offices and a park, and the Paris Nord-Est development (in progress), which plans to create housing and offices over 500 acres between Porte de la Chapelle and Porte de la Villette.

Finally, and insofar as the future of Paris hinges on a stronger integration of its inner suburbs, portions of the Paris ring road have been or will be covered over (Porte des Lilas, Porte de Vanves, and Porte des Ternes), creating new gardens and public green spaces in the neighboring municipalities. The debate about a larger Paris including its inner suburbs has thus been sparked, and is already causing some controversy. The question "How can we enlarge Paris?" is shifting to "Why do we want to enlarge Paris?" A political *patate chaude*...

## "Grand Paris"

In this context, in 2009, President Nicolas Sarkozy commissioned 10 international, multidisciplinary teams (architects, urban planners, sociologists, etc.) to develop "ideas" on the **major challenge of the Parisian agglomeration**. "Ideas" because these are not proposals in the operational sense of the term, but a presentation of the vision these experts have of the French capital in decades' time. The aim is to create a continuous urban and social fabric between the capital and its suburbs, to make it a more efficient economic region, and a more accommodating space for its population, all while strengthening its role as a hub for a high volume of international tourists. A vast transport plan, without which all other goals would be worthless, has long been debated. In May 2011, following a compromise between the state and the regional authority, the **Grand Paris Express** project was green lit. By the 2030s, a new 120-mile automated "super métro" network will be transporting two million passengers a day and easing connections between suburbs, bypassing central Paris altogether. The plan also provides for improvements to the RER network. The work has started, with a gradual commissioning of the wider network planned from 2025-2026. In addition, the extension of métro Line 14 will connect Orly airport to the south. Grand Paris is on track!

### The City of Paris: Its Own Authority

At the head of the City of Paris is a mayor appointed by the Paris Council, composed of 163 councilors, appointed every six years from among the 527 local district councilors elected directly by the Parisian voters in each arrondissement. The mayor holds the same powers as that of any other municipality, with the exception of the police authority (traffic, public order, public safety), which falls under the police prefect (a state official, appointed to the Council of Ministers by the President of the Republic).

Twenty arrondissement councils, which each have their seat in the arrondissement city halls, serve as a link between the administration and the population. They do not have any decision-making powers but are there to assist the mayor and the Paris Council. The councils are formed, in equal parts, of councilors elected by the voters of each arrondissement, municipal officers appointed by the mayor of Paris, and members elected by the Paris Council.

Since Paris is both a municipality and an administrative department, its Council meets as a municipal council and as a general council. The prefect of the Île-de-France region is also the prefect of Paris; they are appointed by the government. The first mayor of Paris to be elected by popular vote was Jacques Chirac (1977). In 2001, the Parisians elected their first socialist mayor, Bertrand Delanoë, who went on to be re-elected in 2008. In 2014, his first deputy, Anne Hidalgo, won. She was the first woman to lead the city. The outgoing mayor won a second term following the 2020 municipal elections, which were held in the midst of the Covid-19 crisis and posted a record abstention rate.

# Paris, a Revolutionary City

Paris has been shaken up by revolutions and social movements that were pivotal for the history of France—if not the world! In fact, it was for this reason that the post of mayor of Paris, a city that was something of a tinder box, was abolished in 1794 and only restored in... 1977.

## Saint Bartholomew's Day

The bells of Saint-Germain-l'Auxerrois, ringing in the night of August 23-24, 1572, marked the resumption of the wars of religion with the **Saint Bartholomew's Day Massacre**. Hundreds and hundreds of French Huguenots (Protestants) were savagely killed by traditionalist Catholics fiercely opposed to the marriage of the Protestant Henry of Navarre (the future Henry IV) with the Catholic Margaret of Valois and to the policy of royal amity. Henry IV didn't enter Paris until March 22, 1594, after converting to Catholicism.



## The Storming of the Bastille

In the upheaval caused by the assembly of the Estates General since June 1789, the sacking of the popular Minister Necker on July 12, 1789 was the match to the powder keg. In search of weapons, on the morning of July 14, Parisians stormed the Hôtel des Invalides before making their way to the Fortresse de la Bastille to find more weapons and ammunition. In the late afternoon, the arrival of the French Guards, who had deserted their barracks, disrupted the government, which agreed to capitulate. The Bastille was stormed and it was quickly demolished thereafter. The symbol of tyranny was gone for good. The following year, the people danced on its ruins. Meanwhile, on the night of August 4, 1789, feudal privileges were abolished, and on August 26 the "Declaration of the Rights of Man and of the Citizen" was adopted. Paris had become a universal beacon for revolutionaries all over the world!

## The Three Glorious Days

The Second French Revolution took place on July 27, 28, and 29, 1830. After receiving a vote of no confidence in the July elections, King Charles X refused to submit to the deputies and asserted his power by dissolving the Chamber of Deputies. He also suspended press freedom and changed the electoral system to exclude the commercial middle class from future elections.
There was much public anger.
The next day, journalists printed calls to insurrection. On July 27, people took to the streets and barricades were put up across the city. Charles X was forced to abdicate. The July Revolution inaugurated the so-called "July Monarchy" by putting, on July 29, 1830, Louis Philippe, Duke of Orléans, on the French throne.

## The French Revolution of 1848

The French Revolution of 1848 resulted from the economic crisis that affected farmers and the working classes.
It took place in Paris on February 23, 24, and 25, 1848. On February 22, 1848, a Republican banquet was banned in the 12e arrondissement of Paris, which caused a riot. On the evening of February 23, troops opened fire on the protesters: the riot turned into an uprising. Victorious, the insurgents took over the Tuileries Palace, Louis Philippe's residence. It was a revolution; the king abdicated. The Republicans established a provisional government, replacing the July Monarchy, and founded the Second Republic on February 25, 1848.
Erected on Place de la Bastille, the July Column commemorates the revolutions of 1830 and 1848.

## The Paris Commune

After the people called to dethrone Emperor Napoleon III and end the Second Empire on September 4, 1870, following France's defeat to the Prussians in the Battle of Sedan, the Third Republic was proclaimed. The Prussians took 83,000 prisoners, including the Emperor, on September 2. Faced with the threat of foreign troops surrounding Paris, a Government of National Defense was formed. However, the capital was besieged by the Prussian army during the winter of 1870-1871. The Parisians heroically held off the siege, but the government capitulated on January 28, 1871: the people were incensed and took control of Paris. On March 26, 1871, at the Hôtel de Ville, the "Commune de Paris", a proletarian government established against the Versailles-based government, was proclaimed. However, it was brutally repressed by the Versailles government forces during the week of May 21-28. During this "Bloody Week", the Hôtel de Ville, the Tuileries, and several Parisian monuments were set ablaze and the column on Place Vendôme was destroyed.
Sacré-Cœur, after the defeat of 1870, came in response to build a church in penitence for France's moral errors.

## May 1968

The student and worker revolution against an unyielding, bourgeois society was sparked on March 22, 1968, at the University of Nanterre. From May 13, students were joined by other younger protesters: blue-collar workers. The Latin Quarter was barricaded, striking became widespread, paving stones were ripped up.
The university crisis and social crisis converged to a political crisis. General de Gaulle's authority was called into question. The parliamentary left publicly supported the protesting youth.
On May 30, General de Gaulle announced that he refused to withdraw from political life and dissolved the National Assembly; 100,000 people demonstrated to show their support for the general. In early June, workers returned to their jobs in public companies. On June 30, the Gaullists won the elections.

# Architecture

Each century has left its architectural mark on the city, but two significant periods in particular forged it: the 16th-17th century and the Second Empire (1852-1870).

## For the Greatness of Kings

### Henry IV, Paris' First Urban Planner

Taking possession of a city devastated by religious wars, Henry IV embarked on a series of works to improve it: in 1606, the **Pont-Neuf** became the first direct link between the two banks of the Seine. The king also sought to give more luster to the political center of his kingdom by building and rebuilding its symbols (the Louvre, the Tuileries), using more noble materials (dressed stone replaced cob and timber) and creating more elegant public spaces, such as **Place Dauphine** and **Place Royale** (present-day Place des Vosges). To allow the passage of carriages that now numbered in their hundreds, much wider avenues were developed. They were typically lined with grand mansions, such as the Hôtel de Soubise and Hôtel Carnavalet.



### Louis XIII and Louis XIV

Louis XIII continued his father's work. The population of Paris rose from 275,000 people in 1571 to more than 500,000 by 1680. Under demographic pressure, the suburbs were growing in size. New neighborhoods emerged on **Île Saint-Louis** and in **Faubourg Saint-Germain**.

This urban planning problem was swept aside under Louis XIV, who was more concerned with demonstrating his power than modernizing his cities. The Louis XIV style is irrevocably associated with the words grandeur, harmony, and symmetry, recurring characteristics that emphasize above all the absolute nature of the monarchy. On the eastern facade of the **Louvre**, facing the city, the monumental Colonnade de Perrault (1667), 577 feet long, is symbolic of the Sun King's penchant for classicism. Likewise, the **Hôpital des Invalides**, with its 643-foot-long facade, is accessed via a towering entrance that resembles a triumphal arch in honor of the king. **Place des Victoires** and **Place Vendôme**, both the work of Jules Hardouin-Mansart (1646-1708), present the same rigorous arrangement, extolling the king's virtues even more greatly by placing a statue of him at the center. Nature was not neglected either. It was tamed by the Sun King under the guidance of André Le Nôtre (1613-1700) who, in 1666, lay a wide tree-lined path along the axis of the Palais des **Tuileries**: the French-style garden became fashionable and was the inspiration for the first version of the **Champs-Élysées**.

## Haussmann's Renovation of Paris

Baron Haussmann (1809-1891), prefect of the Seine, was the architect of the metamorphosis that would give the Second Empire a capital commensurate with its prosperity. Under the aegis of Emperor Napoleon III, he created **new axes to improve traffic circulation**. While the north-south axis was easily achievable—Boulevard Saint-Michel and Boulevard Sébastopol were rapidly built and connected to the new railway stations of Gare de l'Est and Gare du Nord—the east-west axis was trickier to extend: the Louvre, the Tuileries, and the Marais contained a high concentration of buildings occupied by the city's aristocracy, less inclined to be moved elsewhere. Haussmann was also concerned with **public sanitation**. Paris was home to a million people, and cholera struck in 1832. Haussmann gutted the city center; Île de la Cité, with its narrow, insalubrious streets, was practically razed to the ground. Around 370 miles of sewers were built. Between 1852 and 1870, as many as **100,000 buildings** cropped up over the city. Perfectly aligned trees appeared with the laying of each new avenue (80,000 trees planted). The **forests** of Bois de Boulogne and Bois de Vincennes, as well as man-made **parks** (Buttes-Chaumont, Monceau, Montsouris), were also part of his plan.

## Preserving the City's Religious Heritage

The 85 churches in Paris, the city's biggest free museum thanks to their artistic riches, are in poor condition. Stonework is supported by netting, and the interiors are dark and gloomy. Decades of lack of maintenance has put this sacred heritage at risk, tarnishing Paris' image. This colossal challenge will take many years to fix.



### The Haussmannian Building

Today, Haussmannian buildings could never be described as inelegant; yet, back in their day, they drew a lot of criticism. Indeed, although they took their cues from aristocratic residences (classical facades, adjoining apartments), their uniform structure seemed undignified for the well-to-do classes they were supposed to accommodate. To let in light, the building had to be as tall as the street was wide, so 59 feet. The buildings were adorned with continuous balconies on the second and fifth floors. On the top floor, the attic rooms housed the domestic staff. In the apartments, the householders' living quarters (lounge, bedroom, dining room) looked out to the street; the communal areas (kitchen, bathroom), to the interior courtyard. Modern innovations (such as the elevator) would desacralize the second story, which had been the noble floor par excellence, courtesy of its balcony and high ceilings. Indeed, it presented a clever compromise between pleasant views, ease of access, and water supply. Various decrees would ease Haussmannian construction regulations: that of 1882, for example, authorized projecting bow windows.

# Cosmopolitan Paris

An attractive city, Paris is a kaleidoscope where all the communities of the world are represented. Some have taken up residence in specific neighborhoods, not always in easy living conditions. They're places to go to market, buy pastries, pick out a particular fabric... Countless restaurants, grocery stores, and delis offer all the scents and flavors from the four corners of the planet. In a matter of a few métro stops, you can feel as if you've traveled half way around the globe.

## Africa and the West Indies

Africans and West Indians are grouped by ethnicity, profession, and neighborhood.
At the Marché Dejean (around Métro Château-Rouge, 18e arr.), moms tout fresh or cooked food; there's also fish, meat, and other products from Africa. Interestingly, more and more grocery stores that offer the staples of African-West Indian cooking are run by members of the capital's Asian community (Belleville, Goutte-d'Or).



## North African Paris

Métro Line 2 runs through some of Paris' biggest North African communities: Barbès and Goutte-d'Or (18e arr.), undergoing significant renovation, and Belleville (19e and 20e arr.). To find the ingredients for North African cuisine, melt into the crowds at the markets of Aligre (12e arr.), Belleville (11e arr.), or Barbès (18e arr.). The Grande Mosquée (5e arr.) promises a flavor of faraway climes, thanks to its Turkish bath, featured in many a movie, and the mint tea ritual you can experience in its café.

## The Jewish Community

The community's historic district is the Marais (4e arr.). Decimated during the Occupation, it was built up with the arrival of Jews from North Africa who settled in Sentier (2e and 3e arr.) and in the suburbs, where half of France's Jewish population now live.
Several places in Paris testify to its history and culture: Musée d'Art et d'Histoire du Judaïsme and Mémorial de la Shoah (3e arr.); Monument à la Mémoire des Déportés, at Père-Lachaise (20e arr.).

## Chinatown

A plaque on the wall at 13 Rue Maurice-Denis (12e arr.) pays tribute to the 120,000 Chinese who came to France during the First World War, telling us that 3,000 of them who chose to stay in Paris after the conflict ended established the first Chinatown near the Gare de Lyon. From 1975, it was mainly Chinese from the Indochinese, Malaysian, and Philippine diaspora who settled alongside the older immigrant community, originating from Southern China.
While it doesn't claim to compete with the Chinatowns of New York or San Francisco, the area of the 13e arr. that lies between Rue de Tolbiac, Avenue de Choisy, and the tower blocks on Avenue d'Ivry certainly offers flavors

of Asia with its vibrant restaurants and grocery stores where you can find all kinds of exotic products. For the full experience, go at Chinese New Year. The Olympiades shopping mall, nicknamed the "Pagoda", is a maze of Asian arcades, stores, and restaurants. Belleville also has a sizable Asian community, with more restaurants and grocery stores to discover.
Not forgetting in and around the picturesque Rue au Maire (3e arr.), where one of the capital's oldest Chinese neighborhoods is still thriving.

## Japanese Paris

The community of Japanese businesspeople, employees of Japanese companies, students, and artists is concentrated in the Opéra district and Rue Sainte-Anne (2e arr.), where there are plenty of opportunities to tuck into specialties the likes of sashimi, sushi, and tempura.
The Maison de la Culture du Japon is a mine of information on the culture of the country of the Rising Sun (7e arr.).
Japanese fashion boutiques are concentrated around Place des Victoires (2e arr.) and in the Saint-Germain-des-Prés district (6e arr.).

## India in Paris

Most of the migrants are not actually Indian at all, but Pakistani, Tamil from northern Sri Lanka, or Bangladeshi. "Little India" in Paris is concentrated along Rue du Faubourg-Saint-Denis: between Gare du Nord and Porte de la Chapelle, Rue Jarry, Passage Brady (10e arr.), Cairo Street, and Place du

Razvan/Getty Images Plus

Chinese New Year in the 13e arrondissement.

Caire (2e arr.). There are scores of grocery stores and restaurants along Rue Gérando, at the foot of Sacré-Cœur, and next to the Lycée Jacques-Decour (high school, 9e arr.).
The Centre Culturel Mandapa (6 r. Wurtz, 13e arr.) puts on around 100 Indian theater, dance, and music shows every year. The Maison des Cultures du Monde (101 bd Raspail, 6e arr.) organizes traditional Indian, Pakistani, and Bangladeshi music, dance and theater productions.

## T



## V





Photo credits p. 4-5
(left to right and top to bottom)

M. Gaspar/Michelin
B. Gardel/hemis.fr
B. Rieger/hemis.fr
GlobalP/Getty Images Plus
gornostaj/Getty Images Plus
D. Thierry/Photononstop
stocklapse/Getty Images Plus
B. Gardel/hemis.fr
danefromspain/Getty Images Plus
R. Mattes/hemis.fr

**Collection supervised by Philippe Orain**

| | |
|---|---|
| **Editor-in-chief** | Florence Dyan |
| **Editor** | Laurent Vaultier |
| **Contributing Writers** | Alejandro Prieto de Vega, Karen Guillorel, Gaelle Redon, Vanessa Besnard, Gautier Battistella, Luc Decoudin, Hélène Bouchoucha, Marylène Duteil, Geneviève Clastres, Sandrine Favre, Michel Fonovich, Sylvie Kempler, Achraf Meddeb, Philippe Pataud-Célérier, Jean-Claude Renard, Nathalie Rouveyre-Scalbert, Emmanuelle Souty, Laurent Vaultier |
| **Contributors** | Ecaterina-Paula Cepraga, Costina-Ionela Lungu, Denis Rasse (**Cartography**), Véronique Aissani, Carole Diascorn (**Cover**), Marion Capera, Marie Simonet, Ilona D'Angela, Margot Santraine (**Picture Editors**), Andra-Florentina Ostafi (**Objective Data**), Bogdan Gheorghiu, Cristian Catona, Gabriel Dragu, Hervé Dubois, Pascal Grougon (**Prepress**), Dominique Auclair (**Production Manager**)<br>City maps : © MICHELIN 2023 |
| **Graphic Design** | Laurent Muller (interior layout)<br>Véronique Aissani (cover) |
| **Advertising Sales and Partnerships** | contact.clients@editions.michelin.com<br>*The content of any advertising pages contained in this guide is the sole responsibility of advertisers.* |
| **Contacts** | Your opinion is essential to improve our products<br>Help us by answering the questionnaire on our website : editions.michelin.com<br>**Published in 2024** |



MICHELIN Éditions
French Simplified Joint Stock Company with Registered Capital of 487,500 Euros
57 rue Gaston Tessier – 75019 Paris (France)
Registered in Paris : 882 639 354


Registration of Copyright : 03-2024 – ISSN 0293-9436
Typography/Photoengraving : MICHELIN Editions (Paris)
Printer : Estimprim, Autechaux
Printed in France : 02-2024

Certified ISO 14001 Facility
Printed on sustainably sourced paper